CHARISMATIC RENEWAL
AND THE CHURCHES

CHARISMATIC RENEWAL AND THE CHURCHES

Kilian McDonnell

A CROSSROAD BOOK

THE SEABURY PRESS / NEW YORK

The Seabury Press
815 Second Avenue
New York, N.Y. 10017

Library of Congress Cataloging in Publication Data

McDonnell, Kilian.   Charismatic renewal and the churches.
"A Crossroad book."
Bibliography: p.   Includes index.
1. Pentecostalism. 2. Glosslalia—Psychology.
I. Title.
BX8763.M28   270.8'2   76–896   ISBN 0–8164–0293–0

To Margie and Peter Grace

CONTENTS

FOREWORD *by Léon Joseph Cardinal Suenens*   ix

INTRODUCTION   1

1. HUMAN EXPERIENCE AND RELIGIOUS
   MEANING   5

2. DISORGANIZATION AND DEPRIVATION:
   MOVEMENTS AND THEIR CAUSES   17

3. ENTHUSIASM AND INSTITUTION:
   THE RESPONSES OF THE CHURCHES   41

4. MARGINAL PEOPLE AND THE DOMINANCE
   OF ABNORMAL PSYCHOLOGY: 1910–1966   79

5. THE MIDDLE AND UPPER CLASSES AND
   THE MOVE TOWARD NORMALITY: 1967–1975   111

6. ASSESSMENT AND RECAPITULATION   145

NOTES   159

BIBLIOGRAPHY   187

INDEX   197

FOREWORD

Kilian McDonnell's new book is a precious contribution to the study of the Pentecostal movement in its different aspects and will usefully complete his previous exploratory works in that field.

It is evident that it is important to have a theological understanding of the meaning and significance of the classical Pentecostal movement as well as of the Protestant and Catholic charismatic renewal. Undoubtedly their primary significance is to be found in the fields of theology and the history of the spiritual life.

Renewals within the churches are precisely that, being in and of the Church. This was true of the classical Pentecostal movement in its beginnings as well as of the charismatic renewal in the historic churches. But the ecclesial and theological aspects are part of a larger cultural history. To understand that history, a cross-disciplinary method is needed.

In this book, Kilian McDonnell examines the Pentecostal-charismatic movement, drawing from history, sociology, cultural anthropology, psychology, and theology. Using the methods proper to these disciplines, he has isolated the significant contribution of each, with special focus on psychological research.

The special character of the book is the way the data of the social and behavioral sciences become the object of theological reflection. He brings a thorough knowledge of the literature in the various sciences. This book condenses, with scrupulous objectivity, the findings of the above named disciplines helping us to grasp the significance of the striking and widespread phenomenon of the Pentecostal movement, in its different forms. One will appreciate how carefully and with what objectivity he enters into each discipline which he uses as an instrument of analysis but, at the same time, how he is not imprisoned in them and can move beyond them to a higher or more complete perspective. He knows also how to bring complementarity where one would see, at first sight, oppositions or contradictions.

The author has done extensive research and, over the last ten years, field work in North America, Europe, and Africa. He has had many contacts with the leaders in the classical- and neo-Pentecostal world in his capacity as co-chairman of the international dialogue between the Secretariat for Promoting Christian Unity in Rome, on the one hand, and the classical Pentecostal churches and the neo-Pentecostal movement, on the other.

As theological advisor to the *"Ad Hoc* Committee on the Charismatic Renewal" of the United States Catholic Conference of Bishops and to the Service Committee of the Catholic charismatic renewal in the United States, he is very well qualified to write on this subject.

I, personally, was able to appreciate his theological competence when, at my invitation, he accepted to be the principal writer of the "Theological and Pastoral Orientations on the Catholic Charismatic Renewal," a study with international collaboration, known as the "Malines Document."

This book will be a help, not only on the scientific level, but also in the ecumenical field. The charismatic renewal is bringing together many different Christian traditions. As such, it will contribute in an important way to build bridges between Christians on the road towards visible unity. Where the Spirit is at work we may expect that brotherhood and communion in depth will follow as a fruit of His loving presence and of His mighty power. This book will be a precious contribution on all those levels.

L. J. CARDINAL SUENENS

CHARISMATIC RENEWAL
AND THE CHURCHES

INTRODUCTION

A theological friend who heard I was writing a book on the Pentecostal-charismatic movement asked me why I would waste my time on something which was so peripheral to the life of the church. His concern was not only for the wasted time but also what such a book would do to my professional reputation, such as it is, as a theologian. When I told him that the focus of the book is tongues, he was shocked. He told me that he was convinced that no theologian could write on tongues and survive professionally. He was genuinely concerned.

I profoundly disagree with my friend's estimation of the charismatic renewal as a peripheral phenomenon. If its basis is Christian initiation (baptism, confirmation, and eucharist), as I believe it is, then its roots are central. In the matter of tongues he may be correct. Certainly one who wishes to promote his professional career would be well advised to seek a topic a little further up on the hierarchy of Christian truths and realities. There is general agreement among researchers on Pentecostalism, no matter what discipline they represent, that the issue is not tongues, even though there may not have been a movement, in the sociological and anthropological sense, without it. If to isolate tongues is to violate the movement, why would a theologian who, above all, should have tongues in perspective, be guilty of such distortion? It was not a passionate conviction that tongues is to be propagated and people recruited into tongues-speaking conventicles that made me pursue my task in spite of my friend's brotherly concern. Actually, if left to my own devices I would not write such a book. Though I would agree with some scholars that from the point of view of cultural anthropology and the dynamics of movement growth, there would have been no classical Pentecostal movement without tongues as the commitment act (the socially unacceptable gesture by which one commits oneself

1

to the movement and identifies with it). But if one approaches the topic as a theologian, one would situate the gift of tongues in the much larger theological context of the nature of the Christian life and ministry. Tongues is still there but it then assumes a very modest and lowly place. Instead of being the distinguishing mark of a certain kind or degree of Christian, it is simply a minor part of the total Christian life.

Even though my theological instincts told me that tongues should not be singled out, even though most (but not all) books exclusively on tongues are not to be recommended, I chose to write such a book. My excuse is that the major portion of the book would be a review of the psychological research on Pentecostals and charismatics. For good or ill that research did not focus on Pentecostals who prophesied or engaged in the healing ministry. The research is in large part a study of people who speak or pray in tongues. I also proposed to study the reaction of the churches from the psychological perspective. Especially in the early days, this was a major preoccupation of church commissions assigned to study the matter. The other chapters in the book, that on the theological understanding of charism as a human experience, that on social theory as applied to the Pentecostal-charismatic movement, have as their function making understandable the dilemma of the churches as they were confronted with the phenomenon in their midst. These chapters also provide some understanding of the framework in which the psychologists carried out their research.

Some clarification of terms is called for. Glossolalia, speaking in tongues, praying in tongues are all synonyms for a charism of the Holy Spirit which is essentially a prayer gift. There is explicit mention of tongues in 1 Corinthians 12–14; Acts 2:3, 4; 10:46; 19:6, and Mark 16:17. Classical Pentecostals refer to those groups of Pentecostals which grew out of the Holiness Movement at the beginning of this century. The emergence of the classical Pentecostal movement is dated either from the outbreak in Topeka, Kansas, in 1901, or the Azusa Street revival in Los Angeles in 1906. Though the classical movement is not coextensive with what have become the Pentecostal churches, these do in some measure typify the movement. Among them are The Pentecostal Holiness Church, Church of God in Christ, The Assemblies of God, Church of God (Cleveland, Tennessee). The terms Protestant neo-Pentecostals or Protestant charismatics are used interchangeably for those Protestants in the historic churches (Episcopal, Lutheran, Presbyterian, etc.) who have embraced a way of approaching the gospel

characterized by emphasis on the lordship of Jesus, personal commitment, the gifts of the Spirit, interiority, devout reading of the Scriptures, and prayer. This is an inadequate description but will serve for
present purposes. In this book the term Protestant neo-Pentecostal is
used most frequently for purposes of clarity, though in recent years
many have come to prefer "Protestant charismatic" or more precisely,
Lutheran charismatic, etc. Catholic Pentecostals has been largely abandoned by those in the Catholic renewal and has been supplanted by
Catholic charismatics. Like their Protestant counterpart, they remain
in their church but have incorporated into their Catholic life those
charismatic elements named above as well as a heightened sacramental
awareness and practice.

In reviewing the research material from the fields of sociology and
cultural anthropology, as well as from psychology, the studies will be
presented chronologically. A more thematic approach has many ad-
vantages, among them the ease of producing a more organic, coherent
text. Because one of the purposes of the book is to relate the research
to the historical experience of the churches, the chronological review
seemed best. In following this research history, the conclusions of the
published research will be reported. The author is a theologian by
training and his ultimate interest is theological. In reviewing the various fields of research, namely sociology, anthropology, and psychology, the norms and methods of those disciplines will be observed. In
the final chapter, the author will revert to form and will reflect, as a
theologian, on the probabilities which seem to him to emerge from the
research.

Although this book is in part about the reaction of the churches to
the Pentecostal-charismatic movement, it is not heavily theological in
content. For those who would like to know what my theological views
are on the charismatic renewal, especially as concerns the broad theological foundations, they may consult "Theological and Pastoral
Orientations on the Catholic Charismatic Renewal," The Communication Center, P. O. Drawer A, Notre Dame, Indiana. This seventy-page
booklet was drawn up by an international team of theologians and
pastoral leaders. I wrote the first draft and was responsible for for-
mulating the final text. It has come to be known by the short title, "The
Malines Document." Quite obviously it represents only a Catholic
point of view.

The doctoral thesis of Benedict J. Mawn, "Testing the Spirits: An
Empirical Search for the Socio-Cultural Situational Roots of the Cath-

olic Pentecostal Religious Experience," Boston University, 1975, appeared too late to be consulted.

I wish to thank my psychologist friends who went over the earlier drafts of my manuscript and made suggestions for revisions: Dr. Gordon Henley, Dr. Anthony Sorem, Dr. William Backus, Dr. John O'-Connor, Dr. Leo Rolls, and gratitude for the care taken by Dr. Roman Paur, OSB. I wish also to thank Dr. David E. Harrell for the careful reading he gave my first draft and for the suggestions he made from the point of view of an historian; Dr. Thomas Thole, OSB, for reading and criticizing chapter two on the social theories as applied to Pentecostal research; and Dr. Hilary Thimmesh, OSB, for graciously translating an extensive French text on short notice. Not only for the typing and re-typing of the manuscript, but for care concerning points of style, my thanks to Sister Dolores Schuh, CHM. Any deficiencies in the book are solely my responsibility.

1 | HUMAN EXPERIENCE
AND RELIGIOUS MEANING

Charism is essentially a theological category and has to do with the religious meaning of specific human experiences. Charism does not exist in the abstract. It only exists in the concrete, more specifically, in persons and in communities. Therefore, a charism has a dimension which is not exhausted simply by its theological definition and investigation. In any Christian community where charisms are exercised there are a multitude of factors which enter into that exercise: historical, cultural, psychological, ethnic, even economic. When a theologian, whose proper function is to theologize, writes of charisms he is drawn into those boundary waters where it is difficult to draw clear lines between the theological and psychological aspects of reality. Any seaman will witness that boundary waters have their own perils. In this book the author has passed over to what is clearly a psychological aspect of speaking in tongues, an aspect which, of course, is not unrelated to its theological meaning.

When psychologists study people who speak in tongues they, too, enter the boundary waters. Since many of the psychologists who are reviewed in this book speak, at least in passing, of the theological dimensions of the phenomenon they have been investigating, some attempt should be made to describe what a theologian might mean by a charism. What is attempted here is not an exhaustive theological definition, but rather one, not the only, theological description. Obviously this description is limited to those theological aspects which will provide points of contact with the psychological considerations under review.

CHARISM AS MINISTRY

In the New Testament charisms are operations or manifestations of the Holy Spirit in and for the Christian community. "To each is given the manifestation of the Spirit for the common good" (1 Cor. 12:7). Like the Holy Spirit itself, the charisms are gifts, that is, they are given by God and are not something a person merits. A person may seek the charisms (1 Cor. 12:31) but they are essentially spiritual gifts. The gifts are without number, as they are the multitudinous ways that the Holy Spirit comes to visibility in the church in service functions. To a greater or lesser degree a charism is a ministry to others. The more immediately a ministry or charism is related to the service of others, the higher it is on the hierarchy of gifts. The less immediately the charism is related to the service of others, the lower it is on the hierarchy of gifts. Paul mentions some of the charisms, but he makes no claims to being exhaustive. In writing to the Corinthians, Paul says: "Now you together are Christ's body; but each of you is a different part of it. In the Church, God has given the first place to apostles, the second to prophets, the third to teachers; after them, miracles, and after them the gift of healing; helpers, good leaders, those with many languages" (1 Cor. 12:27, 28). In Romans 12:5–8 Paul takes up the theme again. "All of us, in union with Christ, form one body, and as parts of it we belong to each other. Our gifts differ according to the grace given us. If your gift is prophecy, then use it as your faith suggests; if administration, then use it for administration; if teaching, then use it for teaching. Let the preachers deliver sermons, the almsgivers give freely, the officials be diligent, and those who do works of mercy do them cheerfully." A charism is a manifestation of the Spirit in a ministry to the other members of the body. It is therefore directed outward to others, rather than inward to self.

The exercise of a charism is a fully human activity and is not under the control of some force outside a person. The charismatic gift of prophecy, for instance, is under the control of the prophet. Both the capacity to give a speech and to prophesy can be used or not used at will. The prophet is never under compulsion to prophesy: "Prophets can always control their prophetic spirits, since God is not a God of disorder but of peace" (1 Cor. 14:32). So a charism does not transform a person into an automaton. How a person uses his gift will, in the Christian perspective, be a matter of accounting. A true gift can be wrongly used. One can abuse a gift. A prophet can utter a true prophecy at the wrong time or in the wrong circumstances. He is responsible for the manner in which he uses his gift. It is further possible that a person with a true prophetic call may, because he acts out of pride on a given occasion, speak a false prophecy. That is one of the reasons why all charismatic activity, prophetic or otherwise, must be submitted to a discerning process (1 Cor. 14:29). In this sense all charismatic activity is, in the first instance, ambiguous. The ambiguity is removed by a discerning process (1 Cor. 12:30; 14:5, 29) which is essentially a community function though certain individuals may play a more pronounced role in such a process.

NEW FACULTY OR NEW FUNCTION

A more precise question can be asked. Does the charism of tongues constitute a gift in the sense that the recipient now has a radically new capacity, a new faculty which was not present before the Holy Spirit gave the gift? For some who would answer in the affirmative, the emphasis is on the action of God equipping the persons with new capacities of an entirely different order. This is not the case of a human faculty yielding to a divine power, acting together with its force so that all is directed to transcendent ends which lie both in the world and ultimately beyond human history. Rather, the basic capacity itself is new and of an order beyond the human. In this view the gift is a new power and is entirely different from a natural faculty. Those who share this view tend to see the gift of tongues as miraculous.

Others would say that the gift of tongues is not an endowment with a new set of faculties independent of or in addition to the faculties which are proper to human beings. The charism of tongues is rather the same faculties proper to human beings which have a new function. The power of the Spirit who is present everywhere is manifested in a new way. Speaking in tongues is new because it is directed toward the building up of the body of Christ, the church. Praying in the power of the Spirit strengthens oneself and the Christian community. In this view, speaking in tongues might not differ phenomenologically from the verbalizations which occur in non-Christian cultures, though this has yet to be demonstrated.

A theologian would wish to point out two extremes. There is the extreme of over-supernaturalizing the charisms, as though each manifestation of the Spirit constituted something miraculous. The other extreme would be to see the charisms purely as expressions of psychological states, or services which are explainable in purely sociological terms. A charism is not just an exercise of a capacity which pertains to the fullness of humanity. A charism is a gift because that capacity has a new function and a new power. In saying this one does not want to fall into a two-level doctrine of the relationship between the human and the divine. The unity of the human and the divine in the concrete exercise of a charism should be recognized. Speaking in tongues does not occur apart from one's own psychological structure and history.[1] This phenomenon has a human side, a complex of psychological mechanisms and personal history which constitute its psychological structure. In addition, speaking in tongues has a religious meaning. These two aspects, psychological structure and religious meaning in a specifically Christian sense, are distinguishable but not in such a way that one adds the Christian dimension to the human. Every authentic exercise of the charism of speaking in tongues has a "saving side," and every "saving experience" has a human side. The psychologist examines the human side of the saving experience and details its mechanisms. The theologian reflects on the "saving side," noting how God's acting presence is manifested sovereignly in humanity in a new way and in a new depth. In no way is such an approach to the charism of tongues a denigrating of the divine.

MIRACLE—INTERVENTION FROM BEYOND HISTORY

A theologian has a special difficulty in talking about the miraculous as the concept of a miracle is not all that clear even among professional theologians.[2] If theologians are generally unhappy with an explanation of miracles as a suspension of the laws of nature, an intervention by God from outside history, some see miracles as God acting sovereignly within nature, an intervention from within history. The author would not want to explain charisms in general in such a way that the miraculous activity of God within nature is completely and totally excluded from every exercise of all the charisms. Without this sovereign act of him who is Lord of the universe, a lordship he exercises from within history, there are events for which we cannot account.

In fairness to the scholars who have engaged in psychological research of those who speak in tongues (glossolalics), it should be said that the great numbers of persons in the Pentecostal-charismatic movement have an exaggerated view of the manifestations, an oversupernaturalized view, with which most theologians in the historic churches would not agree. All of this colors the mental frame in which the psychologist approaches his subjects of investigation. If a person is making claims of miraculous powers, powers he or she has been given by a direct intervention of God from outside time and beyond history, then the psychologist brings a mind set to his investigation which corresponds to what his subjects claim a charism is, but not what in fact a charism is. When the psychologist hears the word "miracle" fall so easily, carelessly and frequently from Pentecostal-charismatic lips, he then may bring a kind of skepticism to his study from which a more mature theology of charisms would free him. Once again, it is not only the theologian who enters the boundary waters when studying tongues. The psychologist also enters them, and the perils exist for him as well as for the theologian.

A TRUE LANGUAGE?

The psychologist also brings certain psychological presuppositions to his research which are determined by the claim made by glossolalics that speaking in tongues is a speaking in a true language which the speaker has not learned. Without entering into this question in a detailed way, the view of the author is that in the vast majority of cases the one who is speaking in tongues is not speaking a real language, but a prayer language or an art language. Speaking or praying in tongues is to prayer what abstract painting is to art. Just as good abstract art is not color and form without order or discipline, but is a non-objective expression of deep feelings and convictions, so also tongues. Those who are praying in tongues are expressing in a non-objective manner deep religious convictions and sentiments which they might have a difficult time expressing in their own native language. Because many involved in the Pentecostal-charismatic movement think of tongues as a miraculous intervention of God from beyond history and time they quite naturally tend to think that the speaker is talking or praying in a true language which he has not learned. There are a number of cases reported in which a person spoke in tongues and was understood by someone to be speaking a true language, a language which the second person had as a native language and therefore immediately recognized as a true language. A scientist as well as the theologian will tend to be extremely skeptical of these instances. They occur in circumstances in which strict scientific verification is not possible. The conditions of control and validation are absent. It is the private opinion of the author, which he cannot verify scientifically, that in the vast majority of cases, speaking or praying in tongues is not a true language.

The older New Testament exegetes thought that glossolalia involved a true language. Some contemporary exegetes hold that Paul himself thought that it was a true language though a number of these exegetes think Paul was mistaken. Many of those in the classical Pentecostal and in the denominational charismatic renewal movements, Catholic and Protestant, also consider tongues to be a true language in the proper sense. George T. Montague, the editor of the *Catholic Biblical Quarterly*, thinks "that the gift of tongues as reported by Paul was essentially pre-conceptual without any connotation of foreign languages."[3] As will be seen, such linguistic anthropologists as Samarin and Wolfram affirm that tongues as a true language has never been demonstrated. The author shares this opinion but does not want to close the door on the possibility of tongues in quite rare instances being a true language. For this, too, the author has no scientifically verifiable evidence. At this point theological instinct tells him that the door should not be irrevocably closed. Not all witnesses to the event of someone speaking in tongues are persons caught in the grip of some religious enthusiasm or mania.

The psychologist as well as the general reader should not over-invest in the question of whether or not tongues is a true language. Though the investigation of the nature of this vocalization is a valid object of scientific inquiry, and persons involved in the Pentecostal-charismatic movement should not feel overly threatened by such investigations, the theologian cannot tie his evaluation of tongues as a gift to the verification or non-verification of the utterance as a true language. From a purely theological point of view the question is interesting, but basically irrelevant. Tongues is essentially a prayer gift, and a theological evaluation is based on its prayer value (1 Cor. 12:14,16), not on its being a true language. Persons who have this gift often say that they are able to pray at a deeper level by using tongues, than by not using tongues. This is the issue for a theologian. He can take this stand because tongues is not meant primarily as a means of communicating messages from God to individual persons or communities. It is essentially the means by which a person engages in the prayer of praise, usually in private. What language is being used is theologically irrelevant and therefore not the primary focus of the theologian.

THE ISSUE IS NOT TONGUES

The isolation of tongues as an object of psychological investigation is a valid procedure for a psychologist. This isolation is also justified by certain expressions of the Pentecostal-charismatic movement. In some cases the literature issuing from the movement gave the impression that it had as its purpose to initiate persons into the practice of praying or speaking in tongues. Any serious student of the Pentecostal-charismatic movement (whether the focus is on the classical, neo-Pentecostal or Catholic charismatic expression), will immediately recognize that the issue is not tongues. The issue is, rather, totality of the gospel, life in Christ through the power of the Spirit, insertion into the body of Christ, where the members exercise a variety of ministries (the lowest of which is tongues). There is general recognition that to concentrate on the gifts of the Spirit and, much more, to concentrate on tongues, can result in a basic distortion of the gospel. In all sectors of the movement there is recognition, for instance, that love (or charity) is more basic to the Christian life than tongues. This is not to deny that tongues plays a role, indeed is highly esteemed. But speaking in tongues is not what the Pentecostal-charismatic renewal is all about. To contend that it is would be to give a caricature of it.

THE MARK OF A SPECIAL CHRISTIAN?

To situate tongues in its proper context in the life of the church, it might help to see how a theologian, in this instance a Cardinal of the Roman Catholic Church representing a very conservative theological tradition, would describe a renewed church. One should note that this appeared first in print in 1936, thirty years before the emergence of the Catholic charismatic renewal. Despite its length it is given here almost in full.

> It is in [the Holy Spirit's] name at the same time as in the name of the Father and the Son that baptism is conferred on the nations (Mt. the end; cf. John 3:5). It is he who comes down upon all on whom the apostles lay hands (Acts 8:17; 19:6). It is he who, in the Eucharist makes the flesh life-giving (John 6:63). It is through him that sins are taken away (John 20:23). In opening to himself a new access to his Church through the

sacraments, the Holy Spirit fills the Church with sacramental graces which shape it from within to the likeness of Christ, leading it collectively and fully along the way to which Christ committed himself: "If the Spirit of him who raised Jesus from the dead dwells in you, He who raised Jesus Christ from the dead will also give life to your mortal bodies through his Spirit who dwells in you" (Rom. 8:2). . . .

He aims to raise [the faithful] higher, to assist them by his own power to do those perfect acts glorified in the Sermon on the Mount and called beatitudes by the theologians. He makes them children of God in the manner constantly more true: "All those who are moved by the Spirit of God are the sons of God" (Rom. 8:14). He comes "in aid of our weakness." He "intercedes for us with groans beyond all utterance" (Rom. 8:26). His grace, which presses in upon us from every side, is like the air we breathe and without which death would come instantly by asphyxiation.

And then have we not said that by reason of omnipresence—which can also be appropriated to the Spirit as creator. . . . God is present by His very substance in every creature and therefore in each member of His Church in virtue of a direct and immediate contact? He is already, by that single fact, closer to us than we ourselves. He communicates to us our deep being; He sustains in existence at every moment the very substance of our soul and body. "He is not far from any one of us for it is in Him that we live and move and have our being" (Acts 17:28).

The Holy Spirit will come to the aid of his church in exceptional ways. At decisive moments of her history, he will provide her with unexpected reinforcement. He will raise up in her miracles of strength, of light, of purity: in the hierarchy or among the faithful, there will emerge men and women—Francis of Assisi or Francis Xavier, Catherine of Siena or Teresa of Avila—who possess such a deep understanding of the eternal treasure of the church that they can discern in it with infallible vision, the remedy for the ills which afflict their times. To proclaim their message they will have such clarity of voice, such purity of heart; they will set in such sharp contrast the fruits of the life of wisdom and the fruits of the death of illusion, that the world, rescued from its lethargy, will believe that it again hears the apostles. They will work miracles, discern spirits, speak in tongues. They will be the true prophets. They will prophesy not outside the Church, not to add some new content to the full revelation made once and for all by Christ and the apostles. But wondrously informed by the understanding of that revelation, they will prophesy to clarify by its light the movement of their epoch and the needs of mankind. In them will appear anew, in a form adapted to the new conditions of the life of the Church, the charismatic graces which, on the witness of Scripture, were extended to the first Christians.

These comings of the Holy Spirit in the Church, these visits of the Holy Spirit will sometimes be limited to miraculous help. But more often the charismatic manifestations of the Spirit will themselves be only the external sign, the perceptible repercussion of a supernatural outpouring, incomparably more precious, of grace and holiness. Newman was right when, searching for some principle which could illuminate the history of the Church, he thought of what happened after the first Pentecost.[4]

Three things should be noted. The first is the unquestionably minor role tongues has in a renewed church. Cardinal Journet can hardly be thought of as proposing the establishment of a tongues movement to renew the church. Second, though a minor expression of the church's life in the Spirit, it is present. Third, tongues is not the distinguishing mark of a special kind of Christian. It is simply one manifestation of the total life of the church.

PROFESSIONAL PREJUDICE

A basic assumption is that a person or persons are to be considered psychologically normal until otherwise demonstrated. Psychologists will generally agree that the outward boundaries of normality are ample and wide rather than restrictive and narrow.[5] These assumptions were not always granted when dealing with persons who speak in tongues. Not only religious leaders, who may be forgiven a certain ineptness in the more scientific aspects of psychology, but also those trained in the behavioral sciences, who are not so easily absolved from guilt in the matter which belongs to the first principles of their science, have at times failed to grant these assumptions to glossolalics. The author knows of a team of anthropologists and psychologists, professors and graduate students at a well-known university in the United States, which was studying glossolalics in the classical and neo-Pentecostal movements during the mid-1960s.[6] They assumed without adequate knowledge of the persons involved that glossolalics were psychologically deprived *because* they spoke in tongues. This they considered self-evident needing no scientific verification. Even those who were trained in the behavioral sciences and therefore aware that in some societies speaking in tongues is considered neither unusual nor abnormal were not able to stand back from the culturally determined attitudes of their society. Rather, they adopted these attitudes.

There is a further, more precise assumption found in both scientific circles and in the general public, namely, that persons who engage in nonrational behavior are psychologically abnormal. Or it is assumed that persons who gravitate toward the Pentecostal-charismatic movements make up a certain psychological type. In a more general religious framework there is the assumption that religious needs and interests typify the more anxious, insecure members of society.[7] Or, finally, the presuppositions are cast in cultural terms. In this framework one says that one expects this kind of religious behavior from the more passionate, excitable peoples, such as the Latins, and this explains adequately the growth of classical Pentecostals in certain countries; for instance in a number of South American countries.

It would be wrong to proceed on the assumption that the results of a psychological study of glossolalics which issues in a negative judgment on their mental health is a manifestation of deep personal bias on the part of the researchers. On the other hand, it should be admitted also that some behavioral scientists have not escaped bias. Some consistently view all religious experience with deep skepticism. This same tendency to evaluate religious behavior negatively has been noted, among others, by Nathan and Louise Gerrard (1966, 1968), Erika Bourguignon and Louanna Pettay (1964), Virginia Hine (1969), and William Samarin (1972).[8] The same bias long obtained in the study of shamanism. Even when it is admitted that glossolalics are not pathological, there is a common assumption that there is some more generalized psychological deprivation, some disordered personality regression, some deep feelings of inadequacy. It is against the background of these common assumptions that the reports of church commissions, reviewed in the third chapter, are to be seen and judged. These assumptions did not arise out of such commissions but rather the commissions reflect the common climate and attitudes.

SOCIAL UNACCEPTABILITY

The force of attitudes which are culturally determined is hard to underestimate. Glossolalics are engaging in behavioral patterns which in our society were, in general, socially unacceptable. In most European and North American societies speaking in tongues is not what most persons expect from mature, well-balanced responsible adults. Those who depart from this norm of social acceptability are looked upon as engaging in deviant behavior and are therefore accepted in polite society with some hesitancy and embarrassment. The social unacceptability of such behavior was more pronounced in the first fifty or sixty years of the classical Pentecostal movement, that is from about 1900 until about the end of World War II. During the war classical

Pentecostals ceased to be identified with the lower socio-economic levels of American society and became middle-class America. It became increasingly difficult to identify speaking in tongues with the kind of sectarian behavior one came to expect from the lower socio-economic groups. In the late fifties and early sixties the Protestant neo-Pentecostal movement emerged in, among others, the Episcopal, Presbyterian, and Lutheran churches. Persons of education, means, and position in the professional and business world were involved. The older theories of economic and cultural deprivation as a way of explaining glossolalic behavior no longer seemed so convincing. This was reinforced when the Catholic charismatic renewal appeared on the scene in 1967. The Catholic movement added a dimension which until recently was generally wanting in Protestant neo-Pentecostalism, that is, public identification with the renewal of trained theologians and scholars, some of international repute. In this regard one could mention Donald Gelpi of the Jesuit School of Theology at Berkeley; Francis Sullivan, former rector of the Gregorian University in Rome; Stanislaus Lyonnet, professor at the Biblicum in Rome and consultor to the Office of the Doctrine of the Faith (the former Holy Office); Heribert Mühlen, professor at the theological faculty at Paderborn, Germany, who is considered by many as the leading theologian on the doctrine of the Holy Spirit in the Roman Church; Paul Lebeau, one of the directors of the catechetical institute in Brussels, *Lumen Vitae*; George T. Montague, editor of the scientific exegetical review, *The Catholic Biblical Quarterly*; Alday Salvador Carrillo, a New Testament scholar from Mexico City; Jan van der Vekan, a professor of philosophy at Louvain University in Belgium; and Peter Hocken, professor of moral theology, Oscott College, England. In the United States four Roman Catholic bishops have publicly identified themselves with the renewal as personally involved, and there are other bishops in South and Central America, Canada, and Europe who have similarly associated themselves. Leo Cardinal Suenens, Primate of Belgium, one of the four moderators of Vatican Council II, who exercised considerable influence on two major documents coming from the Council, namely, *The Constitution on the Church* and *The Church in the Modern World*, has taken a leading role in the renewal. He was the principal patron of the charismatic pilgrimage to Rome in May 1975, which culminated in an audience in St. Peter's where Pope Paul received ten thousand Catholic charismatics.[9] At the end of the audience the Pope, Cardinal Suenens and twelve other bishops involved in the renewal joined in blessing the assembly. Clearly one is less sure of oneself in speaking of the charismatic renewal as a response to economic or cultural deprivation, or as typically sectarian in character. Though many will still not feel comfortable with the practice of speaking or praying in tongues, one cannot talk about socially unacceptable behavior in the manner one did in the past.

But it was not so in the beginning of the classical movement (dated variously as 1901 or 1906), of the Protestant neo-Pentecostal movement (late fifties, early sixties), and of the Catholic charismatic movement (1967). The review of the psychological literature begins with those studies which were associated with the rise of prophetic, revivalist groups toward the end of the last century and the classical Pentecostal movement at the beginning of this century. In early classical Pentecostal meetings the sessions were often disorganized, highly emotional, and many of the early adherents (though not all) came from the lower socio-economic levels.[10] Many of these early Pentecostals were anti-institutional, anticreedal, antiauthoritarian, antibureaucratic, and anti-intellectual. Though even in those days there was recognition that the movement was not simply a tongues movement, the gift of tongues did indeed have a kind of centrality. Speaking in tongues was, and for many classical Pentecostals today still is, the initial evidence that one has received the baptism in the Holy Spirit. The emergence of Protestant neo-Pentecostal movement (or of the Protestant charismatic renewal, as many prefer to call it) will present psychological researchers with a new socio-cultural context for their studies. Some of these shifts will be evident in chapters five and six.

2 | DISORGANIZATION AND DEPRIVATION: MOVEMENTS AND THEIR CAUSES

Only those in want need a redeemer. Those who are full and self-sufficient do not look for a savior. Theology has always held that all men are in want, even those who are not conscious of their situation, and all need a redeemer. That the rise of religion is a product of poverty and distress is not an uncommon opinion among social scientists. Such was certainly the view of Max Weber, who wrote: "The oppressed, or at least those threatened by distress, were in need of a redeemer and prophet; the fortunate, the propertied, the ruling strata were not in such need. Therefore, in the great majority of cases, a prophetically announced religion of redemption has had its permanent locus among the less-favored social strata. Among these, such religiosity has either been a substitute for, or a rational supplement to, magic."[1]

Though the poor in fact as well as the poor in spirit have no exclusive claim to religious sentiments and sensitivity, there is an undoubted affinity between poverty and religious fervor. "It is the lower classes," Ernst Troeltsch contended, "which do the really creative work, forming communities on a genuine religious basis. They alone unite imagination and simplicity of feeling with a non-reflective habit of mind, a primitive energy, and an urgent sense of need. On such a foundation alone is it possible to build up an unconditional authoritative faith in a divine revelation with simplicity of surrender and unshaken certainty. . . . All great religious movements based on divine revelation which have created large communities have always issued from circles of this kind."[2] In *The Social Sources of Denominationalism*, H. Richard Niebuhr asserted that all major religious movements during the Christian era grew up as solutions to lower class frustrations. The simple and direct grasp of faith by the poor has shunned the religious relativity and qualifications which the more sophisticated find necessary. Ethically the religion of the poor "often demonstrates its moral and religious superiority."[3]

The development of the church-sect theory, as well as the related but not identical theory of movement origins and growth, were rooted in the kinds of perceptions Weber, Troeltsch, and Niebuhr, as well as others, had about the confused, frustrated, disorganized and angry poor. To understand how the churches, and to some extent how the psychologists understood the Pentecostal-charismatic movement, some awareness of social theory as applied to church-sect and movement development is necessary.

A brief description of the essentials of church-sect theory will be followed by a description of various social theories developed to explain the origin and growth of movements. Two theories which have been used to describe the rise of Pentecostalism are those of disorganization and deprivation. Though distinct, they are inextricably intertwined. For present purposes they will be treated together. Authors will not be identified as wholly committed to one or the other of the theories, a particularly difficult task because the theories overlap and many authors represent a combination of them. Without attempting to show in detail how these emerged, some elements in their development, especially those related to Pentecostal research will be briefly sketched. John B. Holt's views on social deprivation, with its "culture shock," will be looked at because of its meaning for Pentecostal research. Holt's theory underwent a modification at the hands of David Aberle, a modification which has been applied to Pentecostalism in more recent years. The empirical challenges to theories of social disorganization and deprivation, both economic and social will be reviewed, together with what these challenges mean for the understanding of Pentecostalism. A few recent publications which are more analytic in their evaluations of social theories as applied to Pentecostalism will be reviewed. This became important in the light of the character of both Protestant neo-Pentecostalism and the Catholic charismatic renewal as it emerged in the sixties. The review of the literature which could be classified as following the psychological maladjustment theory will be given in those later chapters devoted entirely to psychological research and will therefore not be found in this chapter. Finally, some conclusions will be drawn about the limitations and continued usefulness of social theory in Pentecostal research.

The purpose of this chapter is not to give a detailed and adequate account of the history of social theories and its relation to Pentecostal research, something which is clearly beyond the competency of the author. Rather, this chapter will give those broad lines of social theory and Pentecostal research helpful to those seeking to understand the larger context in which the churches made their judgments on the Pentecostal-charismatic movement and in which psychologists pursued their research.

CHURCH-SECT THEORY

Much of the thinking on religious movements goes back to the work of Max Weber and Ernst Troeltsch. Their distinction between sects and churches resulted in the church-sect theory. In its original formulation it was an attempt to distinguish types of religious groups. Weber and Troeltsch were not attempting to explain the causes or conditions which gave rise to certain groups. Later scholars did use the church-sect theory as a theory of cause. Why do such groups come into existence? What are the conditions which cause them to emerge? The discussion on the church-sect theory of causation has a long history and in the course of that history the theory has been qualified and refined to the point that only the brave attempt to untangle and make a systematic whole out of the discussions or even say where the discussion is at the moment. Setting aside the many nuances added in the last decades, and confining a description of the theory to the essential points, one could say that the traditional theory maintained 1) that new religious movements begin by being sect-like in character, 2) that they arise by breaking off from church-type bodies, 3) that they are rooted in economic deprivation, and 4) that they generally transform themselves into churches.[4]

Anyone who knows the history of classical Pentecostalism, especially in this country, knows how sect-like in character was its stance over against culture, how it despised what it saw as the rationalism and the lack of fervor in the established churches, how clearly it was identified with the lower socio-economic class, and how early the process of institutionalization began—indeed began while it was still protesting against it. Though the church-sect typology had a much wider application, it seemed particularly appropriate for what was happening to the emerging classical Pentecostals. It was especially their poverty which attracted the attention of early scholars of the classical Pentecostal movement. Anton Boisen (1936, 1939, 1955) will be one of the earliest representatives of this concern.

THEORIES OF MOVEMENT FORMATION AND GROWTH

Sociologists and cultural anthropologists have described the conditions which give rise to new religious groups. Quite predictably these scholars pay particular attention to those class differences which they judge to be at the basis of new religious alignments and movements. Though the thinking concerning the origin and development of religious groups has arisen in large part out of the church-sect discussion, a description of the various theories will be given first. These theories tried to isolate those social factors which gave rise to new religious groupings. The more important of these are social disorganization, economic deprivation, social deprivation, ethical deprivation, and psychological maladjustment.

The Social Disorganization Theory

Movements arise when the times are out of joint, when one culture has contact (sometimes violent contact) with another and culture shock manifests itself, when family structures are disrupted, when rapid social change calls into question the old alignments and the old values, when there is migration from one milieu to another (from a rural setting to the city), when there are extreme distresses, deportations, detribalizations, and catastrophes. Movements arise in these circumstances because they provide instruments for organizing life in meaningful patterns and give purpose to the newly constructed system of relationships.

The Deprivation Theories

1. Economic deprivation: persons who live a marginal existence because of poverty turn to movements to compensate for the harsh realities. Having only limited access to the necessities of life and few of the luxuries, they join movements in order to assuage the hurt and to make up for the want of economic means.

2. Social deprivation: some individuals feel that they do not share the rewards of society in the same manner as do others. These rewards are such things as prestige, power, status, the opportunity to participate fully in the life of public institutions. Social deprivation arises out of a situation in which these rewards are unequally distributed. The bases of distribution are varied: youth is preferred in terms of reward to old age, men to women, the educated to the uneducated, the white to the black, the Protestant to the Catholic. Having been deprived on a basis which is frequently unjust, those deprived tend to form or join movements to redress the wrong.

3. Ethical deprivation: if a person feels that the dominant values of society no longer provide a meaningful framework within which he can find meaning and purpose for his life, if these dominant values do not provide the tools for organizing one's life in a manner that has purpose and pattern, then such a person will look around for an alternative. Such persons are the raw material of movements. Movements provide a structure of meaning, a universe of purpose, and present one with ideals.[5]

Psychological Maladjustment Theory

Certain persons are psychological cripples. They do not fall within the rather ample limits of normality. Because of the predispositions of their deviant, usually neurotic, personality profile, they are attracted to certain kinds of activities or certain types of enthusiastic groups.

In the discussion which follows, social and economic deprivation will, for the most part, be considered together. It is recognized that though not unrelated, they are sufficiently distinct to be experienced independently and therefore can be independent motivational factors in the rise and growth of movements. While the correlation between the two is not perfect, they do tend to go together.

EMERGENCE AND APPLICATION OF SOCIAL DISORGANIZATION AND DEPRIVATION THEORIES

Early in the socio-cultural analysis of the classical Pentecostal movement, Anton Boisen (1936, 1939, 1955) had pointed to economic distress and deprivation as a way of explaining the nature of their religious experience. In general, Boisen believed that religious experience is rooted in the social nature of man and arises spontaneously under the pressure of crisis situations. Both for the individual as well as for the group, the religious experience may be creative and result in a religious quickening. But it may break as well as make. More generally the religious experience is creative, and when it occurs in mental illness it is frequently incidental to the healing process. Boisen's conclusion is that emotion and the vision of the crisis experience as seen in the classical Pentecostal groups are not ends in themselves but must be translated into personal and social organization if their purpose is to be achieved. The Pentecostal sects arise among the most underprivileged, those classes of people who are struggling for economic survival. But the Pentecostal religion does not concern itself with improving the social and economic plight. Quite the contrary, it is content to let it get worse and worse. It has no social vision, no promise of economic salvation—only the hope of joy which is to come miraculously when the Lord returns. "The Pentecostal churches undoubtedly belong in the group of the eccentric and even of the regressive. Their fundamental assumption is highly dangerous. They believe that the divine manifests itself in the unusual and that the prompting which seems to come from without is authoritative."[6] In spite of this, Boisen found that "for the most part . . . their experiences may be regarded as constructive. With all the excesses that characterize the holy roller groups, we must give them credit for helping many individuals to reorganize lives that had been quite unsatisfactory and to make a better job of living."[7] The growth of these classical Pentecostal churches "may be regarded as a direct result of the shared strain due to the economic depression."[8] The sects are manifestations of nature's power to heal as they are spontaneous attempts of the common people to deal constructively with the stresses and trials which have befallen them with particular severity. Boisen was the first to give broad formulation to economic deprivation as applied to classical Pentecostals.

It was John B. Holt (1940) who developed a theory which included economic deprivation but stressed social disorganization as a factor which gave rise to classical Pentecostal churches in the cities.[9] Holt's thesis was that the growth of the Holiness and Pentecostal churches was the product of social disorganization and culture conflict which accompanied the migration of religious persons of a fundamentalist background from a rural setting to an urban one. The transplanted rural culture came into conflict with the urban culture and there resulted a "culture shock." The rural people were accustomed to close ties to family, friends and neighbors. They were at home with a social system which was closely structured and rooted in the soil. These rural people were transplanted into an urban setting which was impersonal, where the former bonds of family, friends and neighbors no longer existed, where coldness and unconcern typified the way persons related to one another. The social system of the city was much looser, and it was not bound in any immediate way to the soil. As a result, contended Holt, the immigrants sought security and social adequacy in the warmth and support of familial religious groups whose public worship was highly emotional. The Pentecostal churches are only one of their escape activities. The main-line Protestant churches do not appeal to the immigrants precisely because they are the embodiment of the isolation and alienation the immigrants are trying to overcome. The historic Protestant churches do not attract them because they represent the cold, formal, unfriendly city with which they are now confronted. The growth of the sects in the cities "is a social movement insofar as it is an attempt on the part of certain groups experiencing acute social maladjustment to recapture their sense of security through religious revival."[10] Less revolutionary and constructive, the movement is rather reactionary and reformist. Holt, like Boisen, noted that little is to be expected of such a movement in eradicating the social maladjustment which brought it forth. Other scholars have adopted similar social theories, among them Wilbur C. Hallenbeck (1951)[11] and Liston Pope (1942).[12]

In his study of millhands of Gastonia, North Carolina, Pope embraced a social deprivation theory. Such sectarian religious groups "thrive wherever a considerable portion of the population exists on the periphery of culture as organized."[13] The rapid growth of the sects is an indicator of the degree to which the mill workers recognize their cultural alienation. "The sects substitute religious status for social status."[14] The theses of Boisen and Holt were accepted by Benton Johnson (1961) who wished to complement the social and economic deprivation theories. Johnson suggested that these sectarian groups motivate their members to adopt an outlook which is similar in many respects to that of higher, more privileged social strata. This outlook would emphasize upward mobility, individualism, democracy, moral respectability—in a word, the dominant values of American society.[15] The sects tend to ape their social betters and therefore they tend to adopt their social ideals as incorporated in dominant American values. This is to educate away from what are the proper ideals of the sect as expressed in its formal ideology. The study of the "miracle ministry" of A. A. Allen brought Howard Elinson (1965) to the conclusion that the groups drawn to Allen's ministry were those which were "the most peripheral to social and economic success—lower class, poorly educated, Negro, 'white trash,' Puerto Rican."[16] In this same tradition Russell R. Dynes (1955) studied the church-sect types of groups in relationship to the socio-economic status of their members. He found that "sectness is associated with low socio-economic status. In other words, as education increases, emotionalism, evangelism and other sectarian characteristics are increasingly rejected."[17]

Emile Durkheim introduced "anomie" into sociological usage. Anomie is a condition in which there is a breakdown in the social structure and a general loss of consensus, a state of society in which the usual normative standards of conduct and belief have been weakened or have disappeared. Using this category, Renato Poblete and Thomas O'Dea (1960) contended that the immigrant Puerto Ricans in New York City are using the formation of sects as a way out of the condition of anomie. The sect represents an attempt "to redevelop the community in the new urban situation."[18] One of the conclusions of William W. Wood (1965) was that the Pentecostalism in the two small southern cities he studied is a potential solution to some of the personality problems which are a by-product of certain conditions, namely socio-cultural disruption, low social status, general dissatisfaction.[19] In these conditions personality disorganization is widespread. Pentecostalism offers the adherents a means of personality reorientation. The same theory of social and economic deprivation of immigrant Italians who became Pentecostal underlies the research of Anne Parsons (1965).[20] In a more general context of crisis movements, Weston La Barre (1970) speaks of them arising among "socially, economically, politically, educationally and otherwise deprived populations."[21] Anomie is likewise the common origin of both the Jesus Freaks and the Catholic Pentecostals, according to Emile Jean Pin (1974).[22] Both movements are seen as conversion from the moral confusion and the religious alienation which typified the 1960s.

RELATIVE DEPRIVATION—
THE MODIFICATION OF HOLT'S THEORY

The theories of economic and social deprivation have come under rather severe criticism in view of which the theories have been further refined. David Aberle (1962) further developed the deprivation theory in relation to cult movements, turning his attention from the reaction to deprivation to the causes of the reaction. He spoke of kinds of deprivation: possessions, status, behavior, and worth. In any of the cult movements there can be a negative discrepancy in any of these four areas between legitimate expectancy and actuality. Relative deprivation exists if a farmer owns one hundred and fifty acres while he legitimately could expect to own three hundred acres. What the standard in measuring deprivation is cannot be the objective state of affairs "but a difference between an anticipated state of affairs and a less agreeable actuality."[23] In this sense relative deprivation is the difference between what one actually has in strong contrast to what one thinks one should have. When persons realize that they are lacking what they think they should have, then the conditions are ripe for a cult movement.

While still contending that deprivation is "a necessary condition for the rise of new religious movements," though not by itself a sufficient condition, Charles Glock (1965) redefined deprivation in much the same way as Aberle had. One judges a disadvantageous condition not in itself but in comparison to other persons or conditions, or in comparison to an internalized set of standards. The experience of deprivation may be either conscious or unconscious, but in either case it tends to be accompanied by a desire to overcome it. "It is primarily the attempt, then, to overcome some deprivation, that leads to social conflict and may ultimately lead to the formation of a new social or religious group."[24]

The deprivation theories of Aberle and Glock were still further refined by Kenneth McGuire (1972, 1976). In his study of one Catholic charismatic covenant community, McGuire perceived that the young university students who made up the covenant community (persons who bind themselves short of a vow to varying degrees of community life) were not deprived in the sense of the social theories developed in the past. Neither socially nor economically nor in terms of social organization were they noticeably deficient. But they were affectively deprived. "Affective deprivation would be the difference between the affection, or emotional satisfaction, one has versus that which he thinks he should have. . . . There is a difference between the love one actually has and what he thinks he should have. The people in this study feel that prior to entering the community they were not receiving as much love as they should."[25] This affective deprivation is one of the factors which constitute favorable conditions for the formation of a crisis movement such as the charismatic renewal.

In criticism of McGuire's position one would want empirical evidence that the members of the community he was studying were in fact very anxious, tense or guilty. The evidence given is largely impressionistic. Further, one wonders if McGuire, when speaking of affective deprivation, is not talking about a universal condition, something which is constant in all human beings. Who among us thinks that he or she receives the love deserved? Where are the persons who have attained a kind of parity between expected love and love received? Since affective deprivation in McGuire is considered a factor in the rise and growth of the community, is he not explaining a variable (the charismatic community) by a constant (affective deprivation)? In social science a constant cannot be used to explain a variable.

The inability of McGuire to use the older theories of movement formation which were so much discussed and so highly refined the last few decades is indicative of a greater unease about their adequacy. There has been some confusion of the church-sect typology from the beginning. Weber's church-sect type is that of a sociologist while Troeltsch's is that of an ethician. The later developments of church-sect theory were concerned with explaining causes—why certain movements arise and take a specific form. Neither Weber nor Troeltsch had been concerned with causes.

The theories were not of major help in explaining the "why" of the Pentecostal movement. When the church-sect theory became a theory of causes—why these sect groups arise and evolve toward churches—the theory had a difficult time validating itself. There were, for instance, groups which showed no signs of evolving from sect to church. There was also a general failure in the research to distinguish the Pentecostal sects from the Pentecostal movement.[26] The movement includes many more bodies than the Pentecostal sects. There are interdenominational groups such as the Full Gospel Business Men's Fellowship International, the considerable number of prayer groups which do not identify with any church or sect, the "hiddens" (who have embraced the Pentecostal experience and orientation but have no wish to declare this openly), the sizeable groups of leaders and preachers who engage in a kind of nondenominational "free ministry," and the thousands of Episcopal, Presbyterian, Lutheran, and Catholic prayer groups and communities. Clearly the church-sect typology will only clumsily accommodate such a disparate collection of groups.

EMPIRICAL CHALLENGE TO HOLT'S THEORY

The theses of Holt and other scholars have been challenged by empirical studies. In research carried out in Columbus, Ohio, Russell R. Dynes (1956) tested whether the sectarians of the city were the recent arrivals in the city. Dynes found that those with sectarian tendencies tended to have the longest period of residence in Columbus. "Instead of producing 'culture shock,' migration may provide an opportunity for an individual to reorganize his values for functioning on a higher socio-economic level, and this may involve rejecting his sectarian ideology."[27] The migration to the city may result not in embracing sectarianism but in rejecting it. This is reinforced in some earlier research. Walter R. Goldschmidt (1944) found a tendency of recent white immigrant workers to drop in church attendance on moving into the new surroundings.[28] That the "movement from farm to city tends to reduce the frequency of church attendance" was also one of the conclusions of the research of Beers and Heflin (1944).[29] More recent research would support this general thesis. In Giffin's (1962) study of immigrants to Cincinnati, "60 per cent of all newcomers reported a decline in their church attendance after migration, and . . . those from the southern Appalachians reported a significantly greater decrease than did those from elsewhere."[30] A further independent study of immigrants to Cincinnati arrived at a similar conclusion.[31] In an attempt to test Holt's thesis Nelsen and Whitt used the data of two well-known studies of immigrants to Detroit. These immigrants did not appear to be suffering from culture shock; there was little evidence of anomie (that condition in which the normative standards of conduct and belief have been weakened). Nor did the immigrants appear to be especially sectarian.[32]

THE RELIGIOSITY OF THE POOR

Nor does all the evidence point to a high degree of religiosity among the poor which one would expect to find if one were turning to religion for solace. Basing his research on fourteen thousand cases, Hadley Cantril (1943) found that contrary to the general assumption, namely that the poor and socially deprived turn to religion as practiced in the churches for solace from their economic desperation, it was the more affluent who became members of churches.[33] The number of church members in a population increases with both the economic and the educational status of the population. "Conversely, the numbers of those without church membership increases as the income or educational levels are descended."[34]

There were indications already in the study of Robert and Helen Lynd (1929) that a myth had been constructed about the tendency of the poor to turn to the churches for consolation. The research found that fifty-five percent of the white collar workers attended church at least three times a month while only twenty-five percent of the blue collar workers attended that frequently.[35] Harold Kaufman (1944) researched a rural community in New York, focusing on various prestige classes which were determined in reference to certain social characteristics (such as ethnic group membership, place of residence, occupation, and years of schooling).[36] On this prestige scale seventy-eight percent of the two highest classes were church members; of the next two classes only thirty-eight percent; nine percent of the next two lower prestige classes; and only one percent of the lowest class. In a similar research project on a middle-western community immediately before World War II, August B. Hollingshead (1947, 1949) studied, among other things, involvement in church activities in relationship to class stratification.[37] In the spectrum of five classes the topmost classes had fully ninety-seven percent who professed to be church members, thereafter there was a consistent decline class by class until the lowest class showed seventy-one percent claiming church membership. In the July 1954 data of the American Institute of Public Opinion, eighty-three percent of the professional and business respondents claimed membership in some church while seventy-seven percent of the manual laborers made the same claim. Of those with college education, eighty-three percent belonged to a church and seventy-three percent of those with only a grade school education. That the lower classes are disaffected from the churches while the upper classes are more aggressive churchgoers was, however, not demonstrated in the research on Madison, Wisconsin, by Louis Bultena (1949).[38] There was a slight tendency for more non-church people to come from the lower status brackets than from the higher, but the tendency was not statistically significant. On the other hand, W. Lloyd Warner's (1949) study of "Janesville" showed a significant variation. Seventy-seven percent of the upper-class families were found on the church rolls while only twenty-eight percent of the lower-lower class were so represented.[39] Using a two-class system (upwardly mobile, nonmobile) Gerhard Lenski (1961) showed that in Detroit, Michigan, the lower nonmobile class had a lower percentage of regular church attendance than the middle mobile class.[40] That there is a direct relationship between social status and church membership and attendance was the conclusion of Lee G. Burchinal's (1959) research in four midwestern states. The higher the educational status the higher the degree of church participation.[41]

Several factors must qualify these findings regarding the consistent underrepresentation of the lower classes in church membership.[42] There is a general tendency of the less affluent and the poorer educated to shun voluntary association, whether that be secular or religious. This group is not a joiner of any organization. Nonparticipation in church life is part of the group's nonparticipation in organizational life in general. Though in the studies quoted the lower classes were less aggressive in their churchgoing, there was no consistency in the middle and upper classes. Some studies indicate that the middle class is more involved in the church than the upper class. The statistical difference between the lower and the upper class is not consistent and not always large, even though the difference exists. This is true, for instance, of the research of Hollingshead and Bultena and of the data gathered in 1954 by the American Institute of Public Opinion. Given this small percentage difference in some of the research, conclusions drawn from the whole body of research cannot be definitive.

It is undoubtedly true that the majority of research projects show those in the upper classes to be more religiously involved than the lower classes. But some attention must be paid to a minority report from another group of researchers which shows that the people of lower socio-economic levels are more involved in religion. Yoshio Fukuyama (1960) decided that church membership was an inadequate category for measuring religiosity and proposed that four categories be used: cognitive (what they know about religion), cultic (attendance at worship and participation in church activities), creed (what a person believes as distinct from what he knows or does), and devotional (what one feels or experiences).[43] Fukuyama showed that the kind of relationship found between socio-economic status and religion depended very much on which index of religiosity was used. He found that the more highly educated and the more affluent scored higher than the less educated and poorer parishioners on the cognitive and cultic scales. These upper-class believers knew more about their religion and went more frequently to church and participated in church activities more than their lower-class counterparts. On the other hand the less educated and poorer parishioners scored higher on the creedal and devotional scales. They were surer of their faith and hewed more surely to the traditional beliefs, and looked to the Scriptures more for its devotional than for its intellectual value. "This suggests that different social classes differ not so much in the degree to which they are religiously oriented but in the manner in which they give expression to their religious propensities."[44]

Following the lead of Fukuyama the research of N. J. Demerath III (1965) reinforced the necessity of distinguishing between the degree and kind of involvement in religion when studying social classes.[45] Although he found that lower-class church members seem to be more deeply involved in their religion, the lower class in general does not have a disproportionately higher rate of church membership per se. But those from the lower class who opted for religion did so with more force and vigor.[46] No new light was shed by the research of Glock, Ringer, and Babbie on the lower class's flight from religion, but they were able to demonstrate that among those who did become church members "parishioners of lower status are the most likely to be deeply involved."[47] Those parishioners whose life situations most deprive them of prestige and gratification in the secular society are the most involved in the church. Gerhard Lenski (1953) studied Indianapolis and found that the middle class (when defined in purely financial terms) exhibited greater interest in religion than either the upper or lower classes, while those who had enjoyed the greatest income gain since marriage expressed the least interest in religion.[48] Lenski recalls the long history of research which studied the relation between religion and economic status, and suggests that the "nature of the relationship has not been made clear."[49] Though he was writing in 1953 his cautionary note seems to be still valid. ". . . at the present time there are but few generalizations about the social correlates of religious interest which sociologists can state with any real assurance. There are even fewer which can be made about the causative factors which lead to intense interest on the part of some and gross indifference on the part of others."[50]

The sociological data which would support the economic and social deprivation theories are not that overwhelming. If one were to take a lead from the general pattern of that data (which indicate that the poor are not notably committed to any church and that they tend not to join voluntary associations), one could not say that those who are economically and socially deprived are turning to the churches for consolation against the harsh realities of their lives, which is not to deny that they are innocent of all religious convictions. At best one can say that the data are not consistent in such a way as to justify erecting social theories which identify causes in the strict sense. Even while denying that the theories identify causes of movements, it must be granted that they do identify those conditions, those social-cultural climates, which favor and encourage the rise of movements. For this reason the theories are helpful in understanding the dynamics of movement growth.

SOCIAL DISORGANIZATION RECONSIDERED

The theory which points to social disorganization as a causative factor in the rise of crisis movements, such as the Pentecostal-charismatic renewal, is indeed not without empirical support. Pentecostalism does spread quickly among the immigrant Puerto Ricans of New York City. And it is true that the usual social alignments are disrupted in these immigrant groups. The family structure is weakened, ties with the larger extended family are largely cut off, new value systems are confronted, there is a clash of cultures. Where such conditions obtain they undoubtedly contribute to the rise of crisis movements. But the theory is limited. It is not helpful in explaining the growth of Pentecostalism in rural Puerto Rico, in South America, and Africa, where the usual family patterns are undisturbed, where the traditional value systems are in peaceful possession, where there is no culture clash in Holt's sense, where lives are led in relative tranquility.[51]

If social disorganization indicates the pattern of factors which give rise to the Pentecostal movement, why then does this same movement emerge and grow where such social disorganization is not present? "Also unfortunately for the social disorganization model, observations indicate that Pentecostalism in the United States and Latin America both, flourishes in small rural communities and villages where ties have not been disrupted, and among family groups whose very solidarity is one of the primary reasons for its 'contagion.' Lack of intimate social relationships or personal ties and disrupted families were *not* characteristic of the Pentecostal pre-converts."[52] It is not the rupture of traditional family and village social structures which caused the rise and growth of Pentecostalism. Quite the contrary, it was the existence and normal functioning of these social relationships which facilitated the spread of the movement. One research project studied an urban neighborhood where American Indians were concentrated. Two Negro Pentecostal churches and one white Pentecostal church in the area attempted unsuccessfully to recruit the Indians. Even though social disorganization and community disintegration were present, the Indians could not be recruited. Thinking that only an Indian could recruit other Indians, the white Pentecostals persuaded an Indian of mixed blood to take up the apostolate. The Indian explained the failure "on the grounds that Indian relationships are so fragmented that no one likes anyone else in the neighborhood; the Indians refuse to get together on anything."[53] Even though social disorganization and community disintegration were present, the Indians could not in this case be recruited even by another Indian.

Those who think of social disorganization or psychological maladjustment theories as models for describing the origin and development of movement growth point to the pressure of personal crisis which either precedes or accompanies the initial involvement in the movement. The research report of Virginia Hine did find a significant correlation between conversion during crises and movement involvement as measured by the frequency of glossolalia. But the data showed that those who spoke most frequently in tongues were those whose entry into the movement occurred less often at a time of personal crisis.[54] Rather than relying on theories of social disorganization, social and economic deprivation, Gerlach and Hine point to recruitment as central. What is decisive is face-to-face recruitment by committed participants along the lines of preexisting social relationships where there is some close bond. The one who is recruiting by committed witnessing may be a brother, sister, father, mother, uncle, neighbor, friend, employer, or employee. It is where these preexisting relationships are relatively undisturbed that the movement grows. "No matter what conditions of social disorganization or social or psychological deprivation facilitate the rise of the movement, the key to its spread is to be found in the process of face-to-face recruitment by committed participants."[55]

A team of anthropologists from the University of Minnesota, under Luther Gerlach, researched four types of Pentecostal groups arranged along an institutionalization continuum. The team found that relatives were responsible for recruiting seventy-one percent of the classical Pentecostal groups, fifty percent of the members of a large independent group which had been in existence for from fifteen to twenty years, forty-two percent of those recently organized independent groups which were smaller in size, and thirty-two percent of the "hiddens," that is, those who do not belong to prayer groups and do not publicly admit to being Pentecostal or charismatic.[56]

Donald McGavran (1963), researching classical Pentecostalism in Mexico, found a similar pattern. Face-to-face recruitment was important for explaining the expansion of the movement in Mexico. "Group decision by two and three families (and by twenty and thirty families, too) became an ordinary mode of conversion. The faith, once lit in a people, has a chance to grow soundly and rapidly along the all-important web of relationships."[57] A study of a small religious group on the west coast by John Lofland (1966) showed that it spread through means of preexisting friendships.[58] Lofland recognizes the role that personality and situational factors play in the growth of the movement but notes that these factors are "woefully inadequate" when attempting to explain either the emergence of the movement or the conversion to it of specific persons. The Japanese religious movement named Soka Gakkai was researched by Robert Lee (1967). He found that relatives, neighbors and colleagues were important in recruitment and in explaining the growth of the movement.[59]

SOCIAL AND ECONOMIC DEPRIVATION RECONSIDERED

The weight of the evidence so far seems to indicate that the poorer and less educated are less involved in the life of the churches. This does not mean that they are less religious, simply that their manner of expressing religious sentiments may be different. Persons from the lower socio-economic levels tend to "do" religion less, that is they tend not to give it public expression in institutional form. Would this include giving public expression to religious sentiments in the framework of a movement? The answer seems to be "Yes." Religion may still be important for them even while church membership and church attendance may not be. Their flight might be less from religion than from organized religion, or even from the kind of organization peculiar to movements. The minority report which questions some of the findings of the majority would indicate that more research needs to be done.

If, however, the majority opinion has any merits it would seem that it is dangerous to erect a theory of social and economic deprivation as causative of religious movements such as the Pentecostal-charismatic renewal. If there is considerable evidence, even though contested, that the lower classes tend not to join churches or other voluntary organizations, then it would be difficult to show how deprivation, social and economic, caused the rise of Pentecostalism. This is not to suggest that deprivation is totally unrelated to the rise and growth of movements. Poverty, marginal existence, the lack of prestige, power, status, and the opportunity to participate in decisions affecting their own lives may well constitute a favorable climate for the rise of crises movements. They facilitate their rise but they are not causative in the determinative sense. To the degree that churches or church members are involved in the dynamics of the Pentecostal movement, one will find a remarkable heterogeneity of social classes, and that to a degree not to be found in any other large voluntary social grouping.[60] The economically and socially deprived will still be drawn to religious movements such as Pentecostalism.

PENTECOSTAL RESEARCH
REASSESSES DEPRIVATION THEORIES

A number of scholars researching the Pentecostal-charismatic movement have expressed dissatisfaction with the disorganization and deprivation theories. Except for Gerlach and Hine (she both in the publications she coauthored and in her own), Pentecostal researchers in this country have not paid much attention to the social disorganization theory. Among those clearly unimpressed with the deprivation theories are Plog (1964), Pattison (1964), Hine (1967, 1974), Gerlach and Hine (1968, 1970), Oates (1968), Samarin (1972), Harper (1974) Harrison (1974), and Meredith McGuire (1974). It will not be necessary to examine each of these but a brief look will be given to the more analytic. A number of them simply note the new Pentecostal-charismatic population: well educated, affluent, in positions of power in business and industry as well as in some churches. Economic and social deprivation theories as used by Boisen and Holt are not thought to apply. Whether the relative deprivation theory of Aberle applies is still an open question.

It was on the basis of the new situation which arose in the early 1960s with the emergence of Protestant neo-Pentecostalism that Stanley C. Plog, in reporting the UCLA research on glossolalics in California, noted that the persons in the sampling were deprived neither economically nor socially. Nor were they socially disorganized.[61] Also in 1964 Pattison, in speaking of glossolalia, remarked that "it is not the malcontent, emotionally disturbed, or socio-economically deprived who necessarily seek out such experiences."[62] Virginia Hine has been especially perceptive in her analysis of deprivation theories as applied to Pentecostalism. If one were to apply Aberle's relative deprivation theory to Pentecostals, that is the dissatisfaction arising out of the differences between an anticipated state of affairs and a less agreeable actuality, between what they think they should have and what they actually have, then Pentecostals are poor subjects. In socio-economic as well as in ethical terms, they are not caught between two value systems, the dominant American value system and their own. A sizeable number of the Pentecostals reported that they were perfectly satisfied with the dominant standards of society and with their own and others' behavior until a committed recruiter in a position to influence their thinking sensitized them to the biblical value system. Therefore, the dissatisfaction with the dominant American value system "is an effect of movement dynamics, not a precondition."[63]

The Pentecostal belief system among classical and Protestant neo-Pentecostals not infrequently includes belief in the imminence of the second coming of Christ. Sociologists of religion see in this belief a desire to withdraw from an unsatisfying social order, looking forward to a new creation and new order issued in by the second coming. In this new order, the sociologists of religion say, the devout believer will have prestige, power, a leadership role to compensate for his deprivation of these in the old order. If the theory holds up, more Pentecostals of lower socio-economic status should hold this belief in the imminent second coming than those of higher socio-economic status. In testing this assumption no correlation was found between economic and social deprivation and belief in the second coming.[64] Testing the amount of movement involvement against five separate measures of socio-economic status (income, occupation, education, age, and sex), those who spoke more frequently in tongues were significantly more involved in the movement, but there was no correlation between frequency of glossolalia on the one hand and annual income or educational level on the other. If the theories of social or economic deprivation are truly helpful in explaining the causes of movements, then those who were the most deprived would tend to be the ones who spoke in tongues more frequently. This was not borne out in the testing. There was, however, a significant correlation between the frequency of tongues and occupational status. The more frequent the tongues, the lower the occupational ratings.[65] Occupation has been used by social scientists (North and Hatt, Warner, Hollingshead) as a more accurate, indeed the single best, scale for social status. While education is an indicator of knowledge and cultural experience and is related to behavioral patterns, occupation is an index of power in the social structure.

It would seem that a particular type of status or power deprivation is relevant to involvement in the movement. Virginia Hine is at pains to point out that a statistical correlation between power deprivation and involvement in the Pentecostal movement is not the relationship of cause and effect. "It would not be correct to assume that power deprivation is causal."[66] But she would see a certain consistency between Aberle's theory of relative deprivation (in reference to power) and the Pentecostal movement. Aberle suggests that in analyzing movements it is important to isolate the relationship between the type of relative deprivation of the participants and the specific character of the movement's ideology. Here deprivation and ideology touch at the point of power. Those whose occupational status is less have less power, as occupation is more indicative of power than education or wealth. In the Pentecostal ideology "the baptism in the Spirit" is specifically an act of empowerment. There is a whole "power vocabulary" in Pentecostalism, in large part borrowed from the Scriptures: "You will receive power when the Holy Spirit comes on you" (Acts 1:8). This power is directed toward the effective witnessing to the gospel and therefore to recruiting. "And you will be my witnesses not only in Jerusalem but throughout Judaea and Samaria, and indeed to the ends of the world" (Acts 1:8). The relationship between relative deprivation in reference to power and the power vocabulary of the Pentecostal-charismatic ideology is still not clearly established and needs further scientific investigation.

Predictably, the earlier study of Gerlach and Hine follows the same argumentation, though it is less specific in its details. They judged the three most common models of systems analysis, namely social disorganization, deprivation, and the psychological maladjustment models, to be inadequate. Too many of the participants "could not be classified as socially disorganized, even relatively deprived, or psychologically maladjusted."[67] The social and economic model was also found inadequate by Charles L. Harper as he analyzed the Catholic charismatic movement on the basis of data gathered from about twenty-five Catholic charismatics.[68] The application of the church-sect theory to the origins of the movement within the Roman Church seems to Harper "almost a contradiction in terms,"[69] and even the continued growth and vitality of the classical Pentecostal movement do not *now* seem to be accounted for adequately by Holt's theory of rural migrants to the city who are suffering from cultural shock. Further, in contrast to the classical Pentecostal movement, the Catholic counterpart began not among the poor and uneducated, but among university students, academics, and Catholic intellectuals. "The movement is not, then, a religion of social or economic deprivation, nor can the Catholic Pentecostal expressive forms be attributed to intellectual unsophistication or lack of formal education."[70] Harper's research demonstrated of Catholic charismatics what Bultena had remarked of church membership in Madison, namely their heterogeneity. Catholics who became Pentecostals, Harper found, were such a heterogenous group that it was almost impossible to describe them in common social, economic, cultural, or demographic categories.[71] To explain involvement in the Catholic renewal Harper develops a process model, which includes the following elements: (1) Growing up in a family which emphasized religious training. (2) Increasing ambivalence toward the church, simultaneous with an increase in personal stress. (3) Groping for solutions through the exploration of various options. (4) A turning point or precipitating event, such as a religious experience, which is the culmination of "stressful experiences." A considerable amount of group support accompanies the religious experience, and the acquisition of knowledge about the chosen option, namely the Catholic charismatic renewal.[72] Harper's rejection of deprivation theories is a little difficult to take seriously, mostly because his own theoretical model speaks of the "powerlessness," "self-estrangement," and "the alienating experiences" which those persons suffer who have ambivalent feelings toward the church. These are all manifestations of that relative kind of deprivation Aberle is talking about. Harper has rejected the older deprivation theories and has created another.

Neither economic nor social deprivation, nor social disorganization typified the research population which Michael I. Harrison studied.[73] These groups of Catholic charismatics did contain some members from the lower class and from the economically marginal strata, but its membership was predominantly middle class in education and occupation. Harrison did not find that Catholic Pentecostalism as studied in 1969 appealed to those suffering either absolute or relative economic deprivation.[74] The charismatic renewal within the Roman Church is seen more as a reaction to strains felt within the church and on college campuses during the 1960s, namely a reassertion of the value of personal piety and loyalty to the church. During the sixties the involvement in social action and the concomitant de-emphasis on traditional beliefs had called piety and loyalty into question. In many respects the members did not undergo what in sociological if not in theological terms would be called a conversion. A remarkable number had a high rate of Mass attendance and private prayer prior to contact with the movement, and the evidence also indicates that loyalty to the church predisposes individuals toward the movement. The data would also indicate that persons looking for solutions to religious problems are more favorable to the charismatic renewal. To give an example, seventy-one percent of those who were lonely also said they were seeking deeper Christian relationships. But others who said that they were not lonely also associated with the movement. Thirty-five percent of those who were not lonely did so. Contrary to the evidence of Kildahl, but in agreement with Gerlach and Hine's findings, Harrison's sampling indicated that "extreme personal disorganization or crisis does not seem to predispose individuals toward Catholic Pentecostalism."[75]

There is a convergence on the importance of recruitment by a committed participant, the research of Gerlach and Hine, Meredith McGuire, and Harrison agreeing on this point. Over fifty-nine percent of all participants first heard about it from close friends. There is some proselytizing by Catholic charismatics of persons with whom they are not on intimate terms, but contacts through close friends are the most successful. "Both qualitative and quantitative data indicate that these personal relationships with members facilitate recruitment."[76]

CONCLUSIONS

The social theories of movements should not be understood as claiming more for themselves than their authors intended. Aberle, for instance, speaks of relative deprivation as falling into four rather rough categories: possessions, status, behavior, and worth. While he sees in these four kinds of deprivation the conditions favorable to the use of movements, they do not necessarily lead to the formation of movements. The same four kinds of deprivation can also "be the basis for apathy, disorganization, despair, or suicide."[77] The fact that deprivation is present is not in itself sufficient basis for predicting which way people will react to it, whether the reaction will go in the direction of movement formation, or in the direction of apathy and suicide. Relative deprivation cannot predict if a movement will arise, where it will arise, or who will be involved. The social disorganization theory is helpful in understanding the growth of Pentecostalism among the immigrant Puerto Ricans in New York City but not why it spreads among those who remain in Puerto Rico. Economic and social deprivation give some understanding why Pentecostalism grew among poor southern whites and the millhands of Gastonia, North Carolina, but not why it spreads among the doctors, lawyers, business executives, college professors of an affluent suburb of Minneapolis.

The same is to be said of the church-sect theory. Though helpful in understanding a process, it falls short as a theory of the origin and evolution of religious groups. The church-sect theory does not account for the fact that not all religious groups emerge as sects.[78] The social theories therefore do not point to necessary conditions nor to causes but to favorable conditions and to facilitating factors. Social theorists have sometimes claimed more than their theories can demonstrate, but the theories are still useful within a more limited framework.

Even when speaking of favorable conditions, facilitating factors, generating circumstances, and of their considerable influence in the rise and growth of movements, it should be recognized that movements have lives of their own, quite apart from generating conditions, factors, and circumstances. After these have spurred and activated the movement, after the "lift-off,"[79] there are operative processes and dynamics which give the movement a life independent of the first impulses. The movement, because it is self-contained in its dynamics, autonomous in the interrelatedness of organization, ideology, recruitment, opposition, and commitment, can spread to other groups and areas where the favorable conditions and facilitating factors do not exist. Its continued existence is not dependent on the continued existence and presence of the favorable facilitating conditions. Important in the growth and spread of Pentecostalism is face-to-face recruitment by a committed witness who is forceful in getting others to believe as he or she does.

Care should be taken that social theories are not too casually discarded simply because a new social situation has arisen to which the theories do not seem to lend meaning. Social theories arise out of observed events, conditions, patterns, and out of conclusions which are drawn therefrom. Because grounded empirically they belong to history and geography. They are rooted in moments and places. Ideally they are not temporal reflections of eternal essences, or earthly specifications of heavenly laws. Because so grounded they must not be universalized, divorced from moment and place. The test of a social theory of movements is not its universal applicability, but its adequacy within a limited framework. The unanswered questions are "What are the horizons and boundaries of that framework?" "Within what limitations does a theory cease to be adequate?" It is quite possible that a social theory will present a model which will help to understand certain behavioral patterns, groupings, alignments. That it is not helpful in understanding these same things forty years later in a quite different place is not to invalidate the theory. Boisen's economic deprivation theory might present a quite adequate, though not perfect, model for understanding the Pentecostal experience of poor southern whites in 1939. It is not necessarily void of meaning and use because it cannot explain the Pentecostal experience of rich northern whites in 1976. Social theories belong to history.

3 | ENTHUSIASM AND INSTITUTION: THE RESPONSES OF THE CHURCHES

When an approach to religious reality is experience oriented and when the group activities of those who have adopted that approach are based on the supposition that everyone is a participator with a song to offer, a message to give, a scriptural passage to read, a prophecy to present, then the psychological health of the participants becomes a question of some urgency. Further, when the participants believe that the Spirit is present at their meetings and in some sense speaks through them, then one asks the question, "What comes from the Holy Spirit and what comes from the human psyche?"[1] At this point the question of the health of the psyche of those involved must be asked. The historic churches were confronted with this question in the 1960s and they responded by appointing commissions to issue reports.

The reports issuing from church commissions should be evaluated with great fairness, especially as they concern the psychological dimensions. One is struck with the major effort made by the various committees and commissions to be impartial in their psychological judgments. They were aware that scientific psychological studies were not at a stage which would permit unassailable positions. The psychological evaluations in the years from 1960–1970 were especially difficult for commissions in the historic churches because of the cultural baggage, fundamentalistic exegesis, and the revivalist doctrine of sanctification which were taken over by many of the early Protestant neo-Pentecostals or charismatics. Many early Protestant neo-Pentecostals adopted a style of religious expression which was already disappearing from classical Pentecostal culture, at least in large parts of the United States. When a Lutheran or Presbyterian takes over not only the central insights and experience of the classical Pentecostal tradition but also its fundamentalistic exegesis, its systematic theology, and its cultural baggage, and then hopes to work effectively within a Lutheran or Presbyterian context, such a person and his denomination are faced with almost insurmountable difficulties.

The Catholic charismatic renewal started in the universities, among graduate students and professors. The beginnings of the renewal within Catholicism, too, had problems of excessive and uncritical borrowings from classical Pentecostalism. But these beginnings were accompanied by a climate of theological reflection which was not found in the beginnings of the Protestant neo-Pentecostal renewal. In many ways the Catholic charismatic renewal was more Catholic than, for instance, the Lutheran and Presbyterian renewals were Lutheran or Presbyterian. Though none of the denominational charismatic groups are without their cultural and theological problems, the general character of Protestant neo-Pentecostalism is quite different today than it was in 1960. There is a growing sense of belonging to a theological, ecclesial, and cultural tradition which helps to identify the charismatic renewal in relation to a rich theological cultural heritage of a particular denomination. This tradition is a liberating instrument because it is a loose framework (not above criticism) within which one organizes and interprets religious events and experiences. This sense of gratitude, not for a narrow kind of denominationalism, but for the riches of a heritage and tradition, was not found in a marked degree in early Protestant neo-Pentecostalism as it appeared in this country in the first years of the 1960s. It is, however, found in an ever increasing degree in the Protestant neo-Pentecostalism of today. All of these factors must be kept in mind when evaluating the reports made by the historic churches on early Protestant neo-Pentecostalism.

EPISCOPAL DIOCESE OF LOS ANGELES (1960)

In April of 1960 a commission appointed by the Episcopal bishop of Los Angeles, Francis Eric Bloy, made its report. The report contended that the charismatic "experiences his own conversion and the resultant spiritual glow rather than Jesus Christ and his Church. When he bears his testimony, it is to speak of his new-found happiness rather than to confess that Jesus Christ is Lord."[2] The commission questioned the normality, in psychological terms, of the phenomena as it is related to Acts 2, and stated a theological opinion now generally abandoned, namely, that the more Pentecostal, prophetic gifts of the Spirit are for the church only in its beginning, not for its continuing existence. The report stated: "The abnormal physical and psychological phenomena, which attracted so much attention on the day of Pentecost, tended to disappear within the Body of Christ, and at the last seemed to have died out. The Whitsunday phenomena could be compared to a scaffolding surrounding a new edifice. Once the edifice (the Church) had been completed, the scaffolding became unnecessary and was discarded. . . . The glossolalia occurred in the infancy of the Church. With her growth and maturity the Church wisely discarded the marks of infancy."[3]

EPISCOPAL DIOCESE OF CHICAGO (1960)

A commission appointed by the Episcopal bishop of Chicago also issued its report in 1960. Though eminently fair, there is an evident unhappiness with the whole matter of tongues and there is the suggestion that the charismatic is psychologically suspect. The report pointed to "the danger of irrationality and emotional excess [which] is to be acknowledged as a real danger and to be shunned. Assessment of phenomena of the type of spiritual speaking cannot rule out the possibility that there is a pathological element in them, and also the possibility that they may have a pathological influence on certain types of personality."[4]

AMERICAN LUTHERAN CHURCH (1963)

A special committee of the Commission on Evangelism of the American Lutheran Church submitted "A Report on Glossolalia" in 1963. The committee of eleven was made up of pastors, seminary professors, officers of church bureaus, and a psychiatrist. Only one member of the eleven-man committee was personally involved in the Lutheran charismatic movement. Though the inclusion of one Lutheran charismatic smacks of tokenism, it is an important development. In some initial way this is recognition that the phenomenon must not be wholly judged from the outside. It was hardly an understatement for the committee to note that "the integration of speaking in tongues into the life of a Lutheran congregation has proved very difficult, for both pastor and people. Divisions and tensions have been found in varying degrees in the congregations where glossolalia is known to exist."[5] It was true that many of the early neo-Pentecostals were excessively aggressive and that many brought with them the cultural baggage and the exegetical tradition of classical Pentecostalism. "It appears to be difficult for persons who speak in tongues to be reserved about it. For a variety of reasons it seems necessary to them to witness to the experience enthusiastically."[6] Accompanying this hard-sell evangelism of the Lutheran charismatics were reflections on the church which left the impression that true Christianity was not to be found within its embrace. Rightly or wrongly, the impression was given that glossolalia was a central New Testament experience. The committee's report therefore stressed that "glossolalia is not normative for salvation. Neither is it normative for the Christian's growth in grace."[7]

The committee felt the need for exposure to some of the Lutheran parishes in which glossolalia was practiced. A psychiatrist, a clinical psychologist, and a New Testament exegete made a ten-day tour of four such congregations. In addition to meeting with church councils and prayer groups, a questionnaire was used and a psychological sampling of fifteen persons was made. This sample, too small from which to generalize, did not bear out the popular assumption that people who speak in tongues are psychologically maladjusted. All but one of the fifteen "represented a broad spectrum of psychological types and represented a cross section of the congregations involved."[8] The commission found that "in thirteen of the fifteen persons interviewed there was a clearly defined anxiety crisis preceding their speaking in tongues. This anxiety was related to such factors as intrapsychic conflicts, depression, marital difficulties, financial concerns, and ill health."[9] In addition to this preexistent anxiety there was a situational anxiety involved in the setting in which the person first began speaking in tongues. Tongues itself produces anxiety because it is not socially acceptable. Other factors in producing anxiety are group pressure, concern for acceptance by the group, the length of the meetings, the pressure of the leader, and the feelings of worthlessness. The commission expressed the conviction that the speaking in tongues which it heard "was not gibberish." The committee's report continued: "The sounds heard appeared to have the rhythm and qualities of language and it was felt that it would not be possible for the average person consciously to duplicate the fluency and structure of the productions heard."[10] The commission suggested "that there has been enough talking about glossolalia in our Church and that further publicity would fan the flames and do more harm than good."[11] This would seem a basically wise recommendation, especially when tongues is taken in isolation instead of being considered in a wider theological and pastoral context.

Based on the report of the special committee of the Commission on Evangelism and the "Report of the Field Study Committee on Speaking in Tongues," the Church Council of the American Lutheran Church issued "A Statement with Regard to Speaking in Tongues." The statement, evidently reacting to the revivalist categories in which the charismatic experience of tongues and the "baptism in the Holy Spirit" were presented, recalled that "the Lutheran Church teaches and believes that the Holy Spirit is given in [water] baptism."[12] Also referring to what it perceived as the revivalistic enthusiastic nature of the charismatic experience, and more specifically to charismatic worship, the statement said that the worship represents "a posture in which the activities of the conscious mind seem to be somewhat suspended for the moment. Any posture where the conscious mind is not in full control is more readily open to the influence of evil spirits as well as the Holy Spirit, and therein lies a danger. In the presence of potential blessing there is also danger and the possibility of much confusion."[13] This raises the problem of trance which will be treated in the next chapter. Most charismatics do not experience a loss of consciousness, orientation, reality contact, or control.

The statement concludes with the request that there be no promotion nor practice of tongues at meetings of the congregation and that "there be no instruction in the technique or practice of speaking in tongues."[14] Those who claim the gift are urged to reserve its use for private devotion. Especially in congregations made up of charismatics and those not involved in the movement this would seem to be wise pastoral advice. However much one sympathizes with the church which is being disrupted by advocates of what seems a new style of Christian life, it does seem that the statement is wholly defensive. If the charismatics have an obligation to leave the structures of parish life undisturbed, including worship, the church has an obligation to be accepting and to take a positive pastoral attitude toward charismatics. Both charismatics and the church at large should attempt in positive terms to work out a theology and practice within the Lutheran framework so that the charismatic renewal within the church is thoroughly Lutheran. This should be done in such a way that the prophetic character of the renewal is not lost. All renewal movements which are in the church and of the church call the church to judgment. Lutheran neo-Pentecostals, the same as other Lutherans, have a right to confront the church with gospel. They have the same right as others to ask questions about the effectiveness of parish life as presently structured.

EPISCOPAL DIOCESE OF CALIFORNIA (1963)

A pastoral letter on the topic of glossolalia was issued by James Pike, Bishop of California, on May 2, 1963. Quite justly the bishop called attention to "the religious categories and practices borrowed from pentecostal denominations. . . ."[15] The large presence of this cultural baggage and the uncritical borrowing of a kind of folk exegesis blurred the real issues and made an objective evaluation all but impossible. Bishop Pike called attention to the lack of scientific psychological research, one of the reasons why he was not at ease with glossolalia or exorcism. He advised his clergy not to place emphasis on speaking in tongues "in distinction from the other gifts and fruits of the Holy Spirit."[16] He leveled no ban on the use of tongues in private but he urged "that there be no services or meetings in our Churches or in homes or elsewhere for which the expression or promotion of this activity [speaking in tongues] is the purpose or of which it is a part." The bishop continued: "Nor do I believe that our clergy should lead or take part in such gatherings under whatever auspices."[17] The most quoted phrase of the pastoral letter was that the doctrine and practice of the movement as it was experienced within the Episcopal Church constituted "heresy in embryo."[18] Bishop Pike is reported to have later changed his mind. In a conversation with J. B. Anderson of St. Cloud, Minnesota, he admitted that he had made a mistake in opposing the movement and assumed the blame himself rather than place it on any of the commissions.[19] This was not an expression of interest in the movement and most certainly not an endorsement of it. This conversation took place in 1967 and may reflect his own interest in a broad range of spiritual experiences, including the contact of the living with the dead.

Bishop Pike's admission that he had made a mistake and that he personally assumed the blame for the content of his pastoral letter is an extremely generous position. The pastoral letter is dated May 2, 1963. On the same day, the study commission submitted its preliminary report to Bishop Pike. It can hardly be a coincidence that the submission of the report and the issuance of the pastoral letter occurred on the same day. Nor can it be a coincidence that the pastoral letter faithfully reflects the tenor of the study commission's report.

The study commission consisted of nine members, two of whom were psychiatrists, and one who was an expert on parapsychology. Among the magazines consulted were the quarterly, *Logos* (later changed to *Trinity*), edited by Jean Stone, an Episcopal laywoman, and the *Full Gospel Men's Voice*, a magazine dominated by categories taken from classical Pentecostalism. The problem of situating the classical Pentecostal theological patterns within an Episcopal context can be seen in Mrs. Stone's adoption of the classical Pentecostal exegesis of that time. She wrote in an article entitled, "What is Happening Today in the Episcopal Church?": "An interesting development is that if they [who have experienced the baptism in the Holy Spirit] have not previously believed the Bible literally, they begin to! The Lord appears to be making a lot of Episcopalian Fundamentalists in these end time days."[20] Mrs. Stone taught the classical Pentecostal doctrine of initial evidence, that is, tongues is the evidence that one has received the baptism in the Holy Spirit.[21] The Full Gospel Business Men's Fellowship International, which publishes *Full Gospel Men's Voice* (later changed to *Voice*), is an interdenominational organization whose theological and cultural style is essentially classical Pentecostal. In addition to these sources the commission consulted other literature, largely classical Pentecostal in origin. Though there was a cultural difference to the way the Episcopal charismatics gave expression to their faith, that is, it was more restrained than what was found in classical Pentecostalism, the dominance of classical Pentecostal influence in the Episcopal movement gave sufficient justification for Bishop Pike's remark about the adoption of "religious categories and practices" borrowed from classical Pentecostalism.

Obviously this made the evaluation within an Episcopal context very difficult. The commission stressed the tentative and preliminary nature of its report, and claimed, with some justification, that "glossolalia is not per se a religious phenomenon."[22] Though not proven that glossolalia in a Christian context is the same as the verbalizations which take place in other cultures, it is at least possible that they are phenomenologically identical. From a theological point of view there can be no essential objection to the position which holds that glossolalia is not per se a religious phenomenon.

The study commission acknowledged that the psychiatrist would "understand how transforming an experience glossolalia might be, and how helpful it could be as an act of release periodically practiced."[23] While not suggesting that those "who speak in tongues must be mentally disordered" the report notes that the same phenomenon appears "among adults who are suffering from mental disorders such as schizophrenia and hysteria."[24]

Despite the fact that the report is highly articulated here as everywhere, one has great difficulty adopting open attitudes if one takes the report seriously. A. W. Sadler (1964), in commenting on the report, notes that divine possession, which in the report is likened to the experience of speaking in tongues, cannot be equated with mental imbalance. "Although there are certain striking parallels between the behavior of the ecstatic and behavior patterns associated with hysteria and other mental disorders, the attempt to explain the one in terms of the other in simple reductionist fashion is not justifiable. The matter is much more complex than this. . . ."[25] Alfred Métraux (1959), also speaking of possession, says that the number of persons subject to possession states "is too large for all of them to be labelled hysterics."[26] Nadel (1946) also evaluates the psychological profiles of most shamans positively: "No shaman is, in everyday life, an 'abnormal' individual, a neurotic, or a paranoiac; if he were, he would be classed as a lunatic, not respected as a priest. Nor finally can shamanism be correlated with incipient or latent abnormality. I recorded no case of a shaman whose professional hysteria deteriorated into serious mental disorders."[27] Though the anthropological category of "possession" is broader than the charismatic category of "baptism in the Holy Spirit," anthropologists consider the charismatic experience of tongues as an indication of a possession state. More will be said of schizophrenia and hysteria in relation to tongues in the next chapter.

Ultimately, the Episcopal report asserts, the psychological evaluation is dependent on how the individual integrates the practice of tongues into his personal and social life. If the practice were not under the control of the person, this could be taken as a sign of impaired mental health. This latter point is generally accepted as valid by all branches of the renewal. The inability to control the practice of speaking in tongues would generally be an indication of hysteria. However, the report indicates that only some of those involved in the movement are able to control the regular practice of tongues.[28] Anyone who has done extensive field work, no matter what his final psychological judgment might be, would question the validity of the commission's sampling. It is comparatively infrequent that one meets a Pentecostal or charismatic who cannot control the habitual practice of tongues. The report supposes that all glossolalics speak for the first time during some kind of prayer meeting and only after considerable time has been spent in hearing testimonies and praying together and after considerable emotional involvement. As will be clear, there are small but sufficiently significant numbers of persons who speak in tongues for the first time when alone. This does not of itself rule out the possibility of suggestions and peer group pressure being operative. Although the report is very carefully worded, it leaves the impression that tongues is a result of suggestion or hypnosis.

The psychiatrists on the Episcopal commission had an affirmative reaction to the contention that the practice of praying in tongues was resorted to because human language can be inadequate for the praise and adoration of God. Tongues becomes the language of the "irrational" making up for the inadequacy of one's own language.[29] Perhaps the word "irrational" is unfortunate in its connotations. Tongues is rather a nonrational expression of prayer in much the same way that an abstract painting is a nonpictorial, nonobjective expression of some deep interior feeling which the artist might not be able to express in pictorial objective forms. Neither "nonrational" nor "nonobjective" are synonyms for irrationality. In the nonrational and the nonobjective there can be both "sense" and meaning.

In its conclusions the report contains a warning, fully justified in any Pentecostal or charismatic context, concerning the psychological dangers of an approach to religious reality dominated by the experiential. Such a one-sided approach "hinders the development of a personality well-balanced in its view of itself and its relationship to the objective realities of life."[30] The report is generally fair, but there still persists that nonspecific impression that glossolalic behavior is highly suspect from a psychological point of view.

CATHOLIC BISHOPS OF THE UNITED STATES (1969)

The report to the meeting of the American Roman Catholic bishops in Washington, D.C., in November 1969, of an episcopal study commission headed by Bishop Alexander M. Zaleski of Lansing, Michigan, marks a turning point in ecclesiastical evaluations of the charismatic renewal. The reports of the commissions up until this Catholic report, for all their qualifications and fairness, have shown that the churches

were basically unhappy with the presence of charismatics among
them. There is a lingering nonspecific suspicion that not all is well
psychologically with charismatics. Up to this date the reports have
been dealing with a phenomenon which had been a major source of
friction and discord in the churches. Though problems were not absent from the Catholic renewal, there is a marked difference between
the history of the charismatic renewal in the main-line Protestant
churches and in the Catholic Church. The disruption and division of
whole parishes, not infrequently with the dismissal of the pastor, was
not the normal pattern in Protestant denominations. However, it occurred with sufficient frequency to distinguish the Protestant experience of the renewal at the parish level from that of the Catholic
Church. Some have suggested that the Roman Church is larger on the
inside than appears from the outside and she is therefore able to accommodate expressions of Christian life which other churches cannot.
Undoubtedly it has to do also with the character of the Catholic
renewal. In the Roman Church the renewal was generally more Catholic than, for instance, the Episcopal, Lutheran, Presbyterian movements were real representatives of their respective traditions. In the
Catholic renewal there were theologians involved from the beginning
who reflected on the theological meaning of the renewal. Generally
this was not true of the neo-Pentecostal movement in the Protestant
churches. The Catholic bishops were able to broaden the scope of their
study and were not forced to concentrate only on baptism in the Holy
Spirit and tongues.

The study of tongues is a valid object of scientific research. Church
commissions, too, are justified in singling out for study a behavioral
pattern which varies so markedly from the expectations of society.
However, the isolation of tongues, even when the report is accompanied with biblical and theological reflections, makes an objective
evaluation difficult. The reports of the commissions up to this date
concentrated almost exclusively on baptism in the Holy Spirit and
tongues. In this they may have only followed the leads of those whom
they interviewed. Or the commissions attributed a kind of importance
to tongues which in fact was not reflected in the lives of those that were
being interviewed. Outsiders make these assumptions with some ease.
In any case, the concentration on tongues distorts the insight and
experience of the broader streams of these movements within the
churches. The issue is not tongues. For good reasons or for bad, the
church commissions focused on tongues and this resulted in a basic

distortion. The church commissions, beginning with the report to the American Roman Catholic bishops, broadened their views of the issues involved. For this reason the results are more positive.

The Roman Catholic report was intended to be open but neutral, neither condemning nor commending. But when the report was read in the context of the other reports which had come from the commissions of other denominations, the Catholic report appeared to be more positive than the bishops had intended. The bishops' attitude in 1969 was one of openness but caution. This changed in a few years. Already by June 1972, Bishop Joseph McKinney could say that ninety percent of the American hierarchy were in favor of the charismatic renewal.[31] But at this early stage they intended to be more noncommittal. Gamaliel best describes the bishops' stance: "If this enterprise, this movement of theirs, is of human origin it will break up of its own accord; but if it does in fact come from God you will not only be unable to destroy them, but you might find yourselves fighting against God" (Acts 5:38, 39).

The whole report is only about six hundred fifty words, the shortest to appear. The commission speaks of the strong reaction that some people have to the movement: "For one reason or another the understanding of this movement is colored by emotionalism. For this there is some historical justification and we live with a suspicion of unusual religious experience. We are also face to face with socially somewhat unacceptable norms of religious behavior."[32] The report then turns to the psychological aspects. "It would be an error to suppose that the emotional, demonstrative style of prayer characteristic of the Protestant [Pentecostal] denominations have [sic] been adopted by Catholic Pentecostals. The Catholic prayer groups tend to be quiet and somewhat reserved. It is true that in some cases it has attracted emotionally unstable people. Those who come with such a disposition usually do not continue. Participants in these prayer meetings can also exclude them. In this they are not always successful."[33]

The report points to the fruits of the movement and then suggests that it not be hindered in its growth. "Perhaps our most prudent way to judge the validity of the claims of the [Catholic] Pentecostal Movement is to observe the effects on those who participate in the prayer meetings. There are many indications that this participation leads to a better understanding of the role the Christian plays in the Church. Many have experienced progress in their spiritual life. They are attracted to the reading of the Scriptures and a deeper understanding of their faith. They seem to grow in their attachment to certain established devotional patterns such as devotion to the Real Presence and the Rosary. It is the conclusion of the Committee on Doctrine that the movement should at this point not be inhibited but allowed to develop."[34] The positive, though not uncritical attitudes of the report helped create a new atmosphere where the renewal movements in both the Catholic and Protestant churches could be evaluated with less concentration on tongues. From this point in history the Pentecostal-charismatic movement in the churches will generally be viewed in a broader theological and cultural context.

UNITED PRESBYTERIAN CHURCH (1969, 1970)

In response to four requests the 1968 General Assembly established a Special Committee on the Work of the Spirit. What is especially significant is the presence on the study commission of a number of members who were personally involved in the charismatic renewal within the United Presbyterian Church. This is a development of some significance. The determination of Dr. William P. Thompson, the Stated Clerk, that the neo-Pentecostals in his church (or Presbyterian charismatics as many of them prefer to be called) would not be evaluated and judged only by outsiders was decisive. The committee also asked the views of Dr. William Menzies and Rev. Hardy Steinberg of the Assemblies of God, Dr. J. Rodman Williams of the Presbyterian Church in the United States, and Rev. David du Plessis, perhaps the most important representative of classical Pentecostalism at the world level. All of these consultants had an intimate knowledge of the matter under investigation. Included in the committee of eleven was a Presbyterian psychiatrist who identified himself as a participant in the charismatic renewal.

Both the structure of the committee and the method of proceeding, namely, calling in consultants acquainted with the phenomena, proceed from a courageous stance. In a preliminary report made to the 1969 General Assembly the committee noted that involvement in the movement "has sometimes led to dissension within our Church." Occasionally where pastors have been involved, "the pastoral relationship has been terminated."[35] As a result, many pastors have found it necessary to take up "independent ministries" and some left the ministry of the United Presbyterian Church. The laity who have associated themselves with the renewal "have often felt alienated from both their pastors and fellow church members. As a result, they have sought other fellowship."[36] Pastors have sometimes failed to be understanding of the laity's experience and the laity have not always been receptive of the pastor's guidance. At this stage of their study the committee recalled to the attention of the assembly Chapter XX of the Westminster Confession of Faith, "Of Christian Liberty and Liberty of Conscience." The silence of the Book of Confessions on any matters of faith or practice does not prohibit the introduction of such beliefs and practices into the life of a congregation "so long as such beliefs and practices are not destructive to the external peace and order which Christ has established in the Church."[37]

The committee felt the necessity of reasserting the principle that all the confessions of the church are subservient to Holy Scripture. Until a final report could be submitted a plea was made for tolerance, good will, and Christ-centered love. "We remind ministers, sessions, and presbyteries of their respective pastoral responsibilities toward those whose spiritual experience may differ from their own."[38] Of immediate application is the theme of reconciliation which dominates the Confession of Faith of 1967.

The final report of this committee was made to the 1970 General Assembly.[39] Though far more extensive than the Catholic report, it follows the same lines, that is, it also evaluates the phenomenon of tongues but in a much broader theological perspective. This Presbyterian report is also the most pastoral. After an exegetical and systematic summary of its findings, the psychological dimensions are treated in some detail. Then follows a section devoted to pastoral guidelines for ministers and laity who are personally involved in the renewal and another section for those who are not, and a final section for presbyteries. The report concludes with two appendices, one a biblical study and the other a review of the psychological literature.

The report calls attention to the proper limitations of psychology. Any scientific discipline has defined limits of its competency. If it is to function properly, it must stay within the ambit of its proper object. A subcommittee made up of those trained in the psychological and psychiatric fields acknowledged the great contribution which psychology can contribute to the question at hand. However, the subcommittee warned that it would be a "dark and tragic day in the life of Christianity if psychological norms are to become the criteria by which the truth or untruth of religious experience is judged."[40] When psychology is used for a decisive answer to the question of whether a man "has or has not experienced the living Christ, it is an aborted and inappropriate use of science."[41] Asking psychology to perform such a task is "an affront to psychology as a science and a scandal to religion."[42]

In reviewing the literature the commission came to the conclusion that "most of the so-called scientific studies and evaluations are based upon psychological models which either a) assume at the outset that such states are pathological, or b) have been prepared subjectively without following normally accepted controls."[43] The commission also notes that opinions and judgments have been rendered by persons who have "only superficial knowledge of the phenomena."[44] The report does not accept the common assumption that suggestibility and group hypnosis play an important role and notes that some of the people interviewed had the experience of speaking in tongues long before they had any contact with a charismatic group, attended a prayer meeting, or had acquaintance with those already involved in the renewal. No great claims were made as to the therapeutic value of the charismatic experience. The experience itself will not change a disoriented neurotic into a well-integrated extrovert. It was recognized by the commission that individuals with neurotic personalities are frequently drawn to the more dramatic religious movements. There is, however, no evidence that neurotics exist in greater proportion in the movement than in the general population of the organized church.[45] It should also be noted that the Presbyterian commission found no personality profile which typified those involved in the renewal. The personality patterns are as varied in the Presbyterian charismatic renewal as in a random sampling of people in the Presbyterian Church.

A summary of the commission's psychological conclusions is cited here in full: "The subcommittee found no evidence of pathology in the movement. The movement was found to be dynamic, growing, and involving persons from practically every denomination, walk and station in life. Varied educational backgrounds and personality patterns are present and the socio-economic status ranges from the uneducated through those in high executive positions carrying great responsibility in major corporations, in federal government and in the space effort. Physicians, psychologists, psychiatrists, scientists, professors of every description, clergy of every denomination including the hierarchy, and professors of religion and philosophy are to be found in the movement."[46]

THE PRESBYTERIAN CHURCH IN THE UNITED STATES (1965–1971)

The Presbyterian Church in the United States, which represents Presbyterianism in the South, also appointed a commission to study the questions raised by the charismatic movement. At the 1964 General Assembly a committee was appointed in response to what is technically called an "overture" from the Presbytery of Central Texas. The committee met three times in the ensuing year and brought in a report to the 1965 General Assembly. A request was published in each of the church papers asking for reports from any members of the church "who would like to share their experiences in this matter."[47] The committee studied direct reports from eight ministers and indirect reports from two. Two charismatic meetings of ten or more persons were attended by the committee. They were permitted to use a tape recorder and other tapes were made available by interested persons. The testimonies heard "came from individuals who are active (and apparently constructive) members of their local churches."[48] The practice of glossolalia in the groups was limited to either private devotion or small groups. There was no speaking in tongues in the public worship of the congregation. Those who prayed in tongues understood it as "an aid to prayer, a means of expressing emotions that cannot be phrased in words."[49]

Referring to the Confession of Faith (VII) and the Larger Catechism (QQ 30–35), the report asserts that the Word and Sacraments are the ordinances in which the covenant is dispensed and administered. By the grace of God they are "more than sufficient to convey to the people of God the full power and fruits of the Spirit. . . ."[50] Prayer, if vocal, should be made in a known tongue as noted in the Confession of Faith XXIII, 3. Though this was originally directed against the practice of the Roman Church, where prayers were offered in Latin, the concern was that the mind be involved in the worship of God. "This would rule out *any* vocal (public) prayer that the congregation cannot understand, whether in Latin, in glossolalia, or in outmoded, pietistic terminology that is now meaningless."[51] The committee notes that Scripture in several cases clearly distinguishes between a baptism with water and a baptism with the Holy Spirit (Matt. 3:11; Mk. 1:8; Lk. 3:16; Acts 1:5). "But both Scripture and the Confessions face the possibility that there may be a lapse of time between the two (Acts 8, 10, 19; Confession XXX:3)"[52]

Two questions were raised: whether it is known what the phenomenon of glossolalia is in the New Testament, and whether there is a clear understanding and precise definition of the modern phenomenon. Further, the committee asked whether it is that clear that the two are the same or somehow directly connected. A phenomenon which is complex and multiform is not so easily identified and defined. "In the range of phenomena under study there are experiences that run all the way from utter simplicity of private devotional practice through public and corporate manifestation to more esoteric experiences usually associated with so-called psychic-phenomena, or extra-sensory perception, and even drug-mysticism."[53] While recognizing the vast differences which separate the varieties of experience, "it is difficult, if not impossible, adequately to isolate a particular set of phenomena to which the name 'glossolalia' may be given and which by definition differ from similar phenomena."[54] This early report has quite correctly pointed to central problem areas. In phenomenological terms two experiences might be identical (in so far as experiences can be) while one may be a true charism and the other not.

The fact of the experience is clear but its nature cannot be determined with any precision or certainty, the report asserts. Even granting that the New Testament is the standard of validation, one does not proceed to assume "that any practice that occurred in the first century church may or must occur in the twentieth century church. . . . We have before us the kind of experience that can never be proved or disproved precisely because it is 'immune' to proof. . . . To speak of 'validity' in this instance would be to say that we *do* know, can identify, and even chart the movements of the Spirit. Thus to standardize and categorize the work of the Spirit would certainly involve us in heresy."[55] One sympathizes with the dilemma of a historic church, especially at this early date, when the Presbyterian renewal had not sorted out the central charismatic insight from the exegetical and doctrinal fundamentalism in which it was almost unavoidably clothed. But the doctrinal suppositions of this report would seemingly wipe out the whole spiritual tradition concerning discernment of spirits. This discerning process did make judgments on something closer to "authenticity" than to "validity."

The committee quite rightly declared itself incapable of making a general statement concerning the experiences of contemporary Christians as "either valid or invalid reproductions of New Testament glossolalia," but it did lay down principles, mostly negative in force, regarding the work of the Holy Spirit. The sovereign freedom of the Spirit to act where and by whatever means he will must be recognized and respected. "Such a recognition eliminates the possibility of manipulating or coercing the Spirit by audible and physical means to act or speak in a particular fashion."[56] This is an obvious reference to "induced tongues." An excessive concentration on spiritual phenomena such as glossolalia to the neglect of the centrality of the once-for-all revelation of God in Jesus Christ is a false spirituality. There is, further, no reason to suppose that forms of utterance voiced at the prompting of the Spirit cannot be initiated or cultivated by persons variously motivated. In a word, the gift may be sought and its counterfeit achieved from wrong motives. "In an era in which the Christian church finds the search for a proper language to express its faith a difficult one, a preoccupation with ecstatic speaking in which the intelligibility of the gospel is obscured can be an escape. The urgent need of the church today is not for glossolalia in which the church talks only to itself or to God, but for a relevant language in which it can communicate with the world."[57]

The report issues from a church which has suffered the loss of several pastors who departed after their involvement in the charismatic renewal. Some parishes had been torn by dissension. The defensive note of the report is therefore understandable. Either because those who witnessed to their charismatic experience focused on glossolalia or because the committee mistakenly perceived the renewal to be a tongues movement, the report is one-sided. An evaluation of the charismatic renewal which limits itself to tongues will of necessity be inadequate.

A more ambitious study project was initiated at the 1967 General Assembly. In 1971 the Permanent Theological Committee submitted its final report to the General Assembly. Unlike its own 1964 report, this more ambitious study is made within a broader context and does not concentrate on the phenomenon of tongues, as is indicated in its title, "The Person and Work of the Holy Spirit, with Special Reference to 'Baptism in the Holy Spirit.' "[58] It is therefore similar in its broad theological perspective to the 1970 report of the United Presbyterian Church (whose membership is mostly in the North).

Like the commission of the United Presbyterians, this particular commission also had in its membership persons who had associated themselves with the charismatic renewal. The theological presentation of the charismatic dimension in this report could hardly have been

more positive though it was criticized by some as being too influenced
by theological categories taken from classical Pentecostalism. Of all
the reports issuing from Protestant churches it is the most pronouncedly theological in its presentation. This report follows the Reformed tradition in linking baptism with water and the grace of salvation conferred by the Holy Spirit. On the other hand, the report is at
pains to stress that "though baptism is a channel of God's grace, this
grace is not automatically efficacious. Accordingly, there may be special need in the Reformed tradition to lay stress on later occasions
. . . on which God's grace may also be appropriated. . . . We need to
be open-minded toward those today who claim an intervening period
of time" between baptism in water and receiving the Spirit.[59] This
makes it possible to accommodate classical Pentecostal theology which
stresses the distinction between conversion and the sanctification experience (the second blessing or the baptism in the Holy Spirit). It also
accommodates an older Catholic theology which stressed the distinction between baptism and confirmation, with the possibility of a con-
ferral of the Spirit at two distinct sacramental moments. Contemporary Roman Catholic thought tends to see these two sacraments as part
of one complex of initiation rites stressing the unity of the one Paschal
mystery, the death and resurrection of Christ, into which the believer
is plunged. The tendency in contemporary Catholic thought is therefore away from a theology which separates baptism and confirmation.

With regard to the psychological dimensions, this report follows a
similar line of argumentation as that of the United Presbyterian report. "An experience of the Spirit can neither be validated as such, nor
evaluated with respect to its theological significance, by any scientific
(i.e., psychological, sociological, etc.) means. It is to be acknowledged
that such events, just as any other human events, may become the
legitimate objects of scientific inquiry without prejudging the results
of such inquiry. But regardless of the scientific conclusions which may
be reached, the question of the theological significance of these
phenomena will remain, and it may be answered only within the
context of the Christian faith. The Corinthians' ability to speak in
tongues, for example, may have a perfectly good psychological explanation; but whether the Spirit of Jesus Christ was active in that phenomenon is a question which neither psychology nor any other science
can answer."[60] Where this report goes beyond the earlier Presbyterian
report is in the extent to which the different competencies between
psychology and theology are pressed. The religious meaning of an

experience is not within the competency of psychology to determine. Theological significance is validated theologically, as psychological factors are evaluated psychologically. Nevertheless, the psychological and the theological aspects of a religious experience inhere in the structures of a human act, and the psychological dimensions have something to say (even though not the decisive thing) to its theological meaning. Conversely, the theological meaning is not unrelated to the psychological dynamics. Both inhere in the structures of life and are different aspects of human experience. There is no theological meaning in this context apart from human acts. The quite valid distinction between the psychological and theological competencies in this report becomes a gulf. Quite rightly the report points out that "the extraordinary or unusual nature of an experience (and the same would apply to gifts) is no criterion by which to judge its significance for faith."[61] Those experiences which are more unusual are not necessarily more theologically significant. Finally, religious experience is, in the first instance, ambiguous and a discerning process will determine whether or not the experience has authentic theological meaning. "Ecstasy is not in itself an unambiguous occurrence. Not every dramatic event, experience, or ecstasy is necessarily a work of the Spirit."[62]

CATHOLIC BISHOPS OF PUERTO RICO (1972)

The statement of the Puerto Rican bishops needs to be seen in the context of three factors. First, the bishops saw the renewal as an import from the United States. Secondly, the strong classical Pentecostal movement on the island put the bishops on their guard. Thirdly, there was strong initial opposition on the part of Catholics who were active in the Cursillo movement. The cursillo is essentially a retreat technique which has many of the same characteristics as the charismatic groups, namely witnessing, emphasis on personal commitment, scriptural reading, a large role for lay leadership, and an experience orientation.

To some extent this accounts for the defensive attitude of the statement, concentrating as it does on abuses and the necessity of remaining fully Catholic. The final remarks concern prudence and precaution. The bishops lamented the "pretended cures even resurrections"[63] which had received much publicity. Some were given the impression that the baptism in the Holy Spirit diminishes the value of sacramental water baptism and that it confirms them in grace. The bishops "condemn anything in the prayer meetings that has the flavor of hysteria, little seriousness, or even ridicule concerning the Catholic faith."[64] Prayer meetings should be characterized "by inner silence and meditation and not by bustle and disorderly noise."[65] They perceived a certain religious indifferentism based on a false ecumenism. Some assert "that all religions are equally true even when religious denominations concerned have doctrines that are openly contradictory."[66]

The bishops do not want to oppose either "the marvelous effects that the Holy Spirit can realize within a soul docile to his inspirations," or "a knowledge, somewhat experiential, of the presence of God in the soul."[67]

The bishops of Puerto Rico refer to the statement of the bishops of the United States as "serious and prudent." Yet because of the differing circumstances on the island they hesitate "to say that the report . . . should be accepted in its totality by the bishops of Puerto Rico."[68] While warning against well documented abuses the bishops are not led "as of now to reprove the movement."[69] But they end on a quote from Pope Paul VI concerning prudence in matters of personal inner religious experience.

Since the publication of this declaration in 1972, the Puerto Rican bishops have shown themselves less defensive and more positive in their evaluation of the charismatic renewal.

LUTHERAN CHURCH-MISSOURI SYNOD (1972)

In 1968 Lutheran Church-Missouri Synod asked its Commission on Theology and Church Relations to study the charismatic renewal with special reference to the baptism in the Holy Spirit. At a meeting of Missouri Synod charismatic pastors in 1968 there were forty-four pastors claiming to have received the baptism in the Holy Spirit. A similar meeting in 1971 showed that the number of Missouri Synod pastors making that claim had risen to two hundred. The commission issued a report (1972) which gave a very brief historical sketch, some sociological and psychological reflections, a presentation of the theological views of Lutheran charismatics, a biblical analysis, and a section devoted to conclusions and recommendations.[70] Though admitting that God could give such a charismatic gift as tongues today, the dominant tenor is that of dispensationalism, that is, that such gifts "occurred only in the apostolic church."[71]

The commission consulted privately with Lutheran pastors who were involved in the movement, but no one involved in the movement was a member of the commission. Although it would be unwise to have such a commission made up of only those personally involved, it also seems to prejudge the matter if no one on the commission is personally associated with the movement. To this degree the Missouri Synod commission falls short of the two Presbyterian commissions which contained members who identified with the charismatic renewal. Predictably, the Missouri Synod report is more pronouncedly negative than the two Presbyterian reports.

Only two studies are cited in this Lutheran report. Gerlach and Hine (1968, 1970) are quoted in favor of the view that glossolalia is not related to mental illness. The report of Dr. John P. Kildahl, principal investigator, and Paul Qualben, coinvestigator (1971), whose major contention is that glossolalics invariably initiate their speech in the presence of a benevolent authority figure is cited on the more negative side. This report contends that unless one turns oneself over to the leader, one cannot begin to speak in tongues. Those who speak in tongues are more dependent on authority figures than nonglossolalics. The psychological section of the Missouri Synod report concludes that the various psychological studies are interesting and helpful but are largely inconclusive. The tenor of the biblical analysis and of the conclusions and recommendations is largely negative.

Judging from the first meetings of the International Lutheran Conference on the Holy Spirit held in Minneapolis, beginning in 1972, there is reason for the theological strictures in the report from the Missouri Synod. From the beginning of the Lutheran renewal there was not the involvement of Lutheran theologians as was true of the Catholic renewal. If the charismatic insight is presented to a Lutheran church (at least in the United States) in revivalist categories, there is very little the church can do but reject that insight. The Lutheran report objects to baptism in the Holy Spirit as a second work of the Spirit in addition to and beyond conversion and santification. Further, it objects to a doctrine of conditions as though the promises of God were dependent on the effort or deed of the recipient.[72] In this country there has been, up until recently, no theological reflection from Lutheran charismatic theologians comparable to that of Arnold Bittlinger, the German Lutheran pastor from Schloss Craheim in Bavaria.[73] This lack has had its effects upon the report of the Missouri Synod. It is undoubtedly true that the theological context colors the psychological evaluation, at least as it comes from ecclesiastical commissions. The

Lutheran renewal in the United States, however, includes Pastor Larry Christenson, Dr. Theodore Jungkuntz, Dr. Mark Hillmer, and Dr. Richard Jensen, among others, who see the necessity of building a theological substructure for the charismatic renewal which is understandable to those who stand in the Lutheran tradition.[74] The author was asked to address a national meeting of Lutheran pastors and laymen involved in the Lutheran charismatic renewal in February 1974. The suggestion that the Lutheran movement must become more Lutheran was loudly applauded, though some thought the movement might become too conformed to institutionalized patterns and thus lose its prophetic character.[75] Dr. Richard Jensen, professor of systematic theology at Wartburg Seminary in Dubuque, who is personally involved in the Lutheran renewal, has attempted to present at a popular level the charismatic insights in a framework which is faithful to the Lutheran confessional tradition.[76] In 1974, LCUSA (Lutheran Council in the U.S.A.), an umbrella organization of the three major Lutheran churches, sponsored a conference at Wartburg Seminary which drew twenty-four Lutheran theologians, the large majority not involved in the Lutheran charismatic renewal, to study the doctrine of the Holy Spirit in the light of contemporary church life. A surprising openness to the charismatic movement was manifested and its potential value for the Lutheran Church was recognized. Explaining that many of the emphases in the charismatic renewal represent legitimate needs which the church has tended to neglect, Dr. Warren Quanbeck of Luther Theological Seminary (ALC) in St. Paul, asserted that "the charismatic movement is collecting on the bad debts of the Lutheran church."[77]

A theologian from the faculty of Valparaiso University who is personally involved in the Lutheran movement, Dr. Theodore Jungkuntz, answered the objection that the renewal emphasizes the "theology of glory" in such a way that Luther's "theology of the cross" is neglected. Rather than oppose the two, Jungkuntz held that the two are integrally related, and that the theology of the cross is the key to understanding some of the dynamics of the charismatic renewal.[78]

Two other consultations on the doctrine of the Holy Spirit and its relevance for contemporary theology were sponsored by LCUSA. The last consultation, held in Chicago, October 24–26, 1975, was attended by twenty-three theologians. Its purpose was to aid the churches relate positively to the Lutheran charismatic renewal and to assist those in the renewal to remain faithful to their Lutheran confession. Dr. Olaf Hansen of Luther Seminary in St. Paul presented a paper entitled

"Spirit Christology: A Way Out of Our Dilemma." Spirit Christology is an attempt of some modern theologians to avoid the difficulties they see in speaking of Christ's two natures. It represents a reformation of the same theological intuition in terms more intelligible to the modern mind. Professor Hansen's paper provided a basis for discussing the work of the Holy Spirit today.

Also significant was the presentation of a paper originally drafted by Pastor Larry Christenson and reworked by a subcommittee. Entitled "A Theological and Pastoral Perspective on the Charismatic Renewal in the Lutheran Church," it dealt with the history of the charismatic renewal within American Lutheranism and with biblical, theological, and pastoral problems. Rather than a consensus statement, it was accepted as a study document. An entirely new document is projected, including a statement presenting the Lutheran context for the doctrine of the Holy Spirit, a presentation of the concerns and challenges which the charismatic movement brings to the churches, and two pastoral sections expressing the more practical concerns of both the churches and those involved in the renewal. Both theologians personally in the renewal and theologians not involved will contribute to the document.

That the more negative stance of the Missouri Synod report was not just an abstract position is seen in the subsequent action of Concordia Theological Seminary, Springfield, Illinois, a Missouri Synod seminary under the presidency of Dr. Robert Preus. In a document issued in early 1975 entitled "Policy Statement Regarding the Neo-Pentecostal Movement," the seminary officials deplored the "distortions" of the neo-Pentecostal movement. Among the distortions were: the assertion "that the Spirit works within the believer today apart from or supplementary to the Means of Grace,"[79] granting the believer such gifts as speaking in tongues and prophecy; the belief that after conversion the Christian, in order to be filled with the Spirit, "must experience a second or subsequent work of the Spirit, commonly called Baptism with the Spirit."[80] In actual practice this belief places the sacrament of baptism in a position subordinate to baptism with the Spirit. The seminary faculty was offended by the tendency of neo-Pentecostals to "see assurance of God's presence in and even base their certainty of salvation on signs such as tongues, prophecy, etc., rather than on the objective promises of the gospel."[81] Finally the neo-Pentecostals, said the officials, abandoned Luther's theology of the cross for a theology of glory. Neo-Pentecostalism embraces a theology of glory which assumes that all forms of sickness, affliction, and pain in the life of the Christian are contrary to God's will since Christ has redeemed us from all ills, physical and spiritual when He gave His life for us on the cross."[82] In view of what the officials contend is the nonscriptural and non-Lutheran character of the movement, all applicants seeking student status will be asked "whether they claim to have received Baptism in the Spirit in the Neo-Pentecostal sense of that term, and whether they claim to possess one of the special charismatic gifts referred to in 1 Corinthians. . . . Those applicants who are identified as Neo-Pentecostal may be admitted as general students in the Master of Divinity program, but are ineligible for the program leading to certification by the faculty for a call into the ministerium of the Lutheran Church-Missouri Synod and hence for placement in a congregation or agency of the Synod."[83] "Before certification by the faculty for a call into the ministerium of the Synod all regular students will repeat this assurance," namely, that they have not received either the baptism in the Spirit in the neo-Pentecostal sense, and that they do not claim the special charismatic gifts of 1 Corinthians 12.[84] A questionnaire was sent out to prospective students in June, 1975, to ascertain their position on these matters.[85]

There is some justification for these rather harsh measures. It is indeed difficult for a Lutheran pastor to be effective within his Lutheran tradition if his theological categories and procedures are taken from a tradition which is incompatible with historic Lutheranism. Teaching in those categories at the level of the local congregation has often enough resulted in severe strains. But the charismatic experience need not be cast in theological formulations foreign to Lutheranism. Rather than speak of receiving the Spirit apart from or supplementary to the means of grace, one can speak of a new openness to the Spirit received at baptism. If the matter is really theological, then a seminary faculty could quite easily find a theological expression consonant with historic Lutheranism. There is no evidence in the documents issuing from the Missouri Synod that such an attempt has been made.

POPE PAUL VI (1973)

In October 1973 the first International Leaders' Conference was held in Grottaferrata, a suburb of Rome, with a hundred and twenty leaders from thirty-four countries attending. The Pope received a Canadian archbishop, an American bishop, and eleven other participants in the conference. In contrast to what the Pope will say in May of 1975, these remarks are more guarded and general. For instance, from the *L'Osservatore Romano* reprint one could not know that the Pope was addressing leaders of a charismatic conference. One would have thought he was speaking to a congress of persons interested in prayer.

The Pope named some of the characteristics of the renewal: "the taste for deep prayer, personal and in groups, a return to contemplation and an emphasizing of praise of God, the desire to devote oneself completely to Christ, a great availability for the calls of the Holy Spirit, more assiduous reading of Scripture, generous brotherly devotion, the will to make a contribution to the service of the Church."[86] He noted that in the best of renewals "weeds may be found among the good seed" and reminded the leaders of the "active pastoral responsibility of each bishop in his diocese"[87] for the spiritual lives of the faithful. To the bishops he recalled the words of Vatican II which taught that discernment of Spirits belongs in a special way to the competence of the bishops.

These words were received as a sign of encouragement. Note should be taken of their nonspecific character and therefore their weight and importance as papal approval of the renewal at this date should not be stressed. One could easily duplicate similar generic papal exhortations to all kinds of groups.

LUTHERAN CHURCH IN AMERICA (1974)

In 1974 the Commission on Worship of the Lutheran Church in America issued a report entitled "The Charismatic Movement in the Lutheran Church in America."[88] This report stands in strong contrast to that which issued from the Missouri Synod. While facing the problems which the charismatic renewal posits for the church, it asks that "the Lutheran Church in America . . . should, through its various divisions and agencies, recognize the Charismatic Movement as a legitimate part of its life and provide educational materials and opportunities both for pastors and lay people to increase understanding of the movement and to help adherents of the movement toward a deeper and more authentic understanding of their experience."[89] No suggestion should be made to imply that a Lutheran "cannot be Charismatic and remain a Lutheran in good standing."[90] The report adverts to the necessity of understanding the charismatic experience in a manner "consonant with the Scriptures and traditional Lutheran theology."[91]

No sympathy is extended to those who attempt to deal with the renewal by discrediting it, that is, by suggesting that those who are involved are suffering from psychological instability.[92] The only psychological study cited is that of Kildahl. No negative judgment, however, is made on the psychological health of participants in the renewal. "All religious behavior is open to psychological analysis, and such studies should be pursued. But their proper function should be kept clear. To demonstrate, for example, that certain types of people are attracted to the ministry does not preclude the theological concept of divine call. Most of the liturgical acts which shape Christian worship can be found in other religions as well. That does not make them unauthentic for Christians.[93] Though many researchers would have difficulty with the supposition that only persons with a certain psychological profile are attracted to and enter the renewal, the report manifests a great openness in this area as in others. This report, drawn up by Dr. Eugene Brand, is a model of discretion, sensitivity, and a willingness to listen coupled with a perceptive critical faculty.

THE CHURCH OF SCOTLAND (1974)

No denominational group, with the possible exception of the Canadian Catholic bishops, have studied the charismatic renewal with the care and diligence of the Presbyterian churches. Two impressive reports have issued from the two major Presbyterian bodies in the United States. In 1972 the General Assembly of the Church of Scotland instructed the Panel on Doctrine to study the doctrine of the Holy Spirit with special reference to the charismatic renewal. The Scottish report was obviously influenced by the two American Presbyterian studies. Like the American commissions, the Scottish Panel on Doctrine included in its working group ministers who identified with the renewal.

The panel is prepared to accept the reality of the experiences which those in the movement refer to as "baptism in the Holy Spirit," but it questions the appropriateness of this phrase to describe those experiences and, in some cases, the manner in which they are interpreted. "There is only one baptism, once and for all, whereby we are made members of the body of Christ and empowered for his service."[94] In the New Testament Spirit baptism may precede, coincide with, or follow, water baptism but these two elements of the one unity should not be allowed to drift apart. The grace given at baptism or conversion "comes variously and successively into the consciousness of the believer, through faith."[95] Of special concern to the panel, both in the explanation of baptism in the Holy Spirit and in the gifts which are interpreted as a special empowering for ministry, is a kind of theological elitism: "If it is important strictly to avoid any suggestion of a Church within a Church it is no less important to avoid as strictly a ministry within the ministry."[96] Severe criticism was leveled against the "theology of subsequence" of classical Pentecostalism which teaches the necessity of a second work of grace subsequent to conversion. "A theology of subsequence implies two or more classes of believers, a distinction being made between the converted and those who have been subsequently baptized in the Holy Spirit."[97] A corollary to this rejection of subsequence and the second blessing theology is the insistence that the religious experience be interpreted as a release of what was already there and as a growth in grace. Likewise, a doctrine of conditions to be fulfilled before one could receive the baptism in the Holy Spirit (rid oneself of sin, acquire a clean heart) would render the doctrine of justification by faith alone meaningless.

The promise of the gifts was seen as "valid for all times, and to the end of time."[98] Also evaluated positively was Edward Irving's teaching that some of the gifts had ceased to be operative in the church "simply because of lack of faith."[99] The neo-Pentecostal movement challenges the church to accept by faith that which has already been granted by grace. "The gifts of the Spirit are to be expected."[100]

This openness to the witness of the charismatic renewal was coupled with the conviction that the gifts which the Spirit gives to the church may change, so that the gifts he gave to the church of the first century are not necessarily those he offers the church of today.

An exaggerated supernaturalism among some neo-Pentecostals, with regard to the gifts was noted by the panel. In this context the panel took what will appear to many in the renewal, as well as to others not so involved, as an extreme position: "Speaking in tongues is miraculous, but so is the gift of reconciliation between God and man."[101] That glossolalia may have a divine as well as a human aspect or that it might be termed "supernatural" in its religious content and meaning seems well established. One can seriously question whether it is "miraculous." According to the report, the Reformed position, namely that the gifts of the Holy Spirit come variously and successively into the consciousness of the believer, "does not exclude the possibility that the believer would then be able to do something he was unable to do before."[102] But preference is given to the view that in a charism "an inborn ability is heightened, or the believer discovers a new way of fulfilling an old task—the way of love."[103] The neo-Pentecostals on the working group were, however, of the conviction that "a natural gift is not a charism."[104] When stated in this way, without qualification, the position is tenable. But were the meaning that a gift is a totally new faculty, a new endowment from above, it would seem less defensible.

The conclusions of the two American Presbyterian reports regarding the psychological profiles of those in the movement, namely that they are essentially well-adjusted and productive members of society were accepted. The word "ecstatic" as applied to tongues in an unqualified way can lead to the conclusion that glossolalia is "frenzied, uncontrolled behavior."[105] On the contrary, its basic meaning "is one of spiritual exaltation, which can appear strange, even bizarre, to the uninitiated onlooker, but which at the same time can still remain 'decent and in good order' (1 Cor. 14:40)."[106] Tongues is considered an extraordinary phenomenon because it is not a normal means of human communication. Therefore tongues, together with healing are often called "para-normal." "They cannot be explained by any known law of nature, or by any known psychological abnormality. They have to be accepted as facts."[107] That glossolalia is not to be understood by categories taken from abnormal psychology is fair enough but the text seems to indicate that as a phenomenon it is without a psychological structure and dynamics and therefore without a psychological explanation. One would neither want to grant that glossolalia takes place in some ahistorical psychological void, nor that what is explainable in psychological terms is of necessity devoid of the "supernatural."

This eminently fair and balanced report ends with some pastoral guidelines. The exercise of glossolalia and prophecy is neither to be "forbidden nor encouraged in public. However, such practices should not normally be expected during the main diet of public worship on the Lord's day. There may be special occasions where a certain experimentation can be carried out in public worship, provided it is not likely to be divisive, and not during the main diet of worship. . . . This should be regarded as an exceptional rather than a normal practice."[108] Finally, "instruction in the gifts of the Spirit should be given a full but not disproportionate place" in the teaching of the local church.[109]

CATHOLIC BISHOPS
OF THE WESTERN PROVINCE OF QUEBEC (1974)

Six bishops of western Quebec issued a document pointing to the need for biblical and theological teaching for all participants in the renewal. To this end and to assure closer ties with the local church charismatic groups are urged to obtain the help of priests and other competent pastoral persons. The bishops are aware that the renewal does not harbor all kinds of errors and strange teachings but they call attention to what are always possibilities: sensationalism, a false ecumenism, a false prophetism, fundamentalism, sectarian tendencies, illuminism, and a want of spiritual discernment. But the weight of their document is positive. They cite the teaching of Vatican II on the gifts of the Spirit. They see in the renewal a source of great good for the church. "We rejoice when we see a more pronounced taste for personal and community prayer, greater thirst for the word of God, a greater availability in response to the call of the Spirit, a more marked concern to carry the good news to all, a greater fraternal care, especially as concerns the service of the poor, a real preoccupation to grow in unity and mutual respect and to bring the gifts into the service of the Christian community and the world."[110]

CATHOLIC BISHOPS OF THE UNITED STATES (1975)

Early in 1975 the Committee for Pastoral Research and Practices of the National Conference of Catholic Bishops issued a "Statement on Catholic Charismatic Renewal."[111] Like the earlier Catholic statement, this document does not issue from the Conference of Bishops but is rather a report of a committee of bishops to the Conference. The document notes that "charisms have been given to the Church from the beginning and cannot be said to belong only to our times."[112] One of the great manifestations of the Spirit in our times was the Second Vatican Council. "Many believe also that the Catholic Charismatic Renewal is another such manifestation of the Spirit. It does indeed offer many positive signs, clearer in some groups than others."[113] In particular the bishops point to the renewed interest in prayer, a greater love of the Eucharist, reverence for Mary, "a heightened consciousness of the action of the Holy Spirit," "a deepening personal commitment to Christ," and a more profound attachment to the church.[114] That new movements face difficulties and "involve a certain mixture of desirable and undesirable elements" is understandable.[115] Some of the dangers are mentioned: elitism, fundamentalism, a false ecumenism, an exaggerated role assigned to healing, prophecy, tongues, and interpretation even when they are genuine. Only an oblique reference is made to the psychological dimension. There is "danger for some involved in this movement to ignore the intellectual and doctrinal content of faith and reduce it to a felt religious experience."[116]

The document contains a number of cautions, yet it is clearly intended to move beyond the 1969 "wait and see" statement to a more positive stance. The bishops "strongly encourage priests to take an interest in the movement."[117] The final sentence reads: "We encourage those who already belong and we support the positive and desirable directions of the charismatic renewal."[118] This sentence was interpreted by Archbishop Bernardin, president of the United States Catholic Conference of Bishops, as an epitome of the document's essentially positive message.

CATHOLIC BISHOPS OF CANADA (1975)

In mid-1975 the Canadian episcopate issued a statement similar to that issued by the United States Catholic bishops a few months earlier.[119] The Canadian statement differs in two respects from that of the United States bishops. The Canadian statement has more force and authority because it is not a report of a subcommittee to the Canadian bishops but is, rather, a statement of the bishops themselves to Canadian Catholics. Unlike the document from the United States, there were bishops on the committee which drafted the document who were personally involved in the Catholic renewal. The Canadian statement was greatly influenced by what has come to be known as the Malines Document.[120]

The renewal "serves as a new witness proclaiming that Pentecost continues."[121] Rather than perceiving the theological foundations as narrowly focused on the gifts, the bishops assert that "at the very base of the Charismatic Renewal we recognize the trinitarian structure of the Christian faith."[122] Within this trinitarian context the mother of God is honored as the one whose "yes" to the Father is the perfectly expressed response to the action of the Spirit.

The renewal has been especially successful in "personalizing community life, where simplicity and spontaneous behavior replace the stereotyped forms of communication and exchange characterizing certain Christian communities."[123] As others have done, the bishops point to the centrality of prayer, more particularly the prayer of praise. The most striking characteristic of praising the Lord in community "is the manifest joy they experience as Christians being together with Christ."[124] Baptism in the Spirit is seen not as a second baptism but as "a symbolic act signifying a new openness in the believer to the Spirit received at baptism."[125]

No hesitancy is shown in pointing out excesses which exist "here and there" though care is made not to generalize. Among the problem areas are a certain unhealthy orientation toward the miraculous, sensationalism, fundamentalism, a tendency to monopolize the charisms and for groups to turn inward on themselves, the lack of biblical and theological preparation on the part of leaders, and a false ecumenism. Like the statement issuing from the United States, it points to "the exaggerated importance placed on emotional experience of God in certain charismatic groups."[126] The bishops concede that "it is in the affective life that the believer meets with God to learn to know him better and to enjoy His presence," but warn lest one "conclude from this that the life of faith is measured by the degree of emotion that the believer experiences in his religious life. . . . The Spirit awakens the entire person to the presence of Christ in his or her life. It, therefore, would be arbitrary to limit His action to the sphere of emotions only."[127]

The total impact of this carefully reasoned, pastorally discerning document is a solid affirmation of the role the charismatic renewal is playing in the life of the church. No more impressive document has issued from any Catholic episcopal source.

POPE PAUL VI (1975)

Not a theological statement in the sense used in this chapter, but of importance in the future for the larger context in which research on the psychological health of charismatics will be carried out, is the address given by Pope Paul VI, on May 19, 1975, to ten thousand Catholic charismatics in Rome for an international charismatic congress. The Pope repeated what he had said a year earlier, namely that the "miracle of Pentecost should continue in history."[128] Asserting that "nothing is more necessary to this more and more secularized world than the witness of this 'spiritual renewal' that we see the Holy

Spirit evoking,"[129] he then singled out the fruits of the charismatic renewal: "a profound communion of souls, intimate contact with God, fidelity to the commitments undertaken at Baptism, in prayer—frequently in group prayer—in which each person, expressing himself freely, aids, sustains and fosters the prayer of others and, at the basis of everything, a personal conviction, which does not have its source solely in a teaching received by faith, but also a certain lived experience. . . . How then could this 'spiritual renewal' not be a 'chance' for the Church and for the world?"[130] The Pope concluded his formal address with the acclamation, "Jesus is Lord! Alleluia!"

In his spontaneous remarks in Italian after his formal address, the Pope said, "We desire nothing more than that Christians, believing people, should experience an awareness, a worship, a greater joy through the Spirit of God among us."[131] He expressed joy that there is now a generation "who shout out to the world the glory and greatness of the God of Pentecost."[132] When greeting the leaders of the conference after his informal remarks, the Pope grasped Cardinal Suenens's hands and said to him, "I thank you not in my name but in the name of Jesus Christ for what you have done and are doing for the charismatic renewal and for what you will do in the future to assure and maintain its place in the heart of the Church in accord with her doctrine."[133]

This audience given to a congress of Catholic charismatics in the presence of a cardinal and twelve other bishops from around the world is the most public sign of recognition and general approval given by any historic church. Not without reason did historian Dr. Vinson Synan, himself a classical Pentecostal of the Pentecostal Holiness Church, call the Rome conference and the papal audience "the single most important event in the history of world Pentecostalism."[134] The papal audience is obviously not a blanket approval of everything that is taught in the Catholic charismatic renewal, much less a blank check for everything charismatics do. Not all the theological problems are solved and the Pope's audience should not suggest that they are. Nonetheless, it is an unmistakably positive act.

CATHOLIC BISHOPS OF PANAMA (1975)

The bishops of Panama issued their joint statement after Pope Paul VI had received the international charismatic congress in an audience given in St. Peter's in May 1975. This, together with the experience of the renewal in Panama, reinforced the positive attitude the bishops took.

They note "a thirst for God, a living and present God" growing out of the disgust for materialism and an exaggerated secularism.[135] This "inquietude emanating from the action of God's Spirit" has given rise to what in Panama is known as the Movement of Renewal in the Holy Spirit.[136] The movement is characterized by its love of prayer, especially the prayer of praise and adoration. For many this renewal prayer in private and in groups is "a special grace characterized by a strong call to conversion, based on adult acceptance, conscious and free, of Jesus Christ as Lord and Saviour of their lives."[137] The bishops reaffirmed the conviction of Pope Paul, expressed three months earlier, that this spiritual renewal "is a grace and good fortune for the Church and the world."

In response to the Pope's suggestion that the renewal needs guidance and theological direction, the bishops "insist" that the renewal be in and of the church in its sacramental life, hierarchical structure, apostolic authority, and in its devotion to Mary and the saints. They see the strong orientation toward personal and community prayer, private or liturgical, not as a turning toward pure inwardness but as manifesting its authenticity in "social and religious movements."[138] All are asked to refrain "from underrating and prejudging this movement of renewal."[139] Priests and religious are asked to lend their services in guiding and supporting, and the wish was expressed that in each place there be only "the prayer assemblies authorized by the hierarchy for which are assured priestly guidance and the direction of competent laypersons."[140]

SOUTHERN BAPTISTS (1975)

One should not read the history of the churches' response to the presence of charismatic Christians among them as a progress from shock to toleration to reluctant acceptance to a warm welcome. There has been increasing acceptance and approval on the part of those in positions of pastoral authority within the Roman Church. To a lesser degree this has also taken place in two Lutheran churches in the United States and in the Presbyterian and Episcopal churches. But not all churches have had the same experience. In summarizing the major religious news stories of 1975, the editor of *Christian Century* remarked on the growth of the movement among Catholics and Lutherans and the problems other denominations, especially the Southern Baptists, continue to have: "The charismatic movement, rather than bringing heightened spirituality to the churches, frequently caused internal tensions in many denominations, especially in the Southern Baptist Convention—SBC-affiliated state bodies either disavowed or took disciplinary actions against churches and ministers who openly favored the charismatic movement. Large charismatic gatherings of Roman Catholics at the University of Notre Dame and of Lutherans in Minneapolis indicated that the phenomenon is thriving."[141]

In June of 1975 the motion to expel charismatic churches was voted down by the national meeting of the Southern Baptist Convention. But autonomous local associations have taken a stronger stand. A Southern Baptist church in Baton Rouge, and two churches in both Cincinnati and Dallas were "defellowshipped," or expelled, from the local associations of churches. The resolution to expel the two Dallas churches reads in part: "Whereas certain churches in our Association, namely the Beverly Hills Baptist Church of Dallas, and the Shady Grove Baptist Church of Grand Prairie, have openly practiced the present-day phenomena of glossolalia and public faith-healing services in which people are declared healed, exercises which mark a radical departure from what Southern Baptists have historically believed are valid Biblical gifts and doctrines, thus indicating that they are in doctrinal error and are no longer in harmony with our historic Baptist practices, and:

"Whereas repeated attempts have been made in the spirit of love, healing and reconciliation . . . for at least six years to resolve these differences without success, and:

"Whereas because of these departures from Historic Baptist practice other churches have been adversely affected resulting in a breach of fellowship among our churches.

"Be it therefore resolved that the messengers of these above named churches be not seated in this associational meeting and that they be no longer considered as cooperative bodies in our association."[142]

Historically such an action is not surprising. From the turn of the century it has been those churches which theologically and historically stand closest to the Pentecostal tradition (Christian Missionary Alliance, Church of the Nazarene) which have taken the strongest stand against Pentecostalism and have been the least influenced by it. The liturgical churches (Lutheran, Presbyterian, Episcopal, Roman Catholic) which theologically and historically are the furthest removed from the Pentecostal tradition have been more open to and more influenced by it. The action of the Southern Baptists fits into this pattern.

The resolution of the Dallas Baptist Association against the charismatic parishes passed 608–401. A large number of the forty per cent who voted against the resolution did so not because they are personally involved in the Baptist charismatic renewal but because they are convinced that Baptists are not true to themselves when they exclude people on nonbiblical grounds. They thought that the Baptist principle of the Bible as the only rule for faith and order was denied. Dr. Douglas Watterson, though not part of the Baptist charismatic movement, said that the passage of the resolution was "an extreme error." Charismatic Baptists "were denied fellowship for what was called heretical doctrine. But we can clearly see by looking at the New Testament that it is not heretical doctrine."[143]

Because local associations are autonomous, the withdrawing of fellowship does not alter the churches' standings in either the state conferences or in the Southern Baptist Convention. But the atmosphere is hardly friendly.

SUMMARY

With the words of Pope Paul VI one is far from the theological and psychological climate out of which issued the early Episcopal statements where the phenomenon was psychologically suspect (also the events of Pentecost as recounted in Acts 2 were suspect), where a justifiably large preoccupation was with the theological and cultural borrowings from other traditions. In the Episcopal statement of the diocese of Los Angeles, tongues was seen as scaffolding necessary for the beginning of the church which was later wisely discarded. Operative here is a theological dispensationalism. These early Episcopal statements reflect a church faced with an experience which at that time was considered psychologically dubious, and a theology whose revivalistic categories are essentially foreign to the major contemporary streams of the American Episcopal church. From Bishop Pike's "heresy in embryo" to Pope Paul's positive evaluation of the fruits of the renewal in the churches is a giant step.

The American Lutheran Church had to deal with the undeniable fact that in many of its parishes the introduction of the charismatic movement had been divisive, partly but not exclusively because of the aggressive hard-sell evangelism of early Lutheran adherents, and also because the American Lutheran Church understood that in the teaching of Lutheran charismatics, tongues was considered normative, though not necessary for salvation. Quite rightly the American Lutheran Church pointed to the traditional Lutheran teaching that the Holy Spirit is received in Baptism.

Something of a turning point was reached when the committee of the Catholic bishops in the United States issued its statement in 1969. For the first time there was an attempt to broaden the perspective both theologically and culturally. Typified by an open but cautious attitude the statement was meant to be a "wait and see" document. This open neutrality, when read against the background of the Episcopal statements and that of the American Lutheran Church had a different ring to it. Charismatics in all the churches, including the Protestant, as well as many outside the charismatic renewal, read it as a ringing affirmation. This misreading of the text undoubtedly created a different climate for the 1970 statement of the United Presbyterian Church. Through the instrumentality of the Stated Clerk, Dr. William P. Thompson, the committee appointed included significant charismatic representation. The psychological sophistication of the report, as well as its realism and deep pastoral concern for those in the parishes who were not personally involved in the renewal, made it a model for future church commissions. An early report of the Presbyterian Church in the United States justly pointed to the complexity and multiformity of the phenomenon. If one is not sure of what glossolalia is in the New Testament context and if the term glossolalia covers a wide range of experiences today, how can one say that the contemporary experience of tongues is the same as that recorded in the Scriptures. The tone of the earliest report was largely unfavorable to the charismatic movement. The later commission of this Presbyterian body included charismatics in its membership. The theological perspective was much broader and the total presentation was much more favorable to the renewal. The final reports of these two Presbyterian churches (1970, 1971) influenced the Scottish Presbyterian church (1974) whose working group included ministers who identified with the renewal. This report evaluated the renewal favorably though critically.

The reports of the three Presbyterian churches opened the Reformed tradition to charismatics in the churches and gave them a kind of acceptance which they had not yet experienced. The opposition could still point to churches and seminaries where the charismatic dimension was the occasion, if not the source, of divisions, but the possibility of charismatics living peaceably within the Presbyterian communion was now a reality.

The Missouri Synod statement is understandable in terms of the conservative theological tradition of the Synod and also in terms of the un-Lutheran theology sometimes found in the Lutheran movement. But it also represents a step backward for two reasons. No creative attempt was made by a theological faculty, which has the resources, to situate the Lutheran renewal within a Lutheran framework. No representative of the Lutheran renewal was on the committee which wrote the Missouri Synod document and therefore the renewal was judged wholly from the outside. The 1974 statement of the Lutheran Church in America recognized, on the other hand, that the renewal could be an authentic expression of Lutheranism and urged that the manner in which it was understood should be consonant with the Scriptures and traditional Lutheran theology. Though it accepted the thesis that certain psychological types are attracted to the renewal, it energetically rejected the position that charismatics suffer from psychological instability. The theological work of LCUSA (Lutheran Council in the U.S.A.) gives hope that the Lutheran churches in the United States will be guided in their relations with charismatics in their midst by two principles: first, the necessity of finding a truly Lutheran theological formulation for the charismatic insight; and secondly, the right of Lutheran charismatics, as Lutherans rather than specifically as charismatics, to confront the churches and the Lutheran confessional history with the gospel. The Lutheran charismatics should not enjoy this right less than other Lutherans.

The Catholic bishops of Puerto Rico had a local situation in 1972 which differed considerably from that which the Catholic bishops found in the United States in 1969. These local conditions evoked a declaration which was less "wait and see" and more "caution, prudence, vigilance, circumspection." But the charismatic renewal was neither forbidden nor hindered.

The 1975 document from the Committee for Pastoral Research and Practices of the Catholic bishops in the United States has something of an enigmatic character. Though positive in its main lines—indeed, interpreted by the president of the national hierarchy as an attempt to go beyond the "wait and see" character of the 1969 statement to a more pronounced approval—it is still heavy with cautionary tones. Without Archbishop Bernardin's authoritative interpretation one could easily read the document as a drawing back of the hierarchy.

Of all the statements issuing from Catholic hierarchies the most impressive theologically and pastorally is the Canadian statement of 1975. Not blind to problem areas, it contains serious theological reflection and a balanced pastoral discernment. Other national hierarchies can look to it as a possible model. The statement of the Catholic Bishops of Panama (1975) understands the renewal as a grace for the church and a movement which needs theological and pastoral guidance. They echo the 1975 statement of the committee of bishops in the United States and call on priests to interest themselves. In both cases this admonition was a measure to insure sound doctrine and correct pastoral practice. Also it was a recognition of those strengths of the renewal which all the Catholic statements enumerate in detail.

The 1973 and 1975 addresses of the Pope show a move from greater reticence to more open approbation of the essential insights of the Catholic renewal. The 1975 address was a major event and will undoubtedly affect the larger context in which charismatics are evaluated in the future. National hierarchies tend to wait for a signal from Rome as Rome tends to wait for a signal from national hierarchies. The positive evaluation of the renewal in Pope Paul's 1975 address will give national hierarchies the signal for which they have been waiting. One can expect a number of other national hierarchies to express themselves in guarded favor of the renewal.

The more "evangelical" conservative Protestant churches still have many problems as seen in the Lutheran Church (Missouri Synod) and in a number of local Southern Baptist associations. A doctrinal fundamentalism and dispensationalism (certain charisms belong to the church only in its beginning) make it difficult for these churches to be open to the charismatic renewal. The fault is not always solely with the churches and associations. They are often presented with a theology of the renewal which is foreign to their theological traditions and with a cultural form which is difficult to take over without qualification.

The charismatics in these conservative evangelical churches, as well as others not in the renewal, point out that the churches and associations are not willing to let the traditions and teachings "be normed" by the Scriptures, which is a primary reformation principle clearly stated in the confessional writings.

4

MARGINAL PEOPLE AND THE DOMINANCE OF ABNORMAL PSYCHOLOGY: 1910–1966

To understand some of the problems the churches faced and face when attempting to say something about the psychological dimensions of glossolalic behavior, it is important to know something of the history of psychological evaluations. What is presented here is not an exhaustive survey of the field, but rather an attempt to indicate some of the studies and to give some kind of tentative evaluation. No attempt will be made to give an extensive critique of each study, but rather an indication of their general direction and how the conclusions are in agreement or at variance with the findings of other studies. An historical rather than a topical method will be followed, the former allowing one to understand better the mentality of the churches which was, in part, a reflection of the state of psychological research at a given historical moment. Before this historical survey is begun, two questions will be briefly examined: What is the relation of glossolalia to trance? Is glossolalia learned behavior? These questions are central to the way psychologists and other researchers look at glossolalia.

TRANCE

In his study of a black classical Pentecostal church, Alexander Alland (1961) admits that the members of this lower-class black group suffered from extreme deprivation, both economic and psychological.[1] The

79

psychological deprivation is associated with the guilt and anxiety which is known to be high in the lower-class black community. The focus of his study is "possession" or trance states, which he approaches not only psychologically, but also physiologically and socio-culturally. This broad approach was also attempted by Werner Cohn (1968), who claims that his own attempt was a failure, and that the relationship between psychological factors and membership in social groups is still a riddle.[2]

Alland rejects the older view that trance states have their origin in hysteria or schizophrenia. "Neither of these theories is acceptable in the light of the socio-cultural data. In fact, it is a general blindness to the social environment associated with trance which leads to these gross over-simplifications."[3] The susceptibility to hypnosis and therefore to trance is to be explained partly in terms of a variety of personality types, even though this variety is limited. "Receptivity to trance is most certainly influenced by personality differences."[4] This susceptibility also depends on specific types of socialization. Alland warns against arguing from the presence of a trance state to the presence of a personality disorder. The evidence with regard to the susceptibility of normal people, neurotics and psychotics to trance is not firmly established, and some of it is contradictory. However, the work of Merton Gill and Margaret Brenman (1959),[5] E. Levitt, H. Persky, and J. P. Brady (1964),[6] and finally of Ernest and Josephine Hilgard (1965),[7] show substantial agreement that "normal subjects are more hypnotizable than those who border on the neurotic or are frankly neurotic."[8] An earlier study by Hull (1933) indicated a slight but positive correlation between suggestibility and intelligence.[9] This should help correct the public image that being susceptible to suggestion, and therefore to hypnosis, is a sign of psychological weakness or instability. Speaking of spirit possession as a paradigm to gauge the potential value of altered states of consciousness, Arnold Ludwig (1967, 1968) contends that "such a state is more highly valued among 'primitive' people or among those who are economically deprived and are leading a frustrated marginal existence."[10] It would be difficult indeed to assert that the total environment has no impact on personality development. Alland considers that the receptivity to trance is influenced by personal differences such as the range of experience, the needs of the individual, and the tolerance level for various physiological stresses (loud, rhythmic music with a simple repetitious beat, fasting, a heated room with low oxygen content). In this atmosphere, with the help of a skilled leader, the seeker after the baptism learns to enter a trance, which, says Alland, is a hypnotic state. In the trance state the seeker begins to speak in tongues.

The trance is therefore learned behavior, and once learned its repetition is assured. "Hypnosis becomes auto-hypnosis and after the first experience it becomes less difficult for members to enter into the trance state."[11] Without attributing to the leader the decisive role which Kildahl does, Alland nevertheless gives him a large role comparable to that of a hypnotist.[12] Also important for the first entrance into the trance state is the suggestive influence of other persons present who are already in the trance state. Though this trance state would be looked upon by the folk psychiatry of the dominant American cultural pattern as exceptional and therefore as deviant and abnormal, it is not considered so by the social environment of this particular black classical Pentecostal church. Here one sees how culture affects psychological judgments. What is normal in one culture may appear abnormal in another. It is clear that the trance state is normal in this particular social context, and that members of the church are well adjusted to the broad social environment of their social class.[13]

In their study of glossolalia Lapsley and Simpson (1964, 1965) speak of a "form of dissociation within the personality, in which a set of voluntary muscles respond to control centers other than those associated with consciousness."[14] Dissociation is a mental mechanism whereby a split-off part of the personality temporarily possesses the entire field of consciousness and behavior but in such a way that it does not necessarily imply the presence of hysteria.[15] Though admitting of large variations, Gary Palmer (1967) holds that "relative disorganization is the essence of trance."[16] Also admitting to extensive variations, Felicitas Goodman (1969, 1972) uses rather strong trance rhetoric. Glossolalia is uttered while in a state of "hyperarousal," Goodman's synonym for trance.[17] Glossolalia is something more than what is uttered while in this state of hyperarousal, but is further "an artifact of the mental state, or rather its neurophysiological processes. . . . In some manner (as in epilepsy) the glossolalist switches off cortical control."[18] Glossolalia is "an event of vocalization uttered while the speaker is in a state of dissociation."[19] For Goodman, then, glossolalia is tied to trance and indeed is something that trance causes. In terms of trance, Goodman's position is similar to that of Lapsley and Simpson.

William Samarin (1968, 1969, 1970, 1971, 1972, 1973, 1974) takes a more guarded position: "... glossolalia is *sometimes* associated with *some* degree of altered state of consciousness, that this *occasionally* involves motor activity that is involuntary or, *rarely*, a complete loss of consciousness, and that in any case subsequent use of glossolalia (that is, after the initial experience) is *most often independent* of dissociative phenomena."[20] For Samarin then, trance is not bound in a necessary way to glossolalia, and that after the initial experience of tongues the use of glossolalia tends to be independent of trance states. When examining the linguistic phonetic aspect of glossolalic behavior, Samarin found that glossolalia is not tied in any necessary way to trance.[21] One can find the same phonetic intonational qualities in glossolalic speech when trance is not present. Therefore glossolalia cannot be caused by trance. There will always be instances of trance-speech but it is not possible to demonstrate that glossolalia is always dependent on trance. Samarin seems to have correctly grasped the ambiguities of glossolalic behavior. James R. Jaquith (1967) maintains that the absence of trance can be demonstrated by the ability to begin and to bring to a termination at will the glossolalic utterance. This voluntary control, says Jaquith, indicates that there is no trance state present.[22]

Much of the confusion stems from the definition of trance. The English and English psychiatric dictionary defines trance as a "sleep-like state marked by reduced sensitivity to stimuli, loss or alteration of knowledge of what is happening, substitution of automatic for voluntary activity. Trances are frequent in hysteria, and they may be hypnotically induced. In extreme form trance resembles (or is) coma. Religious or emotionally marked trances are called ecstacy."[23] In this framework trance as a religious phenomenon is an extraordinary or unusual event. There would be almost universal rejection on the part of all Pentecostals and charismatics of the position that tongues is usually spoken in an ecstatic state or that it represents a product of trance. Except for unusual instances tongues is exercised while the reality awareness and orientation is within the normal range. Arnold Ludwig has noted that hypnotic trance is only one of many different forms of trance, and that "trance phenomena are much more widespread than generally supposed and constitute a normal or common, rather than abnormal or unusual, mental faculty."[24] In this regard two researchers have suggested that the words "trance" and "hypnosis" may no longer be useful in discussing hypersuggestibility or hypnotic behavior.[25] The response to direct suggestions or commands and the performance of acts traditionally associated with hypnosis and trance should rather be spoken of simply as task motivation. Trance and hypnosis may be too strong in their connotations. Hypnotism and trance should be removed from the area of unusual states of consciousness since hypnotism is simply the extension of suggestibility which all people possess.

Palmer, too, did not consider the trances of the glossolalics whom he was studying to have been unusual events: "I infer that these people were entering trance from the fact that they concentrated on their prayers and they were able to 'pray in the spirit' (speak in tongues)."[26] Trance in this definition is as common as the reading of a newspaper. Ronald E. Shor (1959), in speaking of trance in relation to hypnosis, refers to the deeper kind of absorption one has in reading a difficult book. One can have a general awareness which is nonfunctional so that the person reading the book registers the remark of a person in the room even though not aware that another person has spoken. Shor accordingly defines trance as "any state in which the generalized reality-orientation has faded to relatively nonfunctional unawareness. . . ."[27]

Bourguignon and Pettay (1964) are particularly skeptical about using trances to analyze such things as "spirit possession," (which is one term anthropologists apply to baptism in the Holy Spirit as to similar phenomena) because of the lack of any scientific consensus on trance. Trance has been accounted for by reference to hysteria, hypnosis, nonpathological dissociation, cultural learning, social learning, histrionics, and epilepsy.[28] These two authors note, as was earlier remarked with regard to tongues, the "strong cultural bias" on the part of scholars who interpret the meaning of trance.[29] The question of trance becomes tied to the question of whether or not this represents deviant behavior or is evidence of mental illness. After a review of the literature on dissociative states as a cross-cultural phenomenon, Dr. Bourguignon (1965) comes to the conclusion that they are "so inadequately understood that no conclusion can be arrived at as to whether it can be classified as normal, deviant, or as evidence of mental illness."[30]

LEARNED BEHAVIOR

Does tongues represent learned behavior? What is learning in this context? Many classical Pentecostals, as well as charismatics from other streams of the movement, would deny that it is learned behavior.

It seems to them that to admit that it is learned behavior would be to deny that it is a gift of the Spirit. This, however, represents an exaggerated supernaturalism, which is manifested in what the author calls the "zap" theory of all the gifts. That is, God gives a person a gift of the Spirit, speaking in tongues for instance, at a certain moment in time. Before God "zapped" him, he did not have the gift, and after he was "zapped," he possessed the gift. In the mind of these people a gift is a totally new endowment. These Pentecostals and charismatics would apply their exaggerated supernaturalism to tongues, prophecy, and healing. That there are men who have these gifts who are not Christians and may have no religious faith at all suggests to some of these Pentecostals and charismatics that the gifts in these cases have a demonic origin, a quite unwarranted conclusion. There is theologically no reason why a certain ability cannot be both a "natural" ability and a gift of the Spirit. It is the author's contention that tongues is learned behavior in the sense that it is something everyone is capable of doing, is a "natural" ability, and the person uses the phonetic material already in his linguistic treasury. Arnold Bittlinger (1966, 1967, 1968, 1969), a German Lutheran theologian and charismatic, also is convinced that the ability to speak in tongues is a "natural" phenomenon.[31] Looking at tongues from the viewpoint of a psychiatrist, E. Mansell Pattison (1964, 1968, 1974) came to the conclusion that "any of us could 'speak in tongues' if we adopted a passive attitude about controlling our body and speech and had an emotional tension pressing for expression."[32] Speaking from within the Christian tradition, Pattison warns against the "hypersupernaturalism" which postulates a supernatural explanation for behavior in a religious framework which is mysterious, unexpected, and unexplained.

There is, however, a broader meaning of learned behavior, such as used by Goodman. In this sense the initiate obeys "a cultural expectation."[33] A certain type of behavior, tongues in this case, is expected, is looked upon with approval, and is rewarded by the esteem of the group. There may or may not be onlookers present who are urging the initiate to glossolalic utterance. In this sense glossolalia is learned behavior.

There is also present another aspect of learning and that is the pattern of the tongue which is spoken. Goodman contends that "the stereotyped utterance mirrors that of the person who guided the glossolalist into the behavior."[34] In other words it is possible for the person who is speaking in tongues to have learned a certain style or phonetic pattern from the person who has guided him or her into glossolalic utterance. The Lutheran psychologist, John Kildahl came to the same conclusion.[35] For English-speaking subjects, says Pattison, glossolalia is composed of basic speech elements of English and to that extent is learned behavior. Glossolalia is therefore "an aborted formation of familiar speech."[36] The phonetic pattern can be picked up from other glossolalics, says Pattison. From his research Walter Wolfram (1966) concluded that although glossolalia shares characteristics with real languages, "it is highly improbable that glossolalists are speaking an unlearned non-native language."[37] The system of phonemes is closely correlated with the language background of the speaker.

Samarin situates his study less in the cultural environment and attributes less importance to glossolalia as learned behavior in the sense of having a linguistic model to imitate. Glossolalia is a "form of pseudolanguage that is available to every normal human being in a normal state,"[38] and can be learned by drawing from his storehouse of spoken sounds. What is so surprising in Samarin's research is the relative irrelevance of previous instruction. For some who spoke in tongues the phenomenon was "unmotivated."[39] They became glosso-lalics in spite of themselves as they had not been exposed to previous instruction on how to acquire the gift. This is counter to the supposition of researchers such as Kildahl, that there is much proselytizing and coaching.[40] There are persons who have never known others who speak in tongues, who never received instructions from any leaders, and who came to the experience spontaneously. Samarin cites cases of persons who came to the experience of tongues without knowing anyone who spoke in tongues and had no other conscious source of information even about the existence of such a phenomenon. This would indicate "the unimportance if not irrelevance of instruction in the acquisition of glossolalia."[41] Others about to be initiated into the practice of glossolalia who had some limited knowledge of tongues were given no phonetic model to follow and many of them had not heard glossolalia long enough to conceive their own model. They did not know what phonetic elements to use nor how to group them together once they began to appear. Samarin would admit that some who have been exposed to the practice of glossolalia can be influenced phonetically. Aside from this qualification "a person learns, or can learn, a great deal about the charismatic subculture, *but he does not learn to talk in tongues.*"[42] Samarin's finding that coaching plays less a role than had been thought is supported in the Gerlach and Hine research.

One-fourth of the persons interviewed received the "baptism" while alone, that is, without anyone present to instruct, encourage, and coach.[43] These may have had friends who spoke in tongues, or they may have had some instruction and encouragement at some other time, but none at the time when they first began to speak in tongues. Vivier also reports that "many of the test subjects have spoken in 'tongues' for the first time when alone during their private prayers."[44] Even when the factors of group emotionalism and suggestibility, such as hand clapping and rhythmical music were not present, the person came to the experience of tongues. This would suggest that there are mechanisms other than group pressure and psychological manipulation. A preliminary study done by Virginia H. Hine and James Olila (1967) indicated that the two hundred thirty-nine respondents to a questionnaire were not brought to the practice of tongues by psychopathological pressures.[45] In the field work which Wolfram did for his linguistic studies he met some persons who reported that "the inception of glossolalia took place in private without a counsellor."[46] That a person came to the experience of tongues alone, in private, does not, of course, exclude all possibility of suggestion being a factor. It does seem that a person can come to the experience of tongues quite spontaneously, without previous instruction or without previous knowledge of its meaning.

PSYCHOLOGY AND GLOSSOLALIA

The classical Pentecostal movement is dated variously from 1901 or 1906. From its inception tongues played a role of some importance. For large parts of the classical movement speaking in tongues was the "initial evidence" that one had received the "baptism in the Holy Spirit." The early classical Pentecostals in this country came from the lower classes, it will be recalled, and their glossolalic utterances were looked upon as socially unacceptable behavior. They were identified with the lower classes until the Second World War when that social classification no longer typified them, though they still drew from the blue-collar class.

The emergence of Protestant neo-Pentecostalism in the early 1960's meant that persons from the middle and upper classes were associating themselves with behavior which the large part of American society could only consider bizzare. Many of these neo-Pentecostals were well educated, held positions of prominence in business and industry, and some were persons of considerable means. Large numbers of the early Protestant neo-Pentecostals took over not only "baptism in the Holy Spirit," together with tongues as initial evidence, but also the biblical and doctrinal fundamentalism and the cultural baggage of classical Pentecostalism.

Emile Lombard

One of the first studies devoted to glossolalia is that of Emile Lombard (1910).[47] For Lombard glossolalic behavior was the result of mob psychology, "*psychologie des foules.*"[48] Though Lombard emphasizes the role of mass suggestion and revivalistic contagion, he recognizes that one can speak in tongues even though one has never been present when it was practiced. It is sufficient if one hears about it or reads about it in the Scriptures. Suggestion may still be operative here but it is of a subtler kind.[49] People who speak in tongues are "impressionable." For Lombard the causes are psychic. It is a manifestation of a "disorganization of the ego."[50] Speaking in tongues has the character of "infantilism and emotionalism."[51] He wants to avoid the suggestion that glossolalics are hysterical. The adoption of a new language is a result of a change in personality.

Eddison Mosiman

Eddison Mosiman (1911) identifies the psychological condition present in speaking in tongues with the ecstatic condition, which in turn is identified with the hypnotic state.[52] In the ecstatic state two factors play a large role: the dominance of the unconscious and the power of suggestion. The force and effectiveness of the unconscious, pushed by suggestion, bring about those extraordinary phenomena which usually appear in ecstasy. The movement of the tongue, the hallucinations, the prophetic utterances and the other unintelligible utterances in the state of trance are the consequence of the activity of the unconscious. The conscious mind is completely excluded and the phenomenon of tongues is therefore an expression of the unconscious. It is suggestion which activates the unconscious. Suggestion can be some person or some group or it can also be auto-suggestion, either willed and conscious, or involuntary and unconscious. The unconscious, derailed by suggestion, can easily imitate a tongue or language.[53] In his very useful study Mosiman contends that the psychological research does not exclude the possibility that tongues comes from God. In summary, Mosiman holds that "speaking in tongues is an expression of thoughts and feelings through the organ of speech which is temporarily under the dominance of the reflexive nerve centers, and the special forms are principally ascribed to suggestion, which, for the most part, comes from a literal interpretation of the New Testament."[54]

Mosiman's explanation of the psychological structure involved in speaking in tongues is very helpful. No one, not even the most aggressive Pentecostal, will deny that subjective elements play a large role in the exercise of charisms. It would be surprising if the unconscious did not play a large and even an important role. Mosiman can be a link to the later Jungian explanations. In a passing reference Carl Jung described glossolalia as an archetypal "invasion of unconscious contents."[55]

Oskar Pfister

A very brief and limited research using Freudian categories was done by Oskar Pfister (1912). Utilizing the depth analysis of two of his patients, Pfister came to the conclusion that instead of a grammatical structure, one finds in glossolalia a psychological construct which in principle fully coincides with hysterical symptoms and above all with neurotic phenomenon. Tongue speaking is an infantile regression to auto-erotic satisfaction.[56] Behind all tongue speaking Pfister found what he called painful thoughts rooted in infantile experiences which are lived through again and given expression in glossolalia. The infantile roots of speaking in tongues are, for the most part, more pronounced than in dreams. In addition to expressing erotic content, tongues also expresses ambition, longing for a more profitable occupation, etc. "In what is said one finds a multitude of reminiscences which appear to be swirling around without order. Gradually one can recognize in the confused mass of impressions a common theme, until finally the disjointed elements appear as members of one organic expression. In this manner one has an artistic, ordered, and meaningful whole."[57]

George Barton Cutten

The study which has taken on the stature of a classic is the publication of George Barton Cutten (1927). Cutten agrees with Mosiman that there are many common factors between the ecstatic and the hypnotic state, but to identify the two states "is to carry the analogy too far."[58] On the other hand, Cutten says that when dealing with speaking in tongues one is dealing with "a state of personal disintegration," which is abnormal because the "subconsciousness is in control."[59] Tongues is a "childish reaction, showing itself not only by its appearance among the most primitive and untrained in a community, but by its similarity to the reactions of children. . . . Those who speak with tongues are almost without exception devout, but ignorant and illiterate people."[60] Further, those who speak in tongues are characterized by a limited verbal capacity, and little ability for reasoning. Finally, Cutten assumed that glossolalia is linked to catalepsy and hysteria.[61] It was this latter contention that made its way into psychological literature and was repeated. His influence has been great in spite of the dearth of experimental evidence in his book. No other research has ever suggested that glossolalics have little verbal capacity. It was this capacity to verbalize their experience to other members of the historic churches in such a convincing manner which made the neo-Pentecostals such a divisive force in the historic churches.[62] When Cutten wrote, most classical Pentecostals in the United States did come from the lower socio-economic levels. That this is no longer true does not fault Cutten's research.

Anton Boisen

Previously, it was noted how Anton Boisen (1936, 1939, 1945) had related economic distress and deprivation to the religious experience of classical Pentecostals. The growth of these groups "may be regarded as a direct result of the shared strain due to the economic depression."[63] Boisen noted that the years of exceptional growth for the Pentecostal sects roughly coincide with the economic depression of the 1930s and that "there was in this period no demonstrable increase in mental illness."[64] They believe that the divine manifests itself in the unusual and that the promptings which seem to come from without are authoritative. "Even though no personality disorganization may result, and even though there be no commitment to a mental hospital, these false premises are likely to produce all sorts of difficulties in groups as well as in individuals."[65] When the religious experience of this enthusiastic group is induced within a structured and familiar milieu and when the experience follows the accepted patterns, the danger of personality disorder is at a minimum.[66] The group itself may go off on a tangent. When the intense emotion generated in such experiences comes under wise leadership, then, more usually, an important and vital religious movement is likely to result.[67] With all the excesses that characterize the classical Pentecostals, whom Boisen calls "holy rollers," they must be given credit for helping individuals reorganize lives that had been unsatisfactory and make their lives more meaningful.[68] Boisen speaks from his experience as a minister and the founder of a movement for clinical pastoral training. An early proponent of the view that the study of psychiatry and psychology had meaning for theology, he was chaplain for twenty-six years in two important mental hospitals. The views expressed in his writings carry the weight of experience (perhaps too determined by the limited population of mental hospitals) but are impressionistic and cannot be checked.

L. M. Vivier

The most exhaustive psychological research on tongues is that of L. M. Vivier (1960, 1968), the South African psychiatrist.[69] The research design is well articulated though one may want to qualify the results because of a defect in the sampling procedure.[70] Vivier found that psychologically the classical Pentecostals had a poor beginning in life. They had been torn by insecurity, conflict, tension, and emotional difficulties.[71] The research of Bryan Wilson (1961) in England arrived at similar results. Though the sampling of classical Pentecostals in England, who came from the lower socio-economic groups, was no larger than twenty-four, Bryan Wilson was impressed by the frequency of emotionally disturbed backgrounds among the people he interviewed. Among these factors were loss of a parent in early life, mixed marriage of the parents, immigration to England from Ireland and Italy, unhappy home conditions. Since Wilson is approaching his study from a sociological perspective he gives no further psychological data. Wilson concludes: "The general psychological type appeared obvious from these interviews."[72] Though Wilson admits that no evidence concerning the general psychological profile of the Elim (classical) Pentecostals could be deduced from these findings, it does seem an unwarranted leap from unsettled background to the conclusion that the Pentecostals belong to a certain psychological type.

Both Vivier the psychiatrist and Wilson the sociologist start from the same premise, that is, disturbed backgrounds. The sociologist, whose general treatment of Pentecostals is sympathetic and understanding, proceeds, without clinical evidence, from the disturbed background to assertions about the psychological profile. The psychiatrist makes no such leap. Approximately fifty percent of the glossolalics tend to show a history of psychiatric and adjustment problems.[73] However, glossolalics showed marital adjustment similar to that of control groups. Their capacity for marital adjustment did not reflect higher childhood insecurity as one would have expected. Vivier contends that the psychiatric and pathological factors in this sampling cannot be related to the phenomenon of glossolalia as another fifty percent showed no such problems. Persons with adjustment problems would turn to religion as a form of adjustment, would take their religious commitment seriously. They would also tend to gravitate toward religions where group acceptancce and active participation is high. The number of psychologically disturbed personalities in the families of the glossolalics (not the glossolalics themselves) showed that the incidence in the classical Pentecostal families (forty percent) equalled that of the two control groups combined. With this heavy incidence in the family history of classical Pentecostals one would expect that glossolalics would show great signs of anxiety and neuroticism. The Willoughby Test showed that "glossolalia is clearly not associated with neuroticism."[74] The research did show that glossolalia tends to be associated with sensitive people, that is, people who respond to stimuli of low intensity. Vivier, as Boisen, Kelsey, Kiev, and the Gerrards, suggests that glossolalia might serve a therapeutic function and contribute to emotional well-being.[75]

The results of the Rosenzweig Picture Frustration Test show that the glossolalics were less inclined to point out the frustrating obstacle in a frustrating situation than were those in control group B, who were the traditionalists who did not believe in glossolalia. The Pentecostals were more inclined to minimize frustrations. Those who spoke in tongues showed greater ego-effacement, while the traditionalists had their egos more in the forefront of their consciousness. In psychological terms, ego-effacement could either be the condition necessary for speaking in tongues or its result. Vivier relates glossolalia to repression, not in the sense of repressing guilt, but in the sense of self-effacement.[76]

On the suggestibility tests the three groups (one classical Pentecostal group and two control groups) were without significant differences.[77] What differences there were indicated that the Pentecostals were less suggestible than the control groups. There was no difference in suggestibility between those Pentecostals who prayed in tongues frequently and those who prayed in tongues only occasionally.

The 16 Personality Factor Test of Cattell indicated that glossolalics are people who have acquired the habit of renunciation. Their condi-

tioning is such that they accept moral restrictions and are motivated
to seek high goals. "As a group, they are more concerned with feeling
than thought or action—more interested in the humane, and tolerant
of human failings."[78] As a group the Pentecostals do not show any
inherent tendency to dissociate, that is, to lessen control of conscious
acts and to enter states where the perception of their surroundings and
their orientation is diminished. Those who frequently pray in tongues
show a poor capacity for emotional integration and appear to require
some form of catharsis. On the other hand, those who pray in tongues
less frequently show an above normal capacity for emotional integration. Note should be taken that the practice of glossolalia is not related
to either anxiety or tension, but the frequency of the practice is.
Pentecostals have fewer formalized thought processes, are less egotistic and manipulative of the environment, show more preference for
feeling than for thought, and show an interest in the unusual and
extraordinary. The method of repression is used for purposes of adjustment more than for egotistic self-assertiveness. The direction of
aggression issuing from frustration tends to be punitive. Finally, they
are less bound by the traditional and orthodox.[79]

Vivier sums up his findings in this manner:

> It would appear that glossolalia, as practised in its religious context, is
> manifested in normal, non-neurotic persons. It can serve a cathartic
> purpose. . . . we find that glossolalia, as described here, brings about a
> change in the person and a significant change in the ego complex. The
> change tends towards the more mature and tends, furthermore, to add
> quality and enrichment of feeling and depth of meaningfulness. . . . the
> tests in this study serve to discount an inherent weakness in the neural
> organization—the factors of repression and suggestibility. . . . this re-
> search was carried out in a selected group where emotionalism and aids
> to increased states of suggestibility, such as hand clapping, a rhythmical
> music, etc., were not evident. The subjects chosen came from an envi-
> ronment in which Baptism of the Holy Spirit with glossolalia followed
> on quiet prayer and meditation. Many of the test group experienced
> glossolalia for the first time while alone during private prayer.[80]

This is the summary Vivier gave of his research in his 1968 article.
Though he was himself personally involved in the Pentecostal movement by the time he wrote the summary of his dissertation, it is not
as optimistic as his 1968 summary of the very same research. In his
dissertation he wrote:

> Dynamically [glossolalics] can be considered as a group of people who,
> psychologically speaking, have had a poor beginning in life. This has
> been reflected by their difficulty in adjustment in the home situation in

infancy and later adulthood. It can therefore be seen that they have been
torn by insecurity, conflict, tension and emotional difficulties. . . . Being
troubled by doubt and fear, anxiety and stress, they have turned from
the culturally accepted traditional, orthodox and formalized, to something that held out for them the unorthodox, the supernatural; to an
environment of sensitiveness for emotional feelings and a group of people bound with the same purpose and clinging to each other for support.[81]

Together with Kelsey, Vivier relates the phenomenon of tongues to
Carl Jung's view of original primary experience.[82] Jung had said that
traditional Christianity had so organized its dogma, creed, and ritual,
that its members were given only a crystallized reflection of the "original religious experience," not the primal experience itself. For Vivier
glossolalia "appears to bridge the gulf of time and reinstate an original
religious experience which has become lost. . . ."[83]

John B. Oman

John B. Oman's (1963) reflections on glossolalia are no more than
that, without any declared experimental basis. But they represent
views which are held by many, also by other researchers. For Oman,
speaking in tongues is a way of restoring one's "infantile megalomania" in a setting where one feels confident not only of acceptance
but also of approval.[84] "Despite logic and open contradiction to common sense no person is entirely free from the allure of infantile
megalomania and feelings of omnipotence."[85] For that reason alone, to
say nothing of the overpowering need to be rid of guilt, one will
always run across Christians who wish to engage in this activity. One
hears here the echoes of Lombard's and Pfister's views. Tongue speaking becomes to the individual a badge of one's spiritual superiority.
This exhibitionism, said Oman, is "never an original drive, but a
secondary defense."[86] Glossolalia is related to neurotic disorganization. Where there is mental disintegration, there is linguistic disintegration.

Ari Kiev

There has been a lingering suspicion for years that tongues is linked
with schizophrenia. Ari Kiev (1963, 1964) studied this relationship in
West Indian immigrants to London who were classical Pentecostals.
One hundred ostensibly psychiatrically "normal" West Indians
(mostly from Jamaica) were compared with ten West Indian schizophrenics. Though admitting that he has no clinical evidence, Kiev

assumes that participation in their Pentecostal religion can and does serve a therapeutic function. Participation also seems to play a role in anxiety reduction. "Although there is no evidence that emotional instability is a necessary ingredient for participation in the services, behavioral patterns institutionalized in the meetings are sufficiently broad as to provide suitable channels for the expression of a variety of needs and personality traits. For the depressed and guilt-ridden, the sin-cathartic basis of the ideology and services provides a useful guilt-reducing device; for the hysteric a socially acceptable model for acting out; and for the accompaniments of neurotic and real suffering as feelings of inferiority, self-consciousness, suspiciousness and anxiety, the social aspects of the movement would seem of value."[87] This is no more than an informed guess on Kiev's part as he explicitly says that he has no empirical evidence to support his opinion.

Kiev found that the schizophrenics were not able "to maintain sufficient control of autistic and regressive behavior to fit into the prescribed ritual patterns."[88] "The schizophrenic patients differed from the normal groups studied in that they could not distinguish the boundaries of reality and fantasy and could not understand the limits in which culturally meaningful symbols and behavior were meant to operate."[89] T. H. Spoerri (1964) also observed that schizophrenics involuntarily engage in glossolalia, utterances which have no purpose and stem from disordered thought processes.[90] On the other hand, the normal glossolalic constructs his speech system with purpose and planning, uses it at will, and controls it. Studying schizophrenics in a broader context, namely their ecstatic condition, H. J. Weitbrecht (1968) distinguishes clearly between ecstasy in schizophrenics and in normal religious persons.[91]

Morton Kelsey

Morton Kelsey (1964), who had studied at the C. G. Jung Institute in Switzerland, took up some of the issues raised by Mosiman and Vivier. Kelsey asserts that contact with the unconscious is necessary for mental, physical, and moral health. "The ego and consciousness cannot exist cut off from the vast reservoir of psychic reality and power"[92] which is the unconscious. "He who has lost touch with the unconscious has lost contact with an indispensable half of reality."[93] Kelsey considers speaking in tongues "a powerful invasion of the unconscious."[94] Kelsey would interpret Jung as seeing in tongues a positive preparation for personality integration. Because it is a psycho-

logical event of some force it can be dangerous for the weak ego and
no one should be forced into this kind of experience. But he points also
to the therapeutic effects of glossolalia.[95] A number of persons have
told of being healed of physical illness and of emotional and psychological difficulties in conjunction with the experience of glossolalia. In
some cases "tongue speaking may well be an unconscious resolution
to neuroses."[96] Kelsey denies that people who speak in tongues are
emotionally disturbed or abnormal.

Little similarity was found by Kelsey between glossolalic utterance
and the irrational speech of schizophrenia.[97] Both hysteria and tongues
unquestionably arise in the area of man's psyche known as the unconscious. "But hysteria is a sickness which puts the mind and often the
body, as well, out of commission, while tongue speaking is a religious
experience which, from the evidence we have, seems to lead to a
greater ability to function in the world. . . . I have observed no case
in which the individual was more neurotic after the experience of
tongues nor have I any medical or psychological reports suggesting
this."[98]

William W. Wood

William W. Wood (1965) studied two communities of classical Pentecostals from the southern part of the United States.[99] The control
group comprised people of the same socio-economic class living in the
same general cultural surroundings. Important for the understanding
of Wood's research is the highly emotional quality of the religious
services of his test group. In addition to field observation, Wood administered one test to all the participants: the Rorschach. Wood grants
that the validity of Rorschach interpretations is poorly established.
Significant differences appeared only in those grey areas of perceptual
habits which are the most disputed areas among Rorschach authorities
concerning the scoring of responses. Wood asserts that between the
Pentecostal group and the control group "there are differences in basic
perceptual habits and consequently, in personality types."[100] Leaning
heavily on the interpretation of the Rorschach tests, Wood found that
Pentecostals lack an adequately structured value-attitude system; they
establish normal interpersonal relationships in situations which are
secure and have a strong drive to form close fellowships with others.
More importantly, Wood contends that "Pentecostalism attracts uncertain, threatened, inadequately organized persons with strong motivation to reach a state of satisfactory interpersonal relatedness and

personal integrity."[101] On the other hand, Wood holds that Pentecostalism provides patterns of behavior which lead to personality integration, a new depth of interpersonal relations and to a sense of personal confidence. Since Wood is dealing with a certain style of classical Pentecostal church life, namely that determined by the lower-class cultural patterns of the South,[102] it is important to note that the instrument of personality reorientation and integration is an "emotionally intense religious experience."[103] Wood ascribes a therapeutic function to the classical Pentecostal style of life as did Vivier, Boisen, and Kelsey. Wood did not find a "Pentecostal personality" but he did find that the Pentecostals have different ways of perceiving and different ways of organizing thought patterns and personal relationships. He does not suggest that the differences amounted to psychological abnormality or pathology.

There is some real doubt as to the value of Wood's research. The reliance on one psychological test, and that a test, the scoring of which contains large subjective and therefore disputed interpretations, makes Wood's findings of less value. The presentation of his findings was confusing to the present author, as it was to two other researchers.[104]

William Sargant

A word should be said about the role of emotionally intense religious experience in relation to changes in behavior, and personality reorientation. William Sargant (1959), taking as his point of departure Pavlov's psychological theories, asserts that political brainwashing, religious brainwashing (conversion), and psychoanalysis all use physiological techniques to precipitate a physiological breakdown, the reorganization of thought patterns, permanent behavior, and attitudinal changes.[105] In order to explain the dramatic restructuring of thought, attitudes, and behavior, Sargant suggests that a temporary cortical inhibition, that is an interruption of normal brain functioning, occurs. There is in humans the same general kind of alteration, cessation, and renewal of normal brain functioning which occurs in experiments on dogs which have been brought to the point of a physiological breakdown. Psychoanalytic treatment, political, and religious conversion, all come to the point of physiological breakdown so that previous mental, emotional, and behavior patterns are disrupted and the individual is free to adopt those presented by those instigating the breakdown. In the religious sphere Sargant suggests that an emotionally intense religious experience, or snake handling, or speaking in tongues can produce the same changes in thought, attitude, and behavior that psychoanalysis, electric and insulin shock treatments and a brain operation called lobotomy produce.[106] It should be noted that Sargant bases his religious research on religious revivalism of the most extreme kind, namely a highly charged emotional atmosphere where trance behavior, violent motor movements, and both visual and auditory hallucinations are present. Much of his illustrative material is taken from the camp meeting revivals typical of frontier life in the last century.

Jerome D. Frank

Very similar to Sargant's conclusions are those of Jerome D. Frank (1961).[107] Like Sargant, Frank confines his research interest to sudden conversions "characterized by drastic and far-reaching psychic upheavals,"[108] which are usually accompanied with intense emotion. These somewhat violent conversions usually lead to permanent changes in both attitude and behavior. The thought reform effected by these revivalistic conversion experiences is similar to that effected by psychotherapy.[109] In both psychotherapy and in the conversion experience distress is induced as a way of facilitating the indoctrination process and the organization of a new world view.

Wood, Sargant, and Frank all presuppose an intensely emotional religious experience. As Rodney Stark (1971) has shown it is extremely important to distinguish between what can best be called conventional religious commitment and extremist commitment.[110] This is especially true when the focus of the study is psychopathology. Though very likely Wood's sampling is not as extremely emotional as the sampling of Sargant and Frank, it would be considered excessively emotional when judged by the norms of the dominant American cultural patterns. Both Sargant and Frank have something to say about the psychological techniques of "inducing conversion." Neither, however, offers any clinical information on the psychological makeup of persons whose world view has been transformed by the induced conversion. The sampling of Wood, Sargant, and Frank would still be typical of some groups of classical Pentecostals in the United States, Africa, South America, and Indonesia. However, their sampling would not be typical of large areas of the classical Pentecostal world, in Europe, and places like South Africa, and in most parts of the United States. The intensely emotional atmosphere of the groups they studied would be highly untypical of almost all Protestant neo-Pentecostal groups, and would bear no resemblance to Catholic charismatic groups. For this reason their studies have little general significance for vast areas of the Pentecostal-charismatic movement.

Stanley C. Plog

One of the earliest studies after the outbreak of Protestant neo-Pentecostalism in California is the research of the psychiatric department of UCLA which was conducted by Stanley C. Plog (1964).[111] A team of researchers from the UCLA Medical Center conducted individual interviews with approximately eighty persons, and had a return of two hundred seventy two questionnaires handed out at three separate meetings. The sampling indicated that from the beginning of neo-Pentecostalism, the movement was ecumenical in character. Over forty denominations were represented with theologies varying from the conservative to extreme liberal. Also representative of the movement's broad support was the appearance in the sampling of persons from both ends of the financial spectrum, from persons receiving monthly incomes of less than one hundred dollars to those who received more than sixteen hundred dollars (the highest code on the income scale of the questionnaire). The occupational breakdown also cut across most of the major categories utilized in the U.S. census code and the educational level range varying from persons with less than three years of school to those with doctorates and other advanced professional degrees. Speaking out of the experience of his previous research of religious groups having a specific appeal, Plog remarked that "it is truly amazing to watch a new movement which has such a broad base of social support."[112]

There was also almost equal representation of men and women, something which would not be predicted by the observation of other contemporary religious movements or denominations, since women usually outnumber men quite heavily in religious practice. The mean age of the participants was about forty-three. Their political affiliation strongly favored the Republicans, outnumbering the Democrats seven to one at the home meeting in the house of an Episcopal woman leader and by a margin of three to one in two public meetings.

One is disappointed in finding so little psychiatric information in this report. Even the information on class representation is wanting in significant details. This may be due partly to the report appearing in *Trinity* magazine, a publication under the editorship of Jean Stone, the Episcopal leader mentioned above. *Trinity* was a popular family style magazine.

James N. Lapsley and John H. Simpson

The contribution to the field of psychological research by the two professors of Princeton Theological Seminary, James N. Lapsley and John H. Simpson (1964) is very difficult to evaluate. There is no account of their method and no display of their data. They have acquaintance with some of the literature in the field and one surmises from their two-part article that they must have visited at least one Protestant neo-Pentecostal prayer group. Most of their information seems to have come from secondary sources. Like Kildahl, the two Princeton professors emphasize the role of the leader but without attributing to him the decisive role that Kildahl assigns to him.[113] The authors believe that glossolalia verges toward the massive dissociation of all, or nearly all, the voluntary muscles from conscious control, as in sleep walking and trance states.[114] Glossolalia functions as an instrument of conflict reduction arising out of unconscious attachment to parental figures. This attachment is accompanied with both feelings of love and of hate, which the individuals are unable to express, producing tension. Because the authors believe that the demonic "is very close to the dynamic center" of Protestant neo-Pentecostalism, they define glossolalia as "an indirect, though powerful expression of primitive love toward the parent and the demonology [as] a projection of the hate and fear in that childhood relationship."[115] They maintain that if their hypothesis of the relation between tongues and the demonic is true, "glossolalia will seldom, if ever, be found without accompanying demons, though these need not be constantly present."[116] In the earlier expressions of Protestant neo-Pentecostalism there were groups (some of which persist into the present) which were preoccupied with the demonic. It remains true that the whole of the Pentecostal-charismatic has a more vivid sense of the demonic than is found in the main-line churches. It is also true that the early Pentecostals recognized that speaking in tongues could be related to the demonic. They were at pains to distinguish between tongues spoken under demonic influence and tongues as a gift of the Spirit.[117] However, there is strong opposition to an exaggerated preoccupation with the demonic within all sectors of the movement. Since Lapsley and Simpson do not seem to be restricting their interpretation to a definite sampling, but generalize their views, one must note that the close relation they see between tongues and the demonic is unique in the rather extensive psychological literature on the topic. No other research has indicated that the relationship they describe exists.

Lapsley and Simpson hold that glossolalics are not "mentally ill in any clinical sense" but they are "uncommonly disturbed."[118] In contrast to the position of Wood and Kelsey, the authors deny that the practice of glossolalia brings a further permanent integration of personality. Rather, they see glossolalia as a self-aggrandizing and narcissistic component. They would not call glossolalics hysterics, but they do point out that the psychodynamics of glossolalics "may be similar" to those of a person with hysterical symptoms.[119] In short they see glossolalia as "a dissociative expression of truncated personality development."[120]

Lapsley and Simpson have been widely quoted but there is no indication from their two short articles that their research was of such a nature as to merit serious attention. Before one would give credence to the serious implications of their conclusions, one would want both an explanation of their methods and an account of their clinical data.

E. Mansell Pattison

A psychiatrist, E. Mansell Pattison (1964, 1968, 1974), who has a broad acquaintance with the impact of cultural values on the dynamics of personality development, especially as regards the more fundamentalistic religious groups, has done field work among classical Pentecostals and Protestant neo-Pentecostals. In his first publication (1964), the focus of Pattison's attention is more on the nature of human behavior than on the psychological make-up of those who speak in tongues. Pattison suggests that normal people, given the motivation and the appropriate situation can and do react in somewhat stereotyped fashions. This happens at football games and on sales days in ladies' clothing stores. While denying that persons involved in such group behavior are abnormal, sick, mentally ill, or hysterical in the clinical sense, Pattison says that such "mildly hysterical behavior" is given social sanction on certain occasions.[121] One cannot characterize the persons who seek out this experience as malcontent, emotionally disturbed, or socio-economically deprived. With these suppositions in mind Mansell describes glossolalia as "a stereotyped pattern of unconsciously controlled vocal behavior which appears under specific emotional conditions."[122] Normal devout religious people experience glossolalia during states of intense spiritual emotion. Glossolalia itself does not indicate the presence of a valid spiritual experience. In some cases it may be an end in itself rather than the expression of religious experience. Speaking in tongues "is part of a general group of phenomena appearing in cultural groups during periods of stress or change. Such 'charismatic phenomena' are not uniquely religious."[123] The same kind of phenomena can be found in settings which are non-Christian and nonreligious. It is, says Pattison, typical of ecstatic emotional experiences when intense emotional release makes rational speech impossible.

As a psychological phenomenon it is "easy to produce and readily understandable."[124] Any normal person can speak in tongues if he adopts a passive attitude about controlling body and speech and has an emotional tension pressing for expression. Relying on the reports of other researchers he would hold that glossolalia is structurally not a language, but is linguistically a "decomposed form of English."[125]

Two aspects of Pattison's position should be noted. He lays great stress on tongues as an expression of a "crowd situation." As the report of the United Presbyterian Church and the research of Lombard, Samarin, Gerlach and Hine have shown, there is no necessary relationship between glossolalia and either the presence or pressure of a group of people. The intense emotional experience of which Pattison is speaking was indeed to be found not only in groups of classical Pentecostals but among Protestant neo-Pentecostals, especially in the years preceding 1964, the year in which Pattison is writing. But a researcher would be loathe to tie the explanation of tongues with intense emotional experience because field work has shown that many of the meetings are not intensely emotional. This is true not only of Protestant neo-Pentecostal and Catholic charismatic groups but even for large sectors of the classical Pentecostal world. If one ties tongues to intense emotional experience one is in difficulty when explaining the phenomenon when the emotional level of the meetings is obviously no greater than those of the services in the main-line churches. There is then no way of explaining the quiet use of tongues in private when the emotional level is very low. To approach the phenomenon of tongues with the supposition that it represents an expression of intense emotional experience is to forego an explanation of tongues in those unemotional settings which form the largest portion of the sampling.

In a later survey (1968) of the published and unpublished research on glossolalia from the point of view of anthropology, sociology, linguistics, psychology, psycholinguistics, and psychoacoustics, Pattison concluded that glossolalia is a "borderline phenomenon between inner speech and external speech."[126] Inner speech is that "thinking to one-self" which is characterized by the articulation of inaudible sounds. This inner speech is fragmented, underdeveloped and incomplete so that if externalized it would be difficult to understand. Therefore inner speech prepares for and precedes external speech. The person about to enter into glossolalic behavior stores the glossolalic phrases he has learned from other glossolalics. The phrases are practiced over and over in inner speech until an acceptable form of glossolalia is mastered. With the repeated use of his tongue, his glossolalic speech becomes more and more competent and automatic. The glossolalic then no longer needs the mechanism of inner speech. But until the glossolalic reaches that stage glossolalia serves as a mediator between inner and outer speech. The inner and outer speech is a helpful construct to explain certain glossolalic experiences. But it does not explain those cases where the person comes to the experience of tongues spontaneously, without previous knowledge of the phenomenon, and without either counselor or coach.

Pattison contends that glossolalia serves a variety of intrapsychic functions along a continuum which extends from the more "playful" to the more "serious."[127] Both the playful and the serious glossolalia is produced volitionally and with intention. As glossolalia becomes more and more part of one's life-style, one may use it without awareness just as one might blink the eyes or tap the fingers without total awareness. Pattison found that glossolalia "bears no necessarily linear relationship with personality variables.... The phenomenon of glossolalia *per se* cannot be interpreted necessarily as either deviant or pathological, for its meaning is determined and must be interpreted in terms of socio-cultural context."[128] Pattison lays large stress on glossolalia as a socio-cultural variable. In those cultural groups where the theory of spirit possession is a shared ideology, the "delusion" is shared by the whole culture. This means that in analyzing glossolalia one is analyzing culture, not personal pathology. While denying that psychopathology is necessarily associated with social class, Pattison found overt psychopathology of a sociopathic, hysterical, or hypochondriacal nature among glossolalics of the lower and lower-middle class where glossolalic behavior was not the norm; glossolalics whom he interviewed from the middle and upper classes where glossolalic prayer was accepted and approved, were "well integrated, highly functional

individuals who were clinically 'normal'."[129] Alland, too, had interpreted the psychological deprivation of the black church he was studying in a socio-cultural rather than in a purely psychological context.

In 1974 Pattison examined white middle-class Americans holding
what he calls fundamentalist beliefs and engaged in glossolalic behavior.[130] His research was therefore focused on Protestant neo-Pentecostals. Although belonging to the middle class, the Protestant neo-Pentecostals have a religious belief system which is at considerable
variance with dominant middle-class values. This clash of value systems leads to a buttressing of the dissonant fundamentalistic beliefs
with certain religious rituals which include glossolalia. The ego psychology, whose conceptual tools Pattison uses, stresses the role of
culture in the structure and function of personality. The belief systems
of a given culture or subculture are important for psychological development. The ideology of white middle-class neo-Pentecostals is found
in five major tenets: man's basic nature is evil; man is to subjugate the
world; time orientation is futuristic; the valued personality is oriented
to action; and interpersonal relationships are individualistic.[131] Pattison suggests that neurotic personality distortion can arise out of cultural conflict, out of the intraorganismic struggle between two incompatible cultural orientations, two major ways of adapting to life.
Cultural conflict may produce personality disorders. The Protestant
neo-Pentecostals belong to a tradition of "intellectual religion" but are
fundamentalist in their religious views. "They find in glossolalia an
infusion of experience into their intellectual religious life, and an
undeniable affirmation of the 'rightness' and validity of their fundamentalist belief system."[132] These are people in conflict. The practice
of glossolalia reinforces their fundamentalistic belief system and is a
release of psychological tension arising out of the conflict of their value
system with the dominant white middle-class values. "This constituency has widespread neurotic conflicts."[133] Here the ritual is not a rite
of passage (as in the classical Pentecostal churches) but primarily a rite
affirming the fundamentalistic belief system and only secondarily serving psychological needs.

Pattison then distinguishes two groups of classical Pentecostals.
First, there are those who have successfully moved into the middle
class. In these he observed little overt psychopathology. Participation
in glossolalia is a perfunctory religious ritual and is primarily a social
event. Those in this class who speak in tongues frequently have quite
obvious neurotic conflicts. "Thus their glossolalic practice appears to

subserve psychological needs."[134] Second, there is still a group of lower-class classical Pentecostals who have real-life conflicts with their culture and appear to gain considerable emotional release through the practice of glossolalia. They do not use tongues to affirm a value system, but as a personally satisfying experience. Affirmation is not their major need. "I have not been impressed by any manifest neurotic conflict in this constituency."[135]

Nathan and Louise Gerrard

Like Alland, the husband and wife team of Nathan and Louise Gerrard (1966) researched a minority group, a community of classical Pentecostals in West Virginia.[136] This group and other such groups found in the hills of Tennessee, Kentucky, and Virginia, interpret literally Mark 16:18 ("they will pick up serpents . . .") and have the handling of snakes as part of their worship services. In classifying these groups, either by theological or anthropological categories, they would have to be considered classical Pentecostals. This attribution is a source of great embarrassment to ninety-five percent of the classical Pentecostals who want nothing to do with the snake handlers. The Gerrards repeatedly visited the snake handlers to observe their behavior and they also conducted personal interviews. They used the Minnesota Multiphasic Personality Inventory (MMPI) to test forty-six members of a congregation of snake handlers with fifty members of another congregation belonging to a conventional Protestant denomination. This latter served as a scientific control group. Both churches were located in Scrabble Creek, West Virginia. Both the snake handlers and the conventional control group were similar in sex and education distribution. The clinical evaluation of the tests was done by three psychologists at the University of Minnesota who did not know which group of tests belonged to the snake handlers and which to the non-Pentecostal Protestant denomination. The three psychologists knew the two sets of profiles simply as group A and group B.

The results of this study showed that the conventional denomination had scores higher in the hysteria scale while the snake handlers had higher scores on the scale indicating psychopathic deviate and hypomania (hypomania refers to mild forms of manic excitement).[137] The psychologists found that ten out of forty of the non-Pentecostal denomination were neurotics while only four out of thirty-five of the snake handlers tested out as neurotics.[138] With regard to the psychoticism, there was no significant difference between the two groups. The members of the non-Pentecostal denomination were more repressive and dysphoric (dysphoric refers to an abnormal feeling of anxiety and discontent) and were more likely to present more symptoms of psychological stress than the snake handlers.[139] Those belonging to the non-Pentecostal denomination were on the average more defensive, less inclined to admit undesirable traits, and were more depressive. The snake handlers appeared less defensive and restrained. Indeed, they were more exhibitionistic, excitable, and pleasure oriented. They were also more determined to enjoy the present and were less under the control of the patterns of the general culture, particularly middle-class culture.[140]

There was a significant difference between the older church members of both groups. Many older members of the conventional denomination evinced symptoms of clinical depression and, in comparison with the older members of the snake handlers, were more neurotic, more pessimistic, more anxious, more rigid, showed greater hypochondriacal preoccupation, and were more withdrawn. In spite of the higher social status and greater economic security enjoyed by the older members of the conventional denomination, they showed more psychological stresses than the older members of the snake handlers. The conventional denomination was a larger church denomination and was more "intellectual," more programmed, with the younger members having relatively less participation in the life of the church. The old snake handlers possessed greater psychological insight into their own motives, were more optimistic, more socially oriented and more energetic and spontaneous. The conventional denomination offered its older members less comfort and security.[141] Among the snake handlers both older and younger members participated equally in church ritual.

The older snake handlers were participants in an emotionally expressive religion, enjoying the respect and esteem of the younger members of their church. The older snake handlers were more free of psychological stresses than the older members of the conventional denomination. The older members of the conventional denomination participated in a church life which severely limited emotional expression, and they experienced stronger feelings of alienation in relation to the upwardly mobile younger members of their church than did the older snake handlers in relation to the younger members of their church.

The emotional balance of the young snake handlers was only slightly less than that of the young members of the conventional denomination, despite the fact that the social and economic circumstances of the young snake handlers were much less favorable than those of the young members of the conventional denomination. The pleasure orientation of the young snake handlers served to sublimate impulses that otherwise would find expression in antisocial hedonism.[142]

The Gerrards summarize their findings: "Comparison of all serpent handlers with all members of the conventional denomination does not show marked differences with respect to mental health, but whatever differences there are seem to indicate the serpent handlers are a little more normal than the members of the conventional denomination."[143] Given the deprivations and frustrations associated with the conditions of their existence as members of the stationary working class (that is, not upwardly mobile but unskilled and functionally illiterate who will remain poor the rest of their lives) the worship and fellowship of the Scrabble Creek snake handlers "constituted a form of group psychotherapy for individuals who otherwise would be vulnerable to mental and behavioral aberrations."[144]

The Gerrards submitted the psychological tests of the conventional denomination and the snake handlers to a second team of clinical psychologists. The team did not know which profiles belonged to the snake handlers and which to the members of the conventional denomination. They did know that half of the profiles represented people who handled poisonous snakes in their religious services. They were asked to sort out the profiles into two groups, those which they thought belonged to the snake handlers and those which they thought belonged to the conventional denomination. The psychologists assigned most "abnormal" profiles to the category they believed to be the snake handlers and most "normal" profiles to the category they believed to be members of the conventional church. *All* the psychotic profiles were assigned to the snake handlers, though the earlier evaluation, unknown to this team of psychologists, had shown that "there is no systematic difference between the two groups on dimensions of thought disorder," that is, psychosis.[145] The total number of abnormal profiles for the serpent handlers was actually lower (thirty-seven) than that of the members of the conventional denomination (forty-five). This clearly indicates the bias spoken of earlier on the part of those trained in the behavioral disciplines.

The Gerrards went to great lengths to assure the objective, scientific analysis of their data. For instance, the two teams of psychologists from the University of Minnesota who analyzed their findings did not know which specific profiles belonged to the snake handlers and which to the conventional church members. An unavoidable difficulty arose in administering the MMPI. It was administered to the members gathered in the church. There was some merriment and giggling at the questions during the testing period. No other way was open to administer the tests but this general hilarity and the lack of privacy for calm reflection calls into question the complete reliability of the findings. Great care needs to be exercised in interpreting data from a study in which there are no series of longitudinal samples. As James T. Richardson has pointed out, "what the group members were like *before* they joined the cult is an unanswered question that looms for anyone attempting to explain the etiology of such groups and movements."[146] What needs to be studied are the personality changes which occur as persons move toward association with the snake handler congregation, and what changes occur after full involvement. Finally, broad generalizations cannot be drawn from the isolated study of two church groups in Scrabble Creek, West Virginia. The Gerrards are careful not to do this, but the temptation is for interested parties to latch on to what they consider psychological vindication.

SUMMARY

During the period from 1910–1966 the research was, for the most part but not exclusively, concerned with marginal people living on the periphery of society, deprived of goods and status, ignorant and neglected. These people were deprived economically and socially, and were considered, even when they were not, psychologically deprived. The larger part of the research of this period belongs to the field of abnormal psychology. During the earliest research the accents were on suggestion, various forms of infantile regression, auto-erotic satisfaction, and neurotic phenomena. Cutten linked tongues with schizophrenia and hysteria. Those who engaged in glossolalia were of limited verbal capacity.

If there is a turning point in this period it is very likely with Boisen. He was still dealing either with the population found in mental hospitals or with the economically deprived. Though Boisen considered some of the religious tenets of classical Pentecostalism to be dangerous, especially what he saw as the emphasis on the extraordinary, yet on the whole he judged that this style of religious life was, under good leadership, constructive and therapeutic.

The most impressive psychological research to date appeared in

1960, published by a Vivier who had studied classical Pentecostals in his native South Africa. He himself had the experience of tongues in the course of his research and though his conclusions are highly qualified and not all of them are flattering to Pentecostals, he did challenge many of the assumptions of the previous research. He questioned the role of suggestion, and the link which had been established between glossolalia and neuroticism. Further, he saw that speaking in tongues could have a therapeutic effect and judged it a religious expression of normal nonneurotic people.

Up until 1963 most of the psychological research was carried out in the context of economic and social deprivation, even when these theories were not clearly formulated. When the Protestant neo-Pentecostal movement emerged in the early 1960s, there was initially little reflection on the new socio-economic factors in the psychological research. While researchers were still preoccupied with classical Pentecostals, Kiev shed light on the relationship between schizophrenia and tongues which had been repeated in the literature since Cutten. Not only did he indicate the difference between schizophrenic and glossolalic behavior, but he pointed to the possible therapeutic value of tongues. This research at least suggested that perhaps glossolalia should not be studied exclusively under the rubric of abnormal psychology.

The broader cultural approach to the psychological aspects of Pentecostalism was signaled by Alland, who must be given recognition, whatever the other faults of his research design. Kelsey took up some of the issues raised by Mosiman and Vivier, namely the role of the unconscious. He interpreted the phenomenon within a Jungian framework and saw it as a powerful invasion of the unconscious. Kelsey made an important contribution toward removing the study of glossolalia from abnormal psychology. The study of marginal people continued in Wood who helped establish what has become a common assumption, namely, that no one Pentecostal personality type exists. The study of very enthusiastic groups continued in Sargant and Frank with the focus on behavioral and personality change through emotionally intense religious experience. The extreme religious expressions and the high emotionalism found in the groups studied by Sargant and Frank tended to push the research back toward abnormal psychology. Oman and Lapsley and Simpson wrote after the appearance of Protestant neo-Pentecostalism. In the new situation, researchers were no longer dealing only with marginal people but with the affluent and well educated. This new population had no special claims on mental health as over the poor and uneducated who took little part in the life of public institutions or in the decision-making process. The religious experiences of the wealthier and better educated neo-Pentecostals were interpreted much like those of their poorer uneducated forebearers. Oman saw them as restoring their infantile megalomania. Tongues was the badge of persons' supposed spiritual superiority. While Lapsley and Simpson conceded that glossolalics were not mentally ill, they were uncommonly disturbed and their glossolalic behavior was an expression of truncated personality development. This too tended to restore the study of glossolalia to abnormal psychology. Plog marveled at the broad social representation in the new wave and at its ecumenical character, but had nothing decisive to say about their mental health.

In a quite different context from Alland's earlier work, Pattison took a broad cultural approach. Using an ego psychology which stressed the role of a subculture's belief system in psychological development, Pattison contributed to the demystification of tongues. It was, said Pattison, something everyone could do. Pattison stressed glossolalia as a social-cultural variable. Since the character of culture conflicts vary, so does the function of glossolalia, which may or may not be neurotic. Pattison was instrumental in removing the psychological research of persons who spoke in tongues from a narrow analysis of personality structure and development.

The major contribution of the Gerrards was less the psychological vindication of classical Pentecostal snake handlers and more a confirmation of a bias on the part of those trained in the behavioral sciences as they look at religious behavior, especially if it deviates from the norms and values of the dominant American middle-class culture. Historically the final question the Gerrards posed was not one concerning the mental health of religious extremists but the cultural bias of those trained in the behavioral sciences.

This period closes, then, with a question about the objectivity of the researchers.

5 THE MIDDLE AND UPPER CLASSES AND THE MOVE TOWARD NORMALITY: 1967–1975

The Pentecostal-charismatic movement had become middle class long before 1967. During World War II the classical Pentecostals attained the middle-class status they sought for almost four decades; they consolidated that social status in the years that followed. Protestant neo-Pentecostalism has been recognized as essentially middle class with some inroads into the upper class since the beginning of the 1960s. The Catholic charismatic renewal has had the same white middle-class character from its beginnings, with the same beachhead in the upper class. And so, by 1967 the perception of the social character of the three streams (classical, neo-, and Catholic) had clearly established itself in the consciousness of observers. The growth of the three streams after 1967 reinforced that perception.

Protestant neo-Pentecostalism and the Catholic renewal gradually begin to take on new organizational form at the national level. In all the denominational expressions there is a deeper concern for rooting the movement in the theologies of the respective traditions while at the same time rejecting a narrow denominationalism. The charismatic renewal in the historic churches is de facto ecumenical. The growth of these denominational expressions, as well as the growth of what can be called "free ministries" (Pentecostal-charismatic leaders who tend not to be identified with any church but are frequently not antichurch) brought the phenomenon of glossolalia to the attention of researchers

111

in a new way. A sign that the free ministries have attained a certain maturity is the move to establish a master's degree program at the Melodyland School of Theology at Anaheim, California, under a respected theologian, J. Rodman Williams. Classical Pentecostalism, too, has moved closer to the main-line churches. They are more reflective and better oriented theologically. A new generation of classical Pentecostal scholars are taking their places in the lives of their churches. These well-trained scholars are able to hold their own with the professionals of any Christian denomination. Among them one could name Vinson Synan, William W. Menzies, Russell Spittler. They were instrumental in the formation of a scholarly association called the Society for Pentecostal Studies. The Assemblies of God has established a graduate school of theology in Springfield, Missouri.

One could argue whether all of this is good or bad but it at least indicates that in socio-cultural terms one is not dealing with the same phenomenon as Cutten, Alland, Kiev, Wood, and Vivier were researching. One does not want to suggest that the lower classes are identified with psychological maladjustment while the move of Pentecostalism into the middle and upper classes is an inevitable sign of emotional maturity and balance. The question is rather of how the movement is perceived—and those perceptions are in large part determined by the mores of middle-class America. During the period from 1967–1975 glossolalia and other kinds of prophetic behavior became less and less socially unacceptable when judged by the dominant middle-class values. The lower classes are still to be found in Pentecostal-charismatic groups but in the broad movement the spectrum of class representation is wider and therefore social acceptance has changed.

It is against this background that the research reviewed in this chapter is to be read.

PSYCHOLOGY AND GLOSSOLALIA: CONTEMPORARY PERSPECTIVES

Wayne E. Oates

In a brief article Wayne E. Oates (1967) reflects on the psychological aspects of glossolalia.[1] His remarks are based not on clinical evidence and there is no indication that he has done field work or conducted interviews. Rather, he reflects on glossolalia against a background of the language studies of Jean Piaget and Harry Stack Sullivan. The only more serious study of glossolalia he refers to is that of Lapsley and Simpson. His lack of acquaintance with the literature in the field and want of clinical support diminish the significance of his contribution. Oates rejects the theory of economic deprivation as an explanation of glossolalia. Basing his reflections on Piaget's research into the speech of children, he calls glossolalia "cradle speech."[2] "Piaget's description of the early speech of a child is precisely Paul's description of speaking in tongues."[3] It is a "preverbal" kind of religious experience and seems to be a breakthrough of the deepest appeals for help. "As an infant crying without language, the glossolalic seeks to be heard by God and his neighbor."[4] More precisely Oates holds that speaking in tongues "is not solely an autistic, ego-centric expression of childlike language but [is] also an attempt at socialization," that is, is aimed at influencing others.[5] Using a category taken from Sullivan's writings, Oates calls glossolalia "parataxic distortions," like that speech of a child which is unintelligible to others but pleasant and meaningful to himself. Because people are so profoundly inarticulate about the personal dimensions of faith, tongues is a way of communicating religious belief at a quite elemental level.[6] Oates denies that people who speak in tongues are mentally ill, but neither do they "have a unique degree of health."[7] A major factor in the experience of tongues, according to Oates, is "releasing of the voluntary muscular situation of a person."[8] Important as a precondition to this release is the build-up, the hypnotic impact of a group of people, and the ecstatic release of tension. The experience opens the consciousness, releases repressions and communicates underlying unresolved problems. Other ways of releasing tension of voluntary muscles is electric and insulin shock therapy, and the use of tranquilizers. Oates closes his psychological reflections by quoting from an unpublished paper by Andrew D. Lester, who characterized the behavior of glossolalics as childish megalomania and ego-centric (echos of Lombard and Pfister.) The people in the groups which Lester visited had weak egos, confused identities, high levels of anxiety, were unstable personalities and generally showed signs of emotional deprivation. Since no clinical evidence and no interviews are reported in either Oates or Lester, it is difficult to comment on the validity of their positions. Pattison also talks about glossolalia as releasing tension, both when serving a playful function and when serving a serious function.[9] Using a galvanometer for the measurement of skin conductance, Gary Palmer found that one test group, contrary to the prediction, was less relaxed during glossolalic prayer than during silent prayer, while another test group was shown to be no more relaxed during glossolalic prayer than during silent prayer and voluntary relaxation.[10]

There is no problem in admitting that glossolalic prayer is a release of tension as long as one admits that all prayer is a release of tension. Note that the emphasis on tension build-up presupposes the presence of group pressures and an emotionally charged atmosphere. As has been shown, other researchers have indicated that these are not of critical importance. One exercise of the gift of tongues in the absence of a group or without any relation to or knowledge of a group is enough to invalidate such a narrow approach to the phenomenon.

Henri Nouwen

An early commentator on the psychological dimensions of the charismatic renewal within the Roman Church was Father Henri Nouwen (1967).[11] Nouwen's short article arose out of the beginnings of the charismatic renewal at Notre Dame University, which became a fact of campus life in February and March of 1967. Nouwen's article appeared in April of that year. It makes no pretense of being a research report and therefore only comments on the events of the previous two months from a psychological point of view. In this perspective it is understandable that Nouwen quotes none of the previously published psychological research. Nor are his reflections the result of a systematic survey. When faced with the question, "Is the charismatic experience dangerous?" Nouwen answers that "for many people, perhaps even for most, it hardly seems to be dangerous."[12] Nouwen stresses the need for preparation and warns against the danger of unprepared exposure to divine powers. Implicit in his position seems to be the assumption that the charismatic experience is authentic. Some students who came to the experience without sufficient preparation showed signs of anxiety and confusion. In some cases students felt on the edge of a physical or mental breakdown. These, however, were "exceptional cases."[13] Nouwen recognizes that many experience a very sudden relief from their mental and spiritual pains. He asks whether the problems have been cured or merely covered up. This seems to be a well-founded question, as exaggerated claims of instantaneous transformation are frequently found to be illusory. The experience of the Catholic charismatics of "sudden freedom, sudden friendship, sudden happiness and joy"[14] might impede, says Nouwen, the gradual development of the human capacities to establish lasting friendship. The impulse to intimacy may become so central that there is little place for those who want to retain some distance and keep their intimacy for themselves. In this context Nouwen warns against a community which is turned inward upon itself. Finally, a religious orientation which is experiential may cause frustrations in those who wish to be part of the renewal but who do not feel able to come to the real experience.[15] Because of the newness of the phenomenon at the time of the writing, Father Nouwen stresses the tentative nature of his reflections.

William J. Samarin

The approach of William J. Samarin (1968, 1969, 1970, 1971, 1972, 1973, 1974) is socio-linguistic. Over a period of five years he was a participant observer in both Pentecostal and neo-Pentecostal meetings in Italy, Holland, Jamaica, Canada, and the United States. He used both interviews and a questionnaire. Most of the respondents (eighty-four returns out of three hundred questionnaires sent out) were middle-class Protestant members of the neo-Pentecostal movement rather than members of the classical Pentecostal movement. For Samarin, glossolalia is a "simplified form of extemporaneous pseudolanguage."[16] A more comprehensive definition would be "a meaningless but phonologically structured human utterance believed by the speaker to be a real language but bearing no systematic resemblance to any natural language, living or dead."[17] Essentially, it is a derivative phenomenon, depending on the linguistic competence and knowledge of each speaker and reflecting cultural differences. The glossolalic speech of classical Pentecostals is different from that of Episcopalians. Like Ludwig, Samarin judges there to be a higher incidence of altered states of consciousness or trance among classical Pentecostals at the time glossolalia is acquired than is true of Protestant neo-Pentecostals, though the statistics are lacking.[18] It is anomalous speech and is psycholinguistically unique because it consists of a string of generally simple syllables that are not matched systematically with a semantic system.[19] Most glossolalics, though not all, arrive at facility in speaking in tongues gradually and with much practice. Samarin is convinced that glossolalia is not simply gibberish. Seventy-three percent of the respondents to the questionnaire were convinced that their glossolalic utterances were true languages.[20] "Glossolalia is indeed like language in some ways, but this is only because the speaker (unconsciously) wants it to be like language. Yet in spite of superficial similarities, glossolalia is fundamentally not language. . . . Contrary to belief, it has never been scientifically demonstrated that xenoglossolalia (a true language spoken by one who has never learned it) occurs among Pentecostals."[21] Samarin is extremely doubtful and in this author's mind, with justification, that the alleged cases of xenoglossolalia among charismatics are real. Attempts to verify make it evident that the stories have been greatly exaggerated and that the witnesses turn out to be incompetent or unreliable from a linguistic point of view.[22] The belief that it constitutes a true language is not tied in any way to the "peak" in which glossolalia is uttered. There are instances of both peaks and troughs, and "it is certainly not the case that glossolalia occurs only with the peaks. Therefore, if glossolalia can be independent of highly charged psychological states, whatever that might mean for the responsible observer of human behavior, it is not merely the product of such states."[23] Looked upon in anthropological terms the function of glossolalia is to distinguish the person from that great mass of other persons, including Christians, who do not speak in tongues and do not belong to the movement. Learning to use this language is part of the process of becoming integrated into the movement. Symbolically a person who speaks in tongues is saying something: "He is saying that he is involved in something . . . that transcends the ordinary. In short, glossolalia is a linguistic symbol of the sacred."[24] This in part accounts for some of the feelings of superiority which can arise in some charismatic groups.

Samarin reports that many Pentecostals, because they think that glossolalia is a true language, think that it is therefore miraculous. On the contrary, Samarin argues, glossolalia "is not a supernatural phenomenon," but, in fact, a very natural phenomenon.[25] It is not at all unlike other kinds of speech humans produce in more or less normal circumstances, in more or less normal psychological states. "In fact, anybody can produce glossolalia if he is uninhibited and if he discovers what the 'trick' is. Both the commonplace nature of glossolalia and experiments have proven this fact."[26] Samarin is supported in this view by Pattison, Daniel C. O'Connell, and Ernest T. Bryant. The Pentecostal believes that God is there because of a linguistic miracle. It is not necessary to believe in this miracle of language, but even in not believing that a miracle has taken place, one can believe that it symbolizes God's presence. As an artifact of religion and a sign of the sacred, Samarin esteems glossolalia very highly.

The research to date presents no evidence to suggest—let alone prove—that glossolalics are all of a single psychological type and "that this personality of theirs predisposes (some would say *causes*) them to speak in tongues."[27] Samarin would not grant that one has to be abnormal to speak in tongues, but does concede that perhaps people of a certain type are attracted to the kind of religion which uses tongues. According to Samarin this personality type could possibly be identified. Glossolalic behavior is not abnormal, only anomalous, and that because "it departs from the run-of-the-mill speech, not because the tongue speakers are in any way abnormal."[28] The psychopathological explanations of glossolalia tend to oversimplify.[29] Producing tongues is not strange; what is strange is the belief that this pseudolanguage is a true language and miraculous. Together with Kildahl and others, Samarin thinks that glossolalia is learned behavior. It is not learned as a real language is learned, but learned nonetheless. For the most part, the information which the seeker needs to have is already part of his linguistic resources, even if he knows no more than one language.[30] From a purely linguistic point of view no special power needs to take over a person's vocal cords. Everyone is equipped with everything one needs to produce glossolalia. Quite frequently the seeker received "a great deal of guidance and instruction. Much of it contributes nothing to the acquisition of the skill, at least in its linguistic aspects."[31] It is not a learned language in the sense that it is necessary to imitate the phonetic patterns of someone who already speaks in tongues. It is learned behavior because it is a derivative of true language which is learned, because it is usually, not always, the product of considerable instruction, and because it is possible to increase one's competence in the tongue. The fact that many people seem to have "discovered" glossolalia on their own, that is, without having heard it from others,[32] does not mean that it ceases to be learned behavior. Even for those who come to it without awareness of what it is and without having heard of the phenomenon from others, it is still linguistically a derivative of their own linguistic treasury, whatever that is, and is therefore learned. Most glossolalics have conscious control of their utterance, but it is not difficult to illustrate "unconscious" or "involuntary" glossolalia.[33] Statements about this involuntary behavior must be interpreted cautiously. Some quite innocently believe that unless "something comes over a person" one will not speak in tongues. Or a certain person may believe that glossolalia is something one does in the power of the Spirit in private prayer, and therefore cannot demonstrate at will what glossolalia is to an interested researcher. It is both a person's psychological make-up and what he has learned about the nature and function of glossolalia that determines his behavior.[34] For these reasons testimonies about involuntary utterances have to be examined with great care.

Samarin can document a number of cases where the practice of glossolalia is linked to ecstasy defined as a pleasurable state of intense emotion which may be linked with an altered state of consciousness. If, however, ecstasy is linked too closely with dissociation (the escape of certain activities from the control of the individual) and glossolalia is then referred to as "the language of ecstasy" or "ecstatic speech," one would have a generalization which would be misleading.[35] "Glossolalia is not simply a product of some altered state of consciousness. There is absolutely no doubt in my mind that many of the 'ecstatic' experiences of the glossolalists are the same as those nonglossolalists but pious Protestants and Catholics."[36]

Lombard had seen the switch to a new language as an effect of a change in personality. A more reasonable claim, says Samarin, is to see glossolalia as a symbol of such change. As an initiation or rite of passage it both signals and symbolizes a fundamental break with the past. It can either accompany the conversion experience (in the anthropological sense) or it can precede or follow it.[37] With Gerlach and Hine, glossolalia was seen as a bridge-burning act ("you can't go back"), an act committing the person to the beliefs of the Pentecostal-charismatic movement and demanding a change in one's life. Sociologists and psychologists would like qualitative and quantitative measurements of the changes which are alleged to have been effected. Not all of this is measurable in a scientific sense and it is therefore not unreasonable to accept testimonials to change as proof of the reality of some change. "One does not measure a 'deeper prayer life' in any scientific way, but devoutly religious people accept its reality as much as all of us accept the reality of happiness."[38] When it comes to the therapeutic effects of the Pentecostal-charismatic movement, they are not simply inferred from observations of what has happened to people or inferred from statements about these changes. Protestant neo-Pentecostals in particular are quite explicit about how they have been helped in resolving emotional problems. What is not clear and not specific is what contribution, if any, glossolalia in particular made in the therapy.[39] There are a host of other elements which might have been much more effective therapeutically, including such things as the strong personal support system these groups provide. Glossolalics look upon the change as supernatural, by which they mean that it is caused by God. The more dramatic the change the firmer the belief that it is supernatural. Many glossolalics would point to the change in lives to prove that glossolalia is supernatural. "No number of 'miraculous' transformations will make of glossolalia what it is not."[40] This is not to dismiss glossolalia but to define its character.

Not all "word salads," that is, ungrammatical arrangements of sounds, are glossolalia. The kind of word mixtures which characterize schizophrenic babbling is not the same kind of thing which goes on in glossolalia. "The two phenomena are incontrovertibly different."[41]

There is full justification for Samarin's criticism of the exaggerated supernaturalism of many in the Pentecostal-charismatic movement. But he too has a defective view. He equates the supernatural with the miraculous. He contends, rightly in the mind of this writer, that glossolalia is, in its linguistic characteristics, a natural phenomenon. He concludes, wrongly in the mind of this author, that it is therefore not supernatural.[42] If one accepts the natural-supernatural vocabulary (with which the author is familiar but ill at ease), then one has to exercise more care than Samarin does in its use. These are theological terms and in some circles what is a natural phenomenon does not exclude it from being supernatural. Christian marriage in the Catholic scholastic tradition is, in the linguistic framework in which Samarin is speaking, a supernatural state with a natural base. The one informs the other. The same can be said of glossolalia. Though a natural phenomenon, it can have a supernatural function, meaning, and content.

Very little statistical evidence is given to support Samarin's positions. He explains himself by saying that his book is not directed to the specialist but has a broader reading public in view. Some of his inferences are based on carefully collected data which are not, however, displayed. Samarin concedes that statistics do not verify all of his conclusions, and in a number of instances the conclusions he has arrived at are a matter of his considered judgment.[43] Though he has made a very valuable contribution to the field, much of his work is, on his own admission, beyond verification.

Anthony M. Sorem

A study with a quite restricted scope, namely of examining the degree of conceptual concreteness and alienation, was made by Anthony M. Sorem (1969).[44] Three groups were the subjects of the research: classical Pentecostals, Protestant neo-Pentecostals, and a sampling of the general public.[45] Sorem found that male Pentecostals had no more need for structure and order in their lives, a characteristic of conceptual concreteness, than men in the general public, although they scored higher on a measure of religiosity. The study assumed that male Pentecostals are as flexible about nonreligious matters as the general public. This is in keeping with the findings of Ralph Dreger (1952), who found no differences in the rigidity of personality structure between religious conservatives and religious liberals.[46] Female Pentecostals, however, manifested both high religiosity and a strong need for a structured life.

Both male and female Pentecostals scored lower on a scale for anomie than did the general public. Female Pentecostals also scored lower on measures of powerlessness and normlessness, two additional aspects of alienation. Since they manifested greater feelings of religiosity and a strong need for a structured life, this was taken to mean that they have a strong sense of confidence, efficiency, and security in the well-established norms of their Pentecostal experience.[47]

Sorem suggests that a possible interpretation of these findings is that both male and female Pentecostals have turned to the charismatic experience because of a need to experience religious fulfillment to a greater depth and with more personal commitment than is commonly considered appropriate in the main-line churches. "Such a desire is perfectly within the bounds of healthy, normal behavior, i.e., is non-neurotic."[48] Male Pentecostals generally do not express a need for structure, order, and predictability any more than do non-Pentecostals. The males seem no more confident and sure of their goals than the general public, and are more tolerant of ambiguity and less threatened by compromise than female Pentecostals. Males can settle for less than the ideal norms of behavior. However, both male and female Pentecostals participate in the faith as an expression of religious desire. In contrast to the classical Pentecostals, the Protestant charismatics studied showed less dependence on the support of a religious milieu to affirm their religious values and the effects derived from them.[49]

By Sorem's own admission some subscale samplings are too small to be significant. Also one would want to know whether greater rigidity of conceptualization, that is the disinclination to be accommodating in religious matters, is a personality factor present before their involvement in the Pentecostal movement, or is it a result of their charismatic-Pentecostal experience. A deep experience of the presence of God might well be a factor in a greater rigidity of conceptualization. Rigidity in this case is not always a negative factor.

Virginia H. Hine

Virginia H. Hine (1969, 1974) reviewed much of the more important psychological data to 1969.[50] Though she has displayed only small portions of her own data in her article, some is to be found in *People, Power, Change,* which she coauthored with Luther Gerlach.[51] The advantage which Hine shares with Alland and Pattison is a broad cultural context within which to interpret psychological data. After the review and evaluation of the literature, Hine comes to the conclusion that "available evidence requires that an explanation of glossolalia as pathological must be discarded."[52] Even those who accept this position, she notes, have a suspicion that those who engage in glossolalic behavior are in some nonspecific, subclinical manner, anxious, inadequate, or immature. This is especially true of churchmen in whose ranks the number of "Spirit-filled" Christians is increasing.[53] Hine has some reservations about approaching glossolalia from the point of view of suggestibility and hypnosis. The team to which she belonged found, among other evidence, that tongue speaking occurs frequently in solitary situations. Twenty-three percent of those interviewed experienced the baptism in the Holy Spirit and spoke in tongues for the first time when they were alone. "Until we know more about the relationship between suggestibility and type of group interaction, and can measure the degree of suggestibility more accurately, generalizations about glossolalics as suggestible individuals do not seem either very useful or supported by available data."[54] Though Hine considers glossolalia to be learned behavior in a more general sense, and grants that a certain "cognitive set" is a predisposing condition, neither factor explains or adequately interprets the phenomenon. Not all individuals with the same cognitive set become glossolalics. In terms of the dynamics of movement growth, Hine sees glossolalia as one component in the generation of commitment which results in changes in both attitudes and behavior in accordance with the patterns elaborated in the ideology to which the movement has pledged itself.[55]

Luther P. Gerlach and Virginia H. Hine

The research written up by Luther P. Gerlach and Virginia H. Hine (1970) is only obliquely concerned with the psychological profile of Pentecostals and charismatics. But they have commented on certain aspects of psychological research and have asked questions about some generally held assumptions. Their contribution is all the more interesting in that it is combined with a study of another contemporary movement, Black Power. Their results are based on a team study of the Pentecostal movement in the United States, Mexico, Haiti, and Colombia. Data on both glossolalia and the dynamics of movement growth in the United States were collected by means of forty-five case histories, two hundred thirty-nine self-administered questionnaires, and participant-observation in over thirty Pentecostal churches and independent groups.

When researchers turn to the analysis of movements they generally concentrate on the causes, the generating conditions. In order to arrange their data in meaningful patterns researchers often use either the models of social disorganization, social or economic deprivation, or, finally, a psychological maladjustment model. In the early stages of their research an attempt was made to use these various models, all of which were focused on causes, either as determining the emergence of the movement or facilitating it. Gerlach and Hine turned from the models of causation because they found that too many of the participants "could not be classified as socially disorganized, even relatively deprived, or psychologically maladjusted."[56] A second reason why the above mentioned models were deemed inadequate was that they provided no basis on which to predict where a movement would spread or who would become involved. If the models were really isolating causative factors, then they should be more reliable in forecasting where the movement would emerge and what kinds of people would join.

Pentecostalism organizes itself in a weblike network. The various cells are tied together, not through any central bureaucratic center, but through intersecting sets of personal relationships. This web which grows principally by face-to-face recruitment is especially suited to spreading the movement across class and cultural boundaries. This results in a great variety of organizational forms. "They range from the most egalitarian to the most autocratic, and include all sizes and degrees of organizational complexity. . . . This organizational smorgasbord enables the Pentecostal Movement to meet a broad range of psychological as well as sociological needs."[57] Diversity of every kind is typical of the Pentecostal-charismatic movement: social, economic, educational, religious, and psychological.

The researchers were impressed by the attention given in the literature on the Pentecostal movement to types of discontent, both pathological and normal, which predispose individuals to commit themselves to movements. In this context dissatisfaction with their earlier religious experience was mentioned. In particular they mentioned the meaninglessness of most church activities, a feeling that something was missing in the structural rituals of church life, a nonspecific desire for "a closer walk with God," "a hunger in my heart for more of the Lord." While granting that dissatisfaction and searching were present, "neither this discontent nor any of the sociological or psychological determinants which might be attributed to it were sufficient by themselves to cause an individual to become involved in the process of commitment to Pentecostalism."[58] Neither field observation nor empirical evidence made available to date would seem to indicate that conversion and commitment to Pentecostalism can be explained on the basis of psychological maladjustment.[59]

One of the characteristics of the movement is its ideological "dogmatism and certitude on the one hand and adoptive ambiguity on the other."[60] Gerlach and Hine advert to the studies on "authoritarianism," dogmatism," or "closed systems of thinking" which attempt to describe a personality type by rigidity of thinking. Because committed participants tend to display dogmatic certitude, they are sometimes assumed to be a certain personality type. The research of Gerlach and Hine concluded that "there is no evidence that Pentecostals as a group represent any particular personality type."[61] There is, it is true, a dependence which is openly proclaimed. Quite frequently one meets phrases such as "I am powerless without God," or "I am completely dependent on God." Typically, a Pentecostal believes that he or she is acted upon by a power which is external to the self. This orientation toward complete dependence and toward a source of external power is sometimes interpreted as a psychological weakness, a lack of ego strength, an inability to take the initiative. To those not in the movement this appears as fatalism, the passive acceptance of all without recourse to positive action. But the powerlessness is accompanied by a sense of power whose source is not the self. This power is acquired through personal religious experience. Since the believer has a personal access to power he is relieved of a restrictive sense of personal responsibility. If one does all that one can in the power of the Spirit one is still responsible but not in a restrictive sense. If a believer has done all in the service of God the "success and failure are all one, and the individual is free to take positive action in any direction he feels moved or directed."[62] Rather than free the Pentecostals from all responsibility and therefore make them irresponsible, the combination of powerlessness and power frees them from preoccupations about success and failure and gives them a new liberty of action.

Involvement in the renewal does alter the individual's self-under-standing. The individuals also perceive themselves differently in rela-tion to both other believers in Christ and to non-Christians. A manifes-tation of one aspect of this new self-understanding is the change in the direction of a more conservative moral code. One can still find among the Protestant neo-Pentecostals those who drink, smoke, and dance, but sixty-one percent of the total sampling shifted toward the behav-ioral code of their more evangelical brethren.[63] This behavioral shift is in those areas which many Christians consider insignificant in moral content. Many Christians consider dancing to be morally neutral and when done in moderation, drinking to be unobjectionable. The re-searchers are not suggesting that these areas are major moral issues but that involvement in Pentecostalism effects behavior change. In this they are supported by the research among Catholic charismatics by Joseph Fichter who found that behavior was changed not only qualita-tively but quantitatively as a result of participation in the renewal.[64] There is no doubt that those who become participants in the move-ment undergo some degree of personal transformation.

The team of anthropologists recognized that to focus the analysis of the movement on tongues "constitutes a distortion of the phenomono-logical fact."[65] Yet as an act of commitment by virtue of which one identifies oneself with the movement it has a role of importance to play. The phenomenon is learned behavior, contend Gerlach and Hine, and this in no way explains away its supernatural content. This is hardly unusual as "most human behavior is learned behavior."[66] In labeling it in this way one has not yet explained "the lasting changes traceable to the phenomenon in Pentecostalism nor the social conse-quences of the commitment so generated."[67] Because it is learned behavior it can also be induced. While recognizing that the vast major-ity of Pentecostals look upon the "now repeat after me" technique of inducing tongues as a species of hocus pocus and charlatanry, the research of Gerlach and Hine indicated no difference in terms of depth of commitment between those Pentecostals whose tongue speech was originally "induced" and those in whom it occurred more "spontane-ously."[68] Many Pentecostals report having come to the experience of tongues without having heard anyone else do it. But the majority had ample opportunity to pattern their vocalizations after others. Only a minority of the participants described some sort of crisis situation in their lives which they felt predisposed them to involvement. "Even in these cases, involvement usually came about through personal contact with a participant, either before or during the crisis situation."[69] This supports the major conclusion from their data, namely that the movement grows by face-to-face recruitment by committed participants.

A great variety of altered states of consciousness were found in their sampling, from semi-trance states accompanied by involuntary motor activity to quiet prayer in tongues in which there was "no loss of conscious control and little if any dissociation experienced."[70] There were some differences in the frequency with which participants prayed in tongues. The frequent tongue speakers were significantly more often (at the .001 level) from liberal than from fundamentalist or classical Pentecostal backgrounds. Frequency of glossolalia is correlated (.02 level of significance) with being alone at the time of the onset of glossolalia.[71] This would seem to support the view that glossolalia has greater functional importance as an act committing a person to the movement for those whose background and education prepares them the least for engaging in glossolalia. Lutheran, Presbyterian, and Episcopal charismatics speak in tongues more often (at the .05 level) than do second generation classical Pentecostals.[72] There was also a correlation between recruitment to the movement and frequency of tongues. Those classical Pentecostals who had been raised in a Pentecostal church and were recruited by their parents spoke in tongues less frequently than those who entered the movement as adult converts recruited by a friend, neighbor, spouse, sibling, or relative other than parent.[73]

That conditions of social disorganization or social or psychological deprivation facilitate the rise of the movement is granted. But it is clear that the original decision to join required some contact with the movement. "We found few cases . . . in which the original contact was not a personal one."[74] The key to the movement's growth is not due to mass hysteria operating in large meetings, nor to other mass propaganda methods, though these may facilitate entry. In fact, the questionnaire indicated that mass media were at the bottom of the list of those factors which influenced persons to become Pentecostals.[75] "The key to its spread is to be found in the process of face-to-face recruitment by committed participants."[76] Relatives recruited seventy-one percent of those in classical Pentecostal churches, fifty percent of the members of a large independent group of fifteen or twenty years duration, forty-two percent of recently organized independent smaller groups, and thirty-two percent of the "hiddens."[77] Parents were predictably the most important recruiters for the classical Pentecostals and the spouses were the most important for the "hiddens." In testing for the relationship between socio-economic differences and differences of recruiting, it appears that at the lower end of the socio-economic scale most of the recruiting is done by relatives. In the middle and upper classes, nonkin associations are more important for effective recruitment. The team observed the spread of the movement by means of personal recruitment into groups in which, according to the theories of social disorganization, social and economic deprivation, it should not have had the slightest chance of success.[78] The personal face-to-face character of the recruitment should not lead one to the conclusion that the movement is highly atomistic, that is, constituted of individuals each of whom has had a spiritual experience. One of the most important facts about growth is that an individual is not recruited to the movement in general but to a cell in particular.[79] The larger movement would not be able to effect and sustain the attitudinal and behavioral changes which are evident without this emphasis on the group. Only the dynamics of the cohesive cell is able to bring about and perpetuate the personal transformation.

Because of the central role which Kildahl attributes to the leader in bringing a person to the experience of tongues, something should be said about the findings of Gerlach and Hine in the area of leadership. They define the special quality of leadership as charisma understood in the Weberian sense. This involves a source external to and greater than the individual from which he derives his power to influence others. The accent is not simply on power. Rather, charisma is the ability, power if one wishes, to make others think and feel as that individual thinks and feels; in a word, effective influence. In a leader this quality "endows an individual with the power of persuasive influence over others and inspires dependent faith and personal loyalty in his followers."[80] The authors speak of the "absolute authority of the minister," "the authoritarian leaders," "the powerful and almost dictatorial quality of leadership."[81] But they warn of the pitfalls of studies which "attribute the success of the movement to a single charismatic leader," either locally or nationally.[82] Gerlach and Hine adopt the position of Dorothy Emmet. She distinguishes between 1) the leader who possesses an almost hypnotic power of personal authority inspiring devoted obedience, and 2) the charismatic leader who strengthens those he influences, inspiring them to work on their own initiative. Pentecostal leadership is primarily of the second type. The leader makes his followers experience the primary source of his own commitment, which is God. He does not block access to the source of power but opens it up. To this extent "the difference between leader and follower . . . does not depend on the presence or absence of charisma, but on the relative degrees of the quality exhibited by the various participating individuals."[83] Because charisma is not the peculiar prerogative of the leader—all enjoy the power to influence others—political control at the local level is often diffused and quite flexible. "Power and authority tend to be distributed among a council of wise and able men, of whom one is recognized to be just a bit more able than others."[84] Rather than undisputed lord he is *primus inter pares*, the first among equals. The power to influence others which is present in each member enhances the humblest member's leadership potential and contributes to the viability of a decentralized organization. Because all possess charisma, the group maintains a genuine egalitarianism while utilizing individual initiative and leadership capacity. Built-in controls over attempts to usurp authoritarian power are also present.

Similar conclusions were reached by Christian Lelive D'Epinay in his study of Pentecostalism in Chile.[85] Though a classical Pentecostal leader may be very influential and persuasive, he cannot do without the freely given consent of his subordinates. He is not a despot. "He cannot be one, on pain of finding himself at the head of a body of absolutists."[86] The power of a pastor depends on the recognition given him by the members of the congregation. They can always withdraw that recognition and challenge his authority. Therefore, it is necessary for the pastor to seek a consensus for his proposed line of action, and this even though the elders are only advisors. These limitations on the authority of the pastor make ecclesiastical procedures "much more truly collegial than it appears."[87]

A study by cultural anthropologists should be judged by the norms of that discipline. Today anthropology is less impressionistic and more statistically based than it was in the past. For a variety of reasons, cogently presented in the introduction to their volume, Gerlach and Hine have chosen to make their presentation less in reference to "hard data" and more as informed participant observers of the Pentecostal scene.[88] This choice was made even though a considerable amount of statistical information was gathered by the team. There is very little reporting of the psychological data in spite of the fact that psychological testing was part of the team approach. This makes it difficult to evaluate their psychological conclusions. Insofar as they are making psychological conclusions, one regrets the absence of control groups. The team was studying the dynamics of movement growth. For this reason the study concentrated on the heterogeneity of the participants, that is, the classical Pentecostals, Protestant neo-Pentecostals, Catholic charismatics, Pentecostal denominational churches, small independent prayer groups, "hiddens," etc. Without greater attention to differential research—which is not entirely lacking here—it is difficult to verify the conclusions. For instance, the Catholic charismatics are part of the sampling, but they constitute only an extremely small portion of it. More precise differential research would have shown how the conclusions apply to the Protestant neo-Pentecostal and the Catholic movements and possibly why they do not.

Daniel C. O'Connell and Ernest T. Bryant

A professor and a graduate student of the Department of Psychology at St. Louis University, Daniel C. O'Connell and Ernest T. Bryant (1971, 1972), respectively, have done research in speech analysis of glossolalic samples and came to the conclusion that all the sounds (scientifically called phonemes) used in the glossolalic samples are in the normal repertoire of sounds characteristic of the language of the speaker, a conclusion which Samarin also reached.[89] Aside from this linguistic research, O'Connell and Bryant have not engaged in any systematic study of an experimental nature. Their short review of the literature is nonetheless rewarding. Once glossolalic behavior has been isolated, a decision can be made as to whether a behavioral scientist has anything to say about it. Not only is there no agreement on its various sources, meaning, and functions, there is no agreement about what actually happens. Agreement can be found that the behavior in question is vocalized. The speechlike quality of these vocalizations derives from the fact that the glossolalic is using the sound treasury of his own native language. The vocalizations are organized into sequences with the pause, rate, pitch, and stress patterns of natural language. General agreement can be found for the assertion that glossolalia "is not lexically communicative, that is, it is not made up of meaningful vocalizations."[90] Most would agree that some sort of religious setting is required, but in the concrete that might vary from some vague sense of the numinous to participation in a Pentecostal group, to private prayer. Other than this, just about everything else is controversial.

The two authors point to "all sorts of theoretical and inferred impedimenta added to the phenomenon by various writers, mostly by means of a disturbingly inadequate use of scientific data and reasoning."[91] In particular O'Connell and Bryant refer to Kildahl's assertion that glossolalia is a regressive phenomenon in which the aspect of hypnotizability allows the speaker to discard temporarily some of his ego functioning. Because the capacity for hypnotism is the sine qua non for Kildahl, this means that a person who is not a Pentecostal and cannot be hypnotized, cannot duplicate glossolalic behavior. O'Connell and Bryant hold that "there is no evidence whatsoever that such a vocal production is—at any level of analysis—a problem for any human being who has a natural language plus normal, operational speech apparatus."[92] Samarin also mentions experiments in which the vocalizations have been duplicated by nonglossolalics.[93] The positive esteem in which persons in the movement hold tongues, the encouragement that all are given to yield to tongues, the tutoring the new members receive "provides a powerful incentive to learn and engage in glossolalia. And it is just that, a socially learned and initiated behavior."[94] While not discounting the religious meaning, or even its being a gift of the Spirit in the theological sense, the authors assert that "behaviorally, physically, neurophysiologically, phonologically, linguistically, and psychologically, the production of glossolalia is in no sense of the word a superhuman feat."[95] If it also reflects the providential operation of the Holy Spirit "it does so—as do most charisms—in a very ordinary way, through natural causes, and without great ado."[96]

Charles Waldegrave

Charles Waldegrave (1972) studied a sampling of one hundred four students from three New Zealand universities, half of whom identified themselves as Pentecostal Christians (which in this case means someone who has experienced the baptism in the Holy Spirit, no matter to which denominational background one belongs) and the other half identified themselves as non-Pentecostal Christians.[97] A battery of psychological tests was administered.[98] Waldegrave concluded that the entrance into the Pentecostal-charismatic renewal "appears to have been quite unrelated to factors of personality."[99] His research gave no indication that people with psychological abnormalities enter the renewal. Nor was there any indication that social factors such as occupational background, intellectual, and academic attitudes were related to their affiliation with the Pentecostal charismatic renewal. No support was found for theories of socio-economic deprivation, nor were anti-intellectual attitudes to be found. Because there are no significant psychological differences between the Pentecostal and non-Pentecostal students, Waldegrave suggests that the explanation of the spread of the movement is to be found in sociology and anthropology rather than in psychology.

John P. Kildahl

A study which has received wide attention is that of John P. Kildahl's (1972) *The Psychology of Speaking in Tongues.* This book grew out of two earlier studies, in which Kildahl, a psychologist, had the collaboration of Dr. Paul A. Qualben, a psychiatrist. A first study commissioned by the American Lutheran Church was followed by a second funded by a grant from the Behavioral Sciences Research Branch of the National Institute of Mental Health. This research was based on interviews and psychological tests given to twenty glossolalics, with twenty nonglossolalics as the control group. The study was limited to Protestant neo-Pentecostals, thus excluding both classical Pentecostals and Catholic charismatics. The research was completed in 1971 and a report filed with the National Institute of Mental Health.

The Psychology of Speaking in Tongues is based on further research on the part of Kildahl and Qualben among Protestant neo-Pentecostals, and includes psychological interviews and extensive psychological testing.[100] The interpretation of the data given in the book is that of Kildahl alone. This research found that those who speak in tongues are more submissive, suggestible, and dependent in the presence of authority figures than nontongue speakers. "Without complete submission to the leader, speaking in tongues was not initiated. . . . In fact, it appeared absolutely necessary that they have a relationship of continuing trust and confidence if they were to experience glossolalia as spiritually important and meaningful. . . . It is not surprising that a profound sense of trust in a leader is necessary for beginning to speak in tongues, just as it is for the induction of hypnosis."[101] The glossolalics were characteristically less depressed than the control group. Even after a year feelings of well-being continued. They continued to describe themselves after a year as more sensitive and loving toward others. "Many felt they had better marital, including sexual, relationships."[102] In terms of mental health Kildahl did not find that the tongue speakers were any less healthy than the control group.[103] Nor was there a special personality type to be found among them. They represented a cross section of all the usual personality types.[104]

According to Kildahl the principal difference between tongue speakers and nontongue speakers was that the glossolalics developed deeply trusting and submissive relationships to the authority figures who introduced them to the practice of speaking in tongues. They had a strong need for external guidance from some trusted authority. "The adulation accorded the leader was the obvious characteristic of tongue-speaking groups. . . . It was not the speaking in tongues that brought the great feelings of euphoria that these people do experience. Rather, it was the submission to the authority of the leader and to a sense of acceptance that followed the submission."[105] So great is this dependency that whenever a tongue speaker broke off the relationship with the authority figure, the experience of glossolalia "was no longer so subjectively meaningful."[106] Important for Kildahl's understanding of the role of the authority figure is the relationship he sees between the practice of speaking in tongues and the ability to be hypnotized. "It is our thesis that hypnotizability constitutes the sine qua non of the glossolalia experience. If one can be hypnotized, then one is able, under proper conditions, to learn to speak in tongues. While glossolalia is not the same as hypnosis it is similar to it and has the same roots in the relationship of the subject to the authority figure."[107] Paul Morentz (1966), a psychiatrist at Berkeley, found strong similar feelings of dependency and suggestibility among his test group.[108] Morentz noted that glossolalia takes on a different meaning in classical Pentecostal groups where it is expected behavior in contrast to the main-line Protestant churches, where it is considered deviant behavior. If hypnotizability constitutes the sine qua non of the glossolalic experience it would seem that some special qualities or traits should characterize the hypnotic subject. This seems not to be the case according to Peter H. van der Walde, for whom studies "indicate that under scientific investigation, hypnosis does not manifest any unique properties, nor hypnotic subjects any unique abilities."[109]

Through Paul Qualben's interviews Kildahl learned that eighty-five percent of those who spoke in tongues had experienced a clearly defined anxiety crisis preceding the onset of the practice of tongues. Further, the experience was generally introduced under the mass pressures of a group or a crowd, or in an atmosphere which was "contagious" because of the charism of the leader. "Without exposure to a regressive group experience, glossolalia could not be induced. The glossolalia experience was rarely generated in the course of quiet, rational introspection."[110] Kildahl noted that tongue speakers band together in highly visible groups, that they tend to be "cabalistic." The group behavior tended to be divisive, to project anger on those who represent their former way of life, to be turned inward and concerned mostly for persons like themselves, to be given to histrionic display, and to be preoccupied with glossolalia.[111]

Kildahl holds that "speaking in tongues can be learned, almost as other abilities are learned. Whether one calls the practice a gift of the Spirit is, then, a matter of individual choice. Speaking in tongues does make the individual feel better, and theologically it is perhaps possible to claim that anything that makes one feel better is in some way a gift of God."[112] As a "learned phenomenon" speaking in tongues is not "very uniquely spiritual."[113] In judging such a phenomenon one should use both individual and community criteria. On the basis of the individual criterion, speaking in tongues has some positive benefits. But on the basis of community criterion the evaluation must be essentially negative. Kildahl mentions the disruptive effects and the irrational excesses which result in community disintegration.[114]

Much of what this study has reported could be found in other research reports. Kildahl found that those who said they were speaking in tongues "at every moment they were not speaking in English" were in the same psychological condition as those who were obsessive about hand washing.[115] Earlier Vivier had also noted that the frequency, not the practice of glossolalia, was found to be associated with anxiety and tension.[116] Kildahl calls attention to the regressive nature of glossolalia, while not suggesting that regressive behavior is necessarily abnormal.[117] Sleep and sexual intercourse, or the businessman's absent-minded stroking of the soft leather of a chair during a harried confrontation with a client are all normal regressive activities. Samarin and Alland have noted the same regressive characteristics of aspects of glossolalic behavior.[118] Pattison had written that glossolalic behavior seems to involve "a degree of regression in several aspects of the ego function. . . . In some glossolalists the regressive state is pathological, although in most instances of which we are speaking the regression is not pathological, but rather a regression in the service of the ego."[119] According to H. Hartmann, the mechanism of regression in the service of the ego is a mark of maturity.[120] Kildahl asserts that in the history of tongue speaking "there are no scientifically confirmed recordings of anyone speaking in a foreign language which he had never learned."[121] Samarin, too, found that alleged cases of speaking in a true language, unknown to the speaker, were found not to be verified when examined.[122] Wolfram and Pattison have taken the same position. The attempt to verify whether tongues is a true language, especially in view of the assertion by large numbers of classical Pentecostals and charismatics that it is a true language, is a quite legitimate object of scientific investigation. However, it should not be invested with undue importance in a theological context. Since in the theological framework tongues is a prayer gift, the question of whether tongues is or is not a true language is theologically irrelevant. The author is quite convinced that speaking in tongues is not a true language and that true scientific verification of a true language has not been demonstrated. As a theologian, he would not want to close the door on the possibility of this occurring. Quite obviously this is not a scientific but a theological judgment.

Finally, Kildahl maintains, as do many others, that speaking in tongues is learned behavior, as other behavior is learned. In an earlier progress report on the research funded by the National Institute of Mental Health, authored by both Kildahl and Qualben (1971), the authors wrote: "Speaking in tongues, however, always follows some kind of demonstration of the phenomenon."[123] Kildahl draws the conclusion that it therefore cannot be a gift of the Spirit except in a greatly attenuated sense.[124] Samarin's position allows for the case of the person who has never heard of glossolalia, knows no one who speaks in tongues, and yet comes spontaneously to the experience. This, too, can be learned behavior, not as an imitation of an available model, but in the broader sense that all vocalization is learned behavior. Glossolalia is a "derived form of speech; its creation depends on the speaker's ability to abstract from what he hears or knows, the units and the tactics—the rules—of a marginal and simplified form of speech."[125] James Jaquith places tongues in the same linguistic category with scat singing (a singer, backed up by several musicians verbalizes a melodic line via nonlanguage material), double talk, nonshared musical speech (singing opera in a language not understood by the audience).[126] He considers glossolalia to be learned behavior, as does E. Mansell Pattison.[127] Bittlinger holds a similar position, maintaining that glossolalia is a natural phenomenon.[128] For Bittlinger, this in no way suggests that it is not a charism of the Holy Spirit. He would deny that there is in Paul the kind of natural-supernatural framework within which many Christians, and many classical Pentecostals and Catholic charismatics, work. A charism is not a completely new faculty, an endowment which one did not possess before. Rather, it is a new service, a new function of what God has already given us, exercised under the power of the Spirit. One sees that Kildahl's theological framework is too narrow. What is learned behavior for Kildahl is not a gift of the Spirit in any specific sense. This position is theologically untenable. Kildahl might have been unduly influenced theologically by the narrow views of those whom he was interviewing.[129] Many Pentecostals and charismatics of all varieties have exaggerated supernatural views of the gifts. The same capacity can either be a charism or not be a charism, depending on whether it is in the service of the kingdom and is exercised in the power of the Spirit. To be a gift of the Spirit it need not be a totally new faculty given "from above."

The overall judgment on Kildahl's book must be negative. A book which is presented as a scientific evaluation must be judged in scientific terms. On this basis the book fails. There is, for instance, very little indication of the numbers of persons or groups tested or interviewed. There is no way of judging the sampling.[130] One takes for granted that a scientist must safeguard the confidentiality of the persons and groups he has interviewed but one can display research data in such a way that confidentiality is in no way threatened.

Four psychological tests were administered: the Rorschach Test, the Draw-A-Person Test, the Thematic Apperception Test, and the Minnesota Multiphasic Personality Inventory. While safeguarding confidentiality, it would be essential to have the data from these tests displayed. Only one of the many measures applicable to Thematic Apperception Test pictures is reported. Though there are thirteen clinical and validity scales on the Minnesota Multiphasic Personality Inventory only one is reported. A researcher asks about the differences on the other scales. No data is reported from the Draw-A-Person Test or from the Rorschach Test.

In addition to this failure to display data in a professional way, Kildahl is highly selective in the studies he chooses to mention. There are important studies which were readily available at the time Kildahl was writing, some of which do not support his findings and interpretation.[131] He takes no note in the text of the findings of most of these studies. Some of these studies are far more extensive than those Kildahl mentions. There is an appended bibliography but there is no indication in the text that the author is acquainted with the content of the research there mentioned.

A major contention of Kildahl is that "without complete submission to the leader, speaking in tongues was not initiated. . . . There were no loners among the tongue-speakers."[132] There is quite sufficient justification for attributing a dominant role to the leader in the Pentecostal-charismatic movement. This has been noted by researchers studying classical Pentecostalism and the Catholic charismatic renewal.[133] Some expressions of the Pentecostal-charismatic renewal are not only leader oriented but leader dominated. Nevertheless, other researchers (Gerlach and Hine, Samarin and the present author) have met loners who experienced tongues without previous knowledge of the phenomenon and without the aid of a dominant leader. Further, this position of the leader is related to Kildahl's assertion that "hypnotizability constitutes the *sine qua non* of the glossolalia experience." If one gives such importance to the authority figure as the one who leads a person into hypnotic trance, then one is ignoring the "evidence that trance may be produced by such 'impersonal' means as having the subject attend to his own magnified breathing sounds, by attending to stroboscopic light, or by spontaneously lapsing into trance on his own."[134] The major role attributed to the authority figure and his relationship to hypnosis would seem unnecessary to explain glossolalic behavior. Theodore X. Barber and David S. Calverley have shown that an authority figure is by no means necessary to bring about behavior traditionally associated with hypnotic induction by a leader.[135] In some areas the same behavior may be due simply to the fact that the subject sits quietly for a period of time with eyes closed. Arnold M. Ludwig (1966) also called attention to the great variety of ways a trance can be produced.[136] Or if hypnosis is a factor in glossolalic behavior, it might be self-induced rather than induced by an authority figure. "The present data appear to make it incumbent upon those who emphasize the importance of the manipulations involved in formal hypnotic-induction procedures first to demonstrate rigorously what specific effects are produced by hypnotic-induction procedures that are not produced by the simple statement, 'Place yourself in hypnosis' and then delineate empirically which of the many variables included in formal hypnotic-induction procedures are relevant and which extraneous in producing each of the effects."[137] Some support for Kildahl's position comes from Ludwig who speaks of the hypersuggestibility of the person who has been hypnotized, the increased susceptibility of persons to accept automatically or respond uncritically to specific commands of a leader, who represents an omnipotent authority figure.[138] However, Kildahl is speaking of kinds of persons who lend themselves to hypnosis, while Ludwig is speaking of the state of hypnosis (and other altered states of consciousness). The two are not the same.

In a speech given at Wartburg Seminary, Dubuque, Iowa, in May

1972, Kildahl's fellow researcher, Qualben, publicly disassociated himself from the interpretation of the data given by Kildahl. Kildahl interprets the dependency on the leader in a highly negative sense.[139] Qualben, on the other hand, said that the ability to develop a trusting relationship can be a sign of emotional maturity. Qualben further differed with Kildahl on dependency as a prerequisite for speaking in tongues. Qualben said that one cannot know from the research done by himself and Kildahl whether dependency in the sense used by Kildahl was a prerequisite for speaking in tongues. They have no objective data, no longitudinal studies which predate the glossolalic experience of the people who were tested. Some of the characteristics which they noted, among them, dependency, could have been the result of, rather than a precondition to, the experience of glossolalia. One would want to add that some dependency belongs to the very definition of Christianity. "I do nothing on my own authority but speak thus as the Father taught me" (John 8:28). "Without me you can do nothing" (John 15:5). Since those who speak in tongues consider it the Spirit acting in them, would not the dependency be directed toward the Holy Spirit rather than to the authority figure? With this theological qualification in mind, the warning of Kildahl about a dependency syndrome is well taken. Other authors have called attention to the same danger.[140] It is possible for the measure of dependency which belongs to psychological maturity to become an unhealthy, immature dependence on an authority figure. But Kildahl does seen guilty of oversimplification as Walter Smet, a Belgian psychologist, and Dennis Bennett, an Episcopal priest who triggered the neo-Pentecostal movement, have contended.[141]

Other researchers would have problems with Kildahl's assertion that there are no "loners." Hine, Kelsey, Samarin, and William Backus have found that there are some persons, not great in number, who come to the experience of tongues quite spontaneously, without previous knowledge of the phenomenon.[142] This would seem to indicate that the "atmosphere of heightened suggestibility" is not all necessary, a point which has been noted by Hine and Vivier.[143] On the other hand a conducive atmosphere frequently accompanies the onset of tongues.[144] The possibility of suggestion would be heightened if the experience of tongues was preceded by an anxiety state. Quoting Qualben's interviews, Kildahl states that eighty-seven percent of the sampling had a clearly defined anxiety crisis preceding their speaking in tongues.[145] The suffering involved in this crisis is "usually intense," with feelings of confusion or estrangement or isolation.[146] This stands in contrast to the findings of Hine and Olila whose samplings of two hundred thirty-nine indicated that only fifteen percent of the respondents' experience of tongues was related to an anxiety crisis.[147] If anxiety is a prerequisite to speaking in tongues, asks the Belgian psychologist, Walter Smet, why did Kildahl not find indications of it in the MMPI tests he himself administered? "Moreover, anxiety and self-doubt are also mentioned in testimonies as being obstacles to yielding to tongues."[148] How is anxiety both a prerequisite and an obstacle?

The obverse of the role assigned by Kildahl to the authority figure is the necessary capacity for being hypnotized on the part of the person seeking the experience of tongues. Kildahl's findings in this area also stand in contrast to that of Vivier, who asserts that glossolalics test out lower than control groups on suggestibility;[149] of Samarin, who contends that linguistic motivation and instruction is of little importance;[150] of Hine and Olila, whose two hundred thirty-nine respondents indicated that their religious experiences were not the result of psychopathological pressure;[151] of Gerlach and Hine who discount psychological factors as decisive and explain recruitment or involvement in terms of face-to-face recruitment by committed participants (usually on the part of persons already known).[152] The recruitment need not be done by a dominant authority figure or one who invites dependency. Richard A. Roth (1967), in a related but independent study, came to the same conclusion as Gerlach and Hine, namely that in explaining recruitment, great importance is placed on "significant personal relationships."[153] Similar conclusions were reached by the psychological investigations of Charles Waldegrave.[154] He asserts that the explanations of the movement, and therefore of recruitment, probably lie outside the boundaries of psychology and more likely in the fields of sociology and anthropology. In this regard he makes special mention of the work of Gerlach and Hine as a starting point for further research. Malony and his colleagues (1972) found that there was no "significant tendency for glossolalics to feel more internally or externally controlled."[155] This would make it difficult to give to the leader the role which Kildahl assigns to him.

For Kildahl, the leader is an instrument of external control. However, twenty-three percent of the respondents to a questionnaire sent out by the Gerlach and Hine team of anthropologists spoke in tongues when alone. This could be explained by techniques of posthypnotic suggestion employed during the prayer meetings. The Gerlach and

Hine team did not observe such techniques being used,[156] but the author knows of certain circles in which such pressures did exist. The research of L. M. Vivier has shown that Pentecostals tested lower in suggestibility than the control group, members of the traditional reformed church.[157] In a later publication Vivier said that the suggestibility factor was "minimal" in the glossolalic group.[158]

The whole issue is brought into a maze out of which there is no exit if too great importance is placed on suggestibility as a predisposition for experiencing glossolalia. Suggestibility is also the basis for normal processes of socialization, education, and successful psychotherapy. "The only true non-suggestible person is the psychopath."[159] T. X. Barber contends that if waking control subjects are exposed to the proper task motivation, they show about as high a level of suggestibility as subjects who are exposed to hypnotic-induction procedures.[160] There is little difference in terms of response to suggestions between the group exposed to hypnotic induction and the waking control group which is properly motivated, as long as both groups have positive attitudes toward the situation (toward what they are suggested to do), and if they are motivated to respond. This would indicate that the determining factor is not the presence or absence of suggestibility, but the presence or absence of proper motivation.

Fairness must be exercised toward Kildahl's research. A number of studies have been quoted in which conclusions are at variance with those of Kildahl. There is a certain risk in quoting one research project against another. Where the research design is different, the samples are not in every case comparable. Therefore, the Hine and Olila research is not a refutation of the Kildahl and Qualben data. Rather, the first study does not support the second and indicates the need for further research.

In the Final Progress Report of the Kildahl-Qualben research it was announced that in the forthcoming book, that is, *The Psychology of Speaking in Tongues*, a chapter by Dr. William J. Samarin would appear.[161] Though the book in fact contains no contribution by Samarin, reference is made to his research.[162] No indication is given that Samarin's research reached conclusions which stand in opposition to those of Kildahl. Samarin, who is not involved in the Pentecostal-charismatic renewal, thinks that Kildahl's book does not substantiate its generalizations. According to Samarin, the psychological characterization found in the book "is more a reflection of personal bias than empiric fact."[163]

H. Newton Malony, Nelson Zwaanstra, and James W. Ramsey

A research team under H. Newton Malony (1972) from the Graduate School of Psychology at Fuller Theological Seminary studied the frequency of glossolalia as related to personality variables among youth by whom glossolalic behavior was expected and approved.[164] The team gathered demographic data regarding family background and the initial glossolalic experience, and analyzed variances in high and low frequency of the use of glossolalia. No relationship was found between frequency of glossolalia and either introversion or extroversion. Besides finding that there was no significant tendency for glossolalics to be more internally and externally controlled, they also found that there was a significant tendency for high frequency glossolalics to be more intrinsic in their orientation to religion than either nonglossolalics or low frequency glossolalics. This was interpreted to mean that those who pray frequently in tongues are "more likely to perceive religion as meeting personal fulfillment than status needs in their lives."[165] Demographically, glossolalia was related to the religious activity of parents, a finding in keeping with the studies by Gerlach and Hine, McGavran, Hine, and the Gerrards. In this context glossolalia was not related to either sex or to socio-economic factors.

In a second study the team investigated forty Assembly of God youth who went on a social action trip to Mexico with a control group of forty Assembly of God youth who did not. High and low frequency of glossolalic behavior were compared and the data were subjected to analysis of variance. There was a tendency for youth who participated in the social action project to use their glossolalia more frequently than glossolalics who did not take part in the project.[166] There was a significant relationship between frequent use of glossolalia and a negative, sinful view of man. Contrary to Vivier's findings, this team concluded that personality variables are not related to the frequency with which a person engages in glossolalic prayer. But the team found that frequency of use was related to religious attitudes.

The team has done a time-series study on the effects of glossolalia on personality integration by testing persons before and after they began to speak in tongues. This study of the effects of glossolalia on personality integration was carried out by studying Catholics who had entered the introductory "Life in the Spirit Seminars," a course usually lasting about seven weeks. The results showed "a significant decrease in anxiety after becoming glossolalic."[167] Comparisons were made between those who did not become glossolalic and those who did. Those who did not become glossolalic remained more anxious, depressed and hostile than the others (those who became glossolalic and those who were already glossolalic). A further comparison between those who did not become glossolalic and those who were already glossolalic prior to the seminar showed the latter group remained higher in ego strength and in their conviction that religion is important.

This is significant research, but the time-series, though testing for changes before and after the inception of glossolalia, treats glossolalia in isolation from movement involvement. It may well be that the greater changes are to be found not in speaking in tongues by itself, but by the total experience of the movement of which tongues might be considered the commitment act. Those who have entered the Life in the Spirit Seminars have, so to speak, already been contaminated, and cannot be used for this broader application of time-series. The research reviewed in chapters four and five of this book frequently claims to be studying the correlation of personality traits and change to glossolalic activity. A close look will reveal that the focus is much wider than that. The researchers studied the correlation of personality to movement involvement which includes many factors besides glossolalia.

James T. Richardson

Unlike Hine and Pattison, James T. Richardson (1973) has not engaged in either testing programs or in systematic field work. The conclusions he draws, then, are based solely on his review of the psychological literature. He maintains that glossolalia is nonpathological in itself, but would suggest that there may be "a connection between the occurrence of glossolalia and certain psychological states in individuals."[168] Given the quality of some of the psychological research, Richardson contends that "the part played by specifically psychological states in generating and sustaining the tongues movement [sic] is still an open one."[169] A strong plea is made for more research, preferably with longitudinal research designs which allow long term evaluations and assessment of variables not possible in one-shot projects.

Meredith B. McGuire

In her study of Catholic charismatics, Meredith B. McGuire (1974, 1975) finds that they "defy the standard sociological explanations based on social and economic deprivation."[170] Her contribution is important in the way it both reinforces the findings of Gerlach and Hine and departs from them. Like Gerlach and Hine, and also Harrison, she found that the Life in the Spirit Seminars which precede real commitment to the Catholic movement are seen as an acceptable induction mechanism, clearly appealing to the middle class. They are "safe," gradual, and orderly. Conversion in this charismatic sense is more a "drift" than a dramatic shift, and the seminars help to guide that gradual reorientation and reeducation.[171] In the seminars "testimony is a fundamental—if not *the* fundamental—aspect of the induction process."[172] Here the new recruits hear the testimony of those already in the movement, and themselves learn how to give their own witness. A major step in the induction process is taken when the new members begin to witness in the seminar. Gerlach and Hine had focused attention on glossolalia as the bridge-burning act in virtue of which the recruit identifies with the members of the movement and its ideology, as over against the millions who do not. McGuire, on the contrary, maintains that "such attention to glossolalia is overdrawn—at least in the case of Catholic pentecostals."[173] Because glossolalia is primarily a prayer gift for personal devotion, members of the larger prayer groups seldom know exactly which members have received the gift. Not only is tongues not "public" in prayer meetings, but is seldom practiced by Catholic charismatics in a public way in their everyday lives. "Thus, although it might cut the new pentecostal off symbolically from the rest of society, it need not ever 'show' publicly."[174] Glossolalia may serve as a symbol of commitment for the new recruits, but it does not involve the new members sufficiently to be considered a major commitment mechanism. Testimony is a greater commitment mechanism since it includes both involvement (in the prayer group) and abandonment (i.e., risk of cutting off family and friends).[175]

The witnessing which the new recruits learn to do in the seminars has as one of its functions learning to perceive one's experience in the appropriate charismatic framework. To this end recruits learn the appropriate terms for describing their experiences, a new way of interpreting everyday experiences which might have spiritual significance and therefore could be used in their witnessing. "Testimony converts all events, all cognitions, and all history, into *significant* events, *meaningful* cognitions, and a history which converges upon the pentecostals' *special* religious experience."[176]

McGuire also remarks that the seminars are essentially indoctrination and motivation instruments and are not idea oriented. Questions seeking clarification of a point made by a leader are permitted, but the content of the answers is not discussable. The seminar is for shared experiences, not shared ideas. In two groups the leader carefully reframed each member's contribution.[177] Or if the new recruit did not use the "appropriate" terms in giving the testimony, the leader translated the testimony into the acceptable words. In other instances the restatement by the leader changed the significance of the testimony altogether. It would be interesting to discover how widespread these practices are. The seminar more closely resembles a retreat than a classroom situation. It does seem possible to have occasions the purpose of which is not debate, as is the case in retreats and orientation sessions. No objection can be taken as long as some other occasions are provided for more intellectual confrontation.

SUMMARY

In this second period, 1967–1975, there was a growing consensus that glossolalia could not be linked in any immediate way with pathology. But the move away from the categories and preoccupations of abnormal psychology was not without its hesitations. It became increasingly evident that as behavior, speaking in tongues was socially passable, even where it won little positive approval. It was accorded something akin to benign toleration. But even among those who held that it was not pathological, that the Pentecostal personality type was nonexistent, that it was the type of activity in which nonneurotics could safely engage—even among some of these researchers there remained that nonspecific suspicion of emotional imbalance and immaturity. Oates expressed this psychological hedging when he said that persons who speak in tongues are not mentally ill but they do not, on the other hand, enjoy a unique degree of mental health. Nouwen recognized what classical Pentecostals have admitted for decades, namely that the spiritual experience of the baptism in the Holy Spirit and tongues could be psychologically dangerous for some, even though not for the vast majority.

The most influential studies of this period come from Samarin, Gerlach and Hine (and the work Hine did on her own), and Kildahl. Samarin helped to demystify glossolalia by investigating the human side of glossolalic behavior. Within the framework Samarin presents, it is possible to have a deep reverence for the gift of tongues as a prayer activity, as a sign of the sacred, as a response to presence even though it is a "natural" linguistic activity of which all normal people are capable. Many Pentecostals and charismatics will find his insistence that what is uttered is not a true language to be threatening. Theologically and exegetically there is no need to hold that glossolalics speak a true language. It can still be a deeply religious and prayerful activity, having the full "supernatural" content and function.

Gerlach and Hine were able to show that the dynamics of movement growth can be demonstrated without resort to deprivation or disorganization theories. According to this team, these theories explain facilitating, not determining, conditions for the rise and development of movements. They therefore do not point to causes. They did not find models of psychological maladjustment helpful in explaining the rise of Pentecostalism. Behavioral changes and changes in self-understanding were shown to be effects of movement involvement. This would indicate that personality is not left unaffected after personal association with the movement. What is crucial for the history of research is the role in the growth of Pentecostalism of face-to-face recruitment by a committed participant. What is decisive is not just a dominant charismatic leader, but the ability of lesser members, the followers, to speak persuasively and influence the lives of others. If this is true, psychological factors might be less important in bringing about association with the movements.

Kildahl's work remains an important one for the questions it raises and the influence it has exercised. In spite of his protestation that glossolalics are no less healthy than those in the control group, there persists the suspicion that those people who need a strong external guidance of a dominant leader are in some subclinical way neurotic. Kildahl is significant for the movement in all the churches because he points out what could happen to a leadership without checks. His work is important for future research on the issue of leadership and how it is exercised.

O'Connell and Bryant reinforce the positions of Samarin, Gerlach and Hine, and Kildahl that glossolalia is not to be oversupernaturalized, that it is not a superhuman attainment. It belongs to the ordinary rather than to the extraordinary. Theologically, one needs no resort to miracles; psychologically, one needs no resort to categories of abnormality to explain the presence or function of glossolalia.

Waldegrave indicates that entrance into the movement is not related to psychological factors. This is still a disputed position but gaining ground. With Samarin, Waldegrave thinks that more light will be shed on the movement by sociology and anthropology than by psychology —a further indication that glossolalic behavior does not belong to the field of abnormal psychology.

Malony and his coworkers show how cautious one should be about accepting Kildahl's assertion of the need to submit to a dominant leader. They found that glossolalics are not more controlled externally nor internally than control groups. Their research uses for the first time in a significant way the time-series testing which Richardson so eloquently pleads for. In this they may set models for other scholars as they construct their research designs.

McGuire really belongs in a sociological rather than a psychological survey. She is significant for the material at hand because she points to the safe, acceptable middle-class induction techniques used in the Catholic movement. Rather than high profile emotionalism, these techniques represent low profile indoctrination. So low is the profile that McGuire would prefer to call the reorientation of lives a "drift" rather than a conversion.

This period ends not with complete psychological vindication of glossolalics but with the elements which might, in the future, issue in a consensus. A measure of nonspecific suspicion remains and this constitutes the unfinished agenda for further psychological research.

6 | ASSESSMENT AND RECAPITULATION

THE MOVEMENT JUDGES ITSELF

In very general terms one could say that the evidence points to Pentecostals and charismatics falling within the rather extensive expanse of what can be called normality. This should not obscure the fact, witnessed also by classical Pentecostals, that from its beginning, the classical Pentecostal movement attracted its share of unstable persons.[1] An early chronicler of the classical movement recognized that "extravagant, violent characters have tried to identify themselves with the work."[2] This chronicler, himself a participant in the movement, admitted that "crooks and cranks were the first at the meetings" and that there was "much professional, religious quackery."[3] Besides the balanced, normal people was that quite "mixed multitude"[4] who were eager for the "froth and foam," that is, "empty manifestation."[5] Even among the leaders there were those who had "faked Pentecost."[6] "Our great battle from the beginning was with freshly religious fanatics, purporting to be the Spirit of God."[7] Sometimes they attempted, and even now attempt, to assume leadership roles within the Pentecostal-charismatic renewal.

Further, classical Pentecostals as well as others have long recognized the danger in attributing to the Holy Spirit what is only the dynamics of emotions.[8] An early German leader of the classical Pentecostal movement wrote in 1909: "When a person has fasted too much and denied himself too much sleep, strange things can happen. One goes into a service which lasts too long, and then the nerves begin to get feverish, and then comes dreams and all possible things. But this comes from the nerves. . . . And one thinks that all of this comes from the Holy Spirit. But it really comes from nerves."[9] Classical Pentecostals as well as neo-Pentecostals and charismatics have urged those members with emotional problems to seek psychiatric help.[10] There is general agreement among all branches of the movement that to lead a psychologically disturbed person into the experience of tongues and what is called the baptism in the Holy Spirit is at very least imprudent.

To pass over the psychological dimensions of the Protestant neo-Pentecostal movement and come to the Catholic charismatic renewal, it was also recognized that not all who were attracted to the Catholic renewal were psychologically well balanced. Ralph Martin, a national leader, declared: "Any community must soon face up to the fact that not all persons who have been attracted to the community are psychologically and spiritually mature. Indeed, serious psychological and spiritual immaturity, and even sickness, will almost certainly be present in some members."

Given a definition of trance which is sufficiently roomy, which does not necessarily imply the presence of neurosis or psychosis, or a subclinical suspicion that people who pray in tongues are psychologically deprived, Pentecostals and charismatics would not deny that trance states occur at what is called baptism in the Holy Spirit, the initial experience of tongues and its subsequent practice. One of the patriarchs of the classical movement, Lewis Pethrus, who might be expected to be especially sensitive on this point because classical Pentecostals were for years despised as emotionally disturbed people, does not deny that trance states occur among classical Pentecostals.[11] All Pentecostals and charismatics, however, are understandably unhappy when the possibly thirty-five million participants in the Pentecostal-charismatic renewal at the world level are all characterized as psychologically deprived. Virginia Hine rightly notes that many of those writers who do not hold that Pentecostals and charismatics are emotionally unbalanced, still foster the suspicion that there is a nonspecific emotional immaturity, a level of anxiety not measurable by clinical means, a generalized personal inadequacy.[12] Since there is no empirical, scientific evidence for this position, Virginia Hine suggests that future studies of glossolalia "might usefully include an examination of possible bias on the part of non-glossolalic observers."[13] Samarin, who does not speak in tongues, suggests that a psychological profile be made of those researchers who show a bias against glossolalics.[14]

CONVENTIONAL OR UNCONVENTIONAL?

In assessing the research made to date one still has to contend with a tremendous conceptual difficulty. In his article on "Psychopathology and Religious Commitment," Rodney Stark says "there are perhaps no more elusive and value-laden concepts in social science than mental illness, insanity, neurosis, inadequacy, and other terms referring to various forms and degrees of psychopathology."[15]

More precisely, is religiousness related to psychopathology? Is religiosity in any significant way an index of psychological deviation or neurosis? Stark researched the question in relation to conventional religion and sought to verify the hypothesis: the various mental conditions referred to by such terms as psychopathology or being mentally ill or ill-adjusted are negatively related to conventional forms of religious commitment.[16] He concluded that psychological abnormalities typically did not motivate people toward increased religious commitment. Quite the contrary, as in the case of other conventional activities and institutions, psychopathology and neuroses will motivate toward religious isolation, estrangement, and apathy.[17] The question which, for present purposes, still remains is whether one may consider involvement in the Pentecostal-charismatic movement as conventional. Undoubtedly there are still forms of Pentecostalism which are excessively sectarian, wildly emotional, and accompanied by strange beliefs and practices. However, for large portions of the neo-Pentecostal and the Catholic charismatic renewal, and one must also add for large sections of the classical Pentecostal world, their form of religious life cannot be called unconventional. There was a time when it was. Here in the United States that lasted up until the end of World War II. Or if one was inclined to be very conservative one would say that it ceased to be unconventional by the beginning of the 1960s. Given the broad social spectrum of those involved, persons from every economic, educational, and occupational strata (and that in considerable numbers), given the growing acceptance by the historic churches, given the entrance into the movement of theologians and scholars who are in the process of elaborating a sophisticated theology of the renewal, and given the presence in the Catholic movement of prominent lay leaders, priests, bishops and, in Belgium, a cardinal, it seems highly inappropriate to suggest that this form of religious expression is unconventional. There seems to be some basis for suggesting that the Catholic charismatic renewal cannot be called unconventional religion. Highly sectarian and deviant movements tend to recruit people who exercise marginal roles in society or whose careers are at a turning point. Although the Catholic movement attracts some marginal individuals, the recruitment seems to be successful among people who are secure in their familial, academic, and occupational careers, who, unlike recruits to sectarian and deviant movements, do retain their ties with outsiders, those not in the movement.[18] Those are the best prospects for recruitment who do such conventional things as show loyalty to the church and who attend Mass. This would point not to a sectarian deviant character but to conventionality. The research of Meredith McGuire also points to how little Catholic charismatics differ from other Catholics, although "Pentecostal manifestations" are virtually unknown to American Catholics.[19] This, too, is a mark of conventionality.

PERSONALITY FACTORS AND TONGUES

It does not seem to this author that there is any significant correlation between psychologically deviant patterns and involvement in the Pentecostal-charismatic movement. Whether there is any significant correlation between psychologically deviant patterns and glossolalia is one question. A quite different question is whether there is any significant correlation between personality factors and glossolalia. This is still an open question. It would indeed be strange if something which plays such a central role in life is not related to psychological factors. To deny this would seem to postulate a religious existence which takes place in a psychological void. If one grants that involvement in the Pentecostal-charismatic renewal and psychological factors are significantly related, what is the nature of that correlation? What psychological factors are significant in a patterned way to such association? There seems to be general agreement that there is no such thing as a Pentecostal psychological personality type. If the psychological dynamics of movement involvement do not reach the degree or the pattern so that they constitute a psychological type, what are they? To date these factors have not been isolated and identified in any way as to constitute a scientific consensus.

Or is one dealing with a psychological constant, a pan-human capacity which belongs to the psychological structure of all who fall within the ample outer limits of normality? The capacity for this kind of religious experience might be interpreted differently, various mechanisms might be developed to encourage or discourage it, the forms in which it is expressed might differ in a cross-cultural examination. But if the capacity for this religious experience is a psychological constant, then how can one use this constant capacity to explain a variable, namely association with the Pentecostal-charismatic movement? Every social scientist knows that constants do not explain variables.

WHERE ARE THE ANSWERS TO BE FOUND?

These questions remain open. There is still room for disagreement, and such disagreement in fact exists. In 1972 William J. Samarin gave a paper on "The Bankruptcy of Psychologizing about the Gift of Tongues,"[20] in which he said that significant answers to the origins and growth of the charismatic renewal have not been forthcoming from psychologists and psychiatrists. He suggested that glossolalia cease being treated as abnormal behavior. What is needed, he suggested, is a sociolinguistic and cultural approach. In his major published work he repeated his conviction that "the attempt to explain glossolalia psychologically is not an impressive one. For one thing, prejudice has prevented many observers from seeing all that they should have seen."[21] One of the problems has been that psychologists and psychiatrists, occupied as they are with abnormal human behavior, have tended to see glossolalia in terms of aberrant behavior, ignoring or simply not knowing the "normal" base of glossolalia as a linguistic phenomenon.[22] Charles Waldegrave, as has been seen, also found that entrance into the Pentecostal-charismatic renewal was apparently not related to factors of personality.[23] Because psychology does not seem to have made a significant contribution in this area, Waldegrave suggests that the explanation of its origin and growth is to be found rather in sociology and anthropology. Virginia Hine tends to look elsewhere than to psychological factors, emphasizing that cross-cultural studies support the assumption that the capacity for ecstatic experience and trance and other associated behaviors is pan-human. Only the interpretation of it, the techniques designed to facilitate or inhibit it, and the form it takes differ cross-culturally.[24] Other researchers would take a quite different position. Though Kildahl does not find a specific Pentecostal personality type, according to him personality factors play a major role, specifically the need to submit to the external guidance of some trusted authority.[25] James T. Richardson, taking rather strong exception to the evaluation of recent literature by Virginia Hine, would give more weight to psychological factors. As he reads the research the weight of opinion "seems to be in favor of some sort of psychologically based explanation for the phenomenon."[26] What is one to think of this conflict of informed opinions?

FUTURE RESEARCH

With the exception of Vivier most of the psychological studies reviewed in this book are seriously defective in research design. On this point Richardson must be supported: much is without control groups and utilizes a "one-shot" design (without a time-series design, that is repeated testing of the persons along a time continuum). Indeed the research design in which a single group is studied only once, or studied without any other group with which it is compared—such a research design does not add to scientific knowledge. Some comparison is necessary, for instance, either before and after involvement in the Pentecostal movement, or a comparison of a group of Pentecostals with non-Pentecostals. The process of comparison is basic to scientific evidence and a research design in which there is not at least one comparison is defective. Many of these "one-shot" designs involve the collection of large amounts of specific detail, careful observation, and testing, but the care is labor lost and is what Campbell and Stanley call "misplaced precision."[27] Pentecostal research has its share of one-shot designs. Many of these only confirm prescientific wisdom.

It should be recognized that serious scholars of international repute do use such designs for Pentecostal research. Joseph Fichter's *The Catholic Cult of the Paraclete* is a case in point.[28] At the other end of the spectrum one finds exaggerated claims for the rate and degree of progress in knowledge which would result from truly scientific experiments—claims which are grandiosely overoptimistic and are accompanied by an unjustified depreciation of nonexperimental wisdom.[29]

There are some special problems those engaged in Pentecostal research must face. A time-series of experiments which would be directed toward testing persons before they associate themselves with the movement and again after association is obviously the ideal. The execution of this particular kind of time-series in Pentecostal research

faces serious difficulties as regards time, location of a suitable population, size of sampling, and, of course, financial resources. To some
extent the researcher must be able to predict from which group or
groups recruits for the movement will come. This kind of well-defined
situation is difficult to isolate. There are testing situations in which
researchers can engage in time-series testing without engaging in
prophecy. A case in point would be college students. With some ease
one can isolate and test those who have decided to go to college before
they actually enter and begin to be changed by the experience. In so
testing the Pentecostal movement one is faced with an entirely different situation. How does one locate those who will at some future date
decide to join the movement? How does one predict? In the Catholic
renewal it is not sufficient to test those in Life in the Spirit Seminars
since those involved have already been affected. The relatives, friends,
and acquaintances of those already in the movement would be a good
place to start. Though recruitment comes from these groups, they are
very extensive. Further, many friends and relatives do not join even
after being exposed to a committed witness. There are groups in which
such testing could take place, such as in a college town where a large
charismatic community exists. Here the student body constitutes a
probability population from which one could rightly expect recruits.
And it is rather well defined. If the testing situation is one in which
there is no limited population that might supply new adherents to the
movement, then the sampling has to be so great that by chance the
researcher snares a sufficient number who do, as a matter of fact,
decide to associate with the movement. Clearly there are research
designs, including control groups, short of this kind of time-series
testing, which are manageable and do more than confirm prescientific
knowledge.

To Samarin's remarks concerning the bankruptcy of the psychological investigation, the author would give partial assent. Psychological
research has not been highly successful. To some extent this is because
of the preoccupation of some psychologists with abnormal behavior.
Though not impressive the psychological research history is not a
blank. Some insights into the psychological dynamics of glossolalic
behavior have been gained, new perspectives have been opened, new
questions are being asked, some old myths have been laid to rest.

With Richardson's recommendation of longitudinal (time-series) research designs that allow for some assessment of change over a period
of time, the author would fully agree. If one can isolate the source from

which the glossolalic population is coming, as Vivier has in part done, then a time-series, including testing before and after involvement, is possible. How often such a situation arises is problematic.

Obviously the research done to date is not without meaning but the author would say that the most significant psychological research has still to be done. Hopefully, the research in this area will continue. The contributions psychology has and will make should not be lightly dismissed. Nor should it be suggested that in this one area of behavior the psychologists have nothing to contribute. The author, while not suggesting that the questions raised in this book have been answered in any definitive way, appends here what seem to him to be the assessments one might make at this point in the research history. If the most significant psychological research is still to be done, then at this stage one can only indicate in the most tentative way what seems to be emerging. What follows are not so much conclusions as the assessments proper to way-stations, to half-way houses. The assessments are made in view of the research presented in the preceding pages but also include the author's theological reflections on the data.

1. Evidence exists which seems to indicate a persistent and widespread suspicion that glossolalics are psychologically deprived. This suspicion is to be found not only at the level of folk psychiatry but among persons trained professionally in the behavioral sciences.

2. Religious needs per se must not be identified with neurotic insecurity or abnormal dependency.

3. The working assumption for those engaged in diagnostic work of a psychological or psychiatric nature should be that certain behavior patterns are within the rather liberal expanse of normality, unless there is interview or clinical evidence to the contrary. It seems unscientific to assume from the beginning that glossolalic behavior belongs to the field of abnormal psychology.

4. To date the evidence would indicate that the practice of speaking in tongues is found among mature, normal, well-adjusted persons. Every social, economic, or educational class is to be found represented in the Pentecostal-charismatic renewal. At this point in the research it has not been demonstrated that glossolalia as a psychological phenomenon is related in any immediately direct manner to personality variables. Though some glossolalics may be suffering from some neurotic or psychotic form of pathology, there is not sufficient evidence to show that glossolalia should be interpreted as per se deviant or pathological.

5. There is no stream of the movement which does not admit that

among those attracted to it are the emotionally unstable or the psycho-logically marginal members of the community. Emotional instability does not seem to characterize the Pentecostal-charismatic community.

6. In explaining why the movement begins and grows, psychological factors seem to be facilitating, not determining, factors. This is to say that certain psychological characteristics make entrance into the renewal easier but they do not determine that entrance.

7. Various theories have been developed to explain the growth of the movement. The theory of social and economic deprivation suggests that those who belong to the lower classes, and are without cultural and economic resources, are drawn to the Pentecostal-charismatic movement as compensation for their social and economic pains. The theory of social disorganization suggests that after disasters, when the patterns of society have been disrupted in a major way (e.g., after a war), people turn to the Pentecostal-charismatic movement for solace. Though these theories have been useful as partial explanations of the growth of the Pentecostal-charismatic movement in certain given cultural and historical situations, they cannot adequately account for its growth. The research would indicate that deprivation and social disorganization are facilitating, not determining factors.

8. Psychological factors such as suggestion and trance may be present either at what is called baptism in the Holy Spirit, the first experience of tongues, or at subsequent exercise of tongues. A light trance is not unusual the first time a person begins to speak in tongues. Sometimes there is a deep trance.

9. The presence of trance does not deprive the experience of its religious meaning. The ability to enter a trance seems to be a common, normal faculty rather than an abnormal and unusual one.

10. There is insufficient evidence to indicate that trance is present in every exercise of tongues. The more likely position is that trance is not always present.

11. Suggestion is part of the total process of socialization and this must be considered when evaluating the role of suggestion in the onset of tongues. Susceptibility to suggestion is more likely a sign of normality than of the presence of most neurotic and psychotic states. Dissociative states (trances), which may or may not be present, seem to be found within the range of normal behavior.

12. A leader and a group may use suggestion and social pressures to such an extent that the religious quality of the experience of tongues may be greatly diminished.

13. The experience of tongues does not seem to be related in any

necessary way to a leader or a group. There are sufficient instances to indicate that one can experience tongues without previous acquaintance with the phenomenon and without previous acquaintance with persons who speak in tongues. These experiences may take place either in the presence of a group or alone.

14. That a phenomenon has a psychological explanation does not exclude it from being a gift of the Spirit. One does not proceed on the assumption that that alone is spiritual and a gift of the Spirit which is without psychological dynamics and explanation. To proceed on such an assumption would remove religious experience from the human condition.

15. Cultural factors must be taken into consideration in evaluating psychological phenomenon. What might be considered deviant behavior in one culture may be considered normal in another. Even granting this principle, experiences in a religious context are more psychologically suspect of being neurotic or psychotic behavior the greater their emotional content. The more suspect they are psychologically, the less credence one gives to their religious content.

16. One would not want to divorce completely cultural phenomena, the subjects' interaction with the total socio-cultural environment, from psychological development. It seems that not only instinctual drives but also the beliefs and values of a culture constitute the data which are used to organize behavior.

17. Convincing evidence that there is such a thing as a Pentecostal personality type has not yet been brought to light. All types seem to be found within the movement. There is no determined cultural pattern or social group out of which Pentecostals and charismatics recruit new adherents.

18. Glossolalia is very likely learned behavior. This does not mean that a glossolalic necessarily learns a pattern of glossolalic utterance from someone else, though that is possible and happens in some Pentecostal-charismatic groups. It is learned behavior in the much more general sense that patterned vocalization is learned behavior and sounds which are already in one's language treasury are used. Some glossolalics come to the practice of glossolalia spontaneously, without having heard of the phenomenon, without having heard anyone speak in tongues.

19. That speaking in tongues is learned behavior does not militate against its being a gift of the Spirit. An exaggerated supernatural view of the gifts should be avoided. A gift of the Spirit is not necessarily a totally new endowment, a new faculty beyond those which belong to

a full humanity. A gift can be a natural capacity, exercised in the power of the Spirit, and directed to the service of Christ's kingdom. Tongues is very likely such a gift.

20. It is not true that what can be described in psychological terms is therefore not a true exercise of a charism, not of the Holy Spirit. This supposition would relegate the Spirit to some Platonic ideal world as it would presuppose that the Spirit operates in a psychological void. On the contrary, only what can be described in psychological terms is a true charism, even though the religious meaning and content is not adequately accounted for in psychological terms.

21. Glossolalics do not understand the meaning of what they are saying in the sense that one understands the meaning of a grammatically structured sentence. This is not an argument against their utterance being a gift of the Spirit.

22. That tongues is a human capacity and experience of which everyone is capable does not mean that it is not supernatural. To be supernatural it does not need to be miraculous and need not be a true language. To be supernatural, it is sufficient if the natural capacity is exercised under the power and inspiration of the Spirit, directed toward the building up of the body of Christ (the church) and toward the kingdom of God.

23. From a phenomenological as well as from a psychological point of view, speaking in tongues is very likely not a uniquely Christian event. It has yet to be demonstrated scientifically, however, that the phenomenon of speaking in tongues as it appears in a non-Christian context is, as a phenomenon, the same as is found among Pentecostals and charismatics. From a theological perspective there is no reason why such identity of phenomena in various religious and cultural contexts should be denied or be a source of embarrassment.

24. What gives speaking in tongues its meaning is not the supposition, here not accepted, of its being a totally new capacity, alien to man and given from above. Theologically the meaning of tongues is to be found in using this phenomenon common to all men for the building up of Christ's body and for the praise of the Father. The phenomenon in a Christian context has both its human dynamics and its religious content and meaning. In brief, what gives tongues its religious meaning is its function. This view in no way belittles what many Pentecostals and charismatics assert is the supernatural character of the gift of tongues.

25. The difference of theological explanation is not to be found in the

presence of God's power in one view and the absence of that power in another. Rather, the difference in theological views is to be found in the broader area of how one perceives the relation of nature and grace.

26. Many Pentecostals and charismatics have a two-level view of the relationship of nature and grace. In this view there is a certain complementarity between nature and supernature but the emphasis is on the distinction to the point of separation between the two. God makes dashes into history, sorties or forays into time but he is essentially at home outside both history and time. The point of departure for this theology is usually re-creation, that is, the Incarnation and Pentecost.

27. If the author accepts to use the nature-supernature vocabulary which Pentecostal-charismatic Christians use (which he does with reluctance), his own theological position would be quite different. He would view the relation of nature and grace as more wholistic, emphasizing the unity of all reality and the presence of God, Father, Son, and Holy Spirit, in the whole universe. God does not make sorties into history. While he is not identified with time and history, they are also his proper home.

28. No less than the other theological view, this view wishes to stress that God's gift of himself in creation and in redemption is free, gratuitous, and unmerited. The point of departure for this view is usually creation, with the Incarnation and the sending of the Spirit seen as further particularities of free gifts given already in creation. It emphasizes not only the unity of all reality but the unity of God's plan of salvation. Therefore a cosmic Christ and the Holy Spirit as the power of unity (Acts 2) are central concerns. Such a theology is essentially cosmic and developmental in its preoccupations.

NOTES,
BIBLIOGRAPHY,
INDEX

NOTES

CHAPTER 1

1. In this area I am indebted to Professor Jan van der Veken of Louvain University.
2. Johann Baptist Metz, "Miracle," *Sacramentum Mundi*, Herder and Herder, New York, 1969.
3. "Baptism in the Spirit and Speaking in Tongues: A Biblical Appraisal," *Theology Digest*, 21 (1973), 353.
4. This first appeared in Charles Journet's article in *Nova et Vetera*, no. 1, (1936), 77–79 and was later incorporated into his major work, *L'Eglise de Verbe Incarné*, D.D.B., Paris, 1951, vol. 2, pp. 504–06.
5. For the various approaches to normality and abnormality, cf. Arnold H. Buss, *Psychopathology*, John Wiley and Sons, New York, 1966, pp. 1–17; Leonard P. Ullmann and Leonard Krasner, *A Psychological Approach to Abnormal Behavior*, Prentice-Hall, Englewood Cliffs, 1969, pp. 9–24.
6. Virginia H. Hine, "Pentecostal Glossolalia: Toward a Functional Interpretation," *Journal for the Scientific Study of Religion*, 8 (1969), 217. The author is indebted to Mrs. Hine not only for the help she gave him as a fellow member of a research team but for the leads found in her article which is the best summary of psychological studies published before 1969.
7. J. M. Yinger, *Religion, Society and the Individual*, Macmillan, New York, 1957, pp. 91–94. Yinger comments on this assumption and rejects it.
8. Nathan L. and Louise B. Gerrard, "Scrabble Creek Folk" (unpublished multilithed manuscript, 1966); Nathan L. Gerrard, "The Serpent-handling Religions of West Virginia," *TransAction*, 6 (May, 1968), 22–28; Erika Bourguignon and Louanna Pettay, "Spirit Possession, Trance and Cross-Cultural Research," *Proceedings of the Annual Meeting of the American*

Ethnological Society (1964), 38–49; Hine, "Pentecostal Glossolalia: Toward a Functional Interpretation," *Journal for the Scientific Study of Religion*, 8 (1969), 211–226; William Samarin, *Tongues of Men and Angels: The Religious Language of Pentecostalism*, Macmillan, New York, 1972, pp. 18–19.

9. "Pope Paul Addresses the Charismatic Renewal," *New Covenant* (July, 1975), 23–25.

10. Walter Hollenweger, *The Pentecostals: The Charismatic Movement in the Churches*, trans. R. A. Wilson, Augsburg Publishing, Minneapolis, 1972, pp. 474–77.

CHAPTER 2

1. *From Max Weber: Essays in Sociology*, ed. H. H. Gert and C. Wright Mills, Oxford University Press: New York, 1946, p. 274. Weber also saw the rich turn to religion because it confirms them in their right to riches. "The fortunate [person] is seldom satisfied with the fact of being fortunate. Beyond this, he needs to know that he has a *right* to his good fortune. . . ." Ibid., p. 271.

2. *The Social Teaching of the Christian Churches*, trans. Olive Wyon, Macmillan, New York, 1931, vol. 1, p. 44.

3. *The Social Sources of Denominationalism*, World Publishing Company, Cleveland, 1929, p. 31.

4. Charles Y. Glock, "The Role of Deprivation in the Origin and Evolution of Religious Groups," *Religion and Social Conflict*, ed. Robert Lee and Martin E. Marty, Oxford University Press, New York, 1964, p. 26.

5. Glock would add two other kinds of deprivation, organismic and psychic. Organismic deprivation would include those deprived of good physical health. Therefore the blind, the deaf, the crippled, and the chronically ill. In Glock's categorization organismic deprivation would also include those suffering from neuroses or psychoses. Psychic deprivation is similar to ethical deprivation in that it is concerned with the meaning and purpose of life, but they are sought for their own sake rather than a source or norm to guide one's moral decisions. Ibid., pp. 26–33.

6. Boisen, "Economic Distress and Religious Experience," *Psychiatry*, 2 (1939), 193. Cf. also Boisen, *The Exploration of the Inner World: A Study of Mental Disorder and Religious Experience*, Harper & Row, New York, 1936; idem, *Religion in Crisis and Custom*, Harper & Row, New York, 1945.

7. Boisen, "Economic Distress and Religious Experience," p. 190.

8. Ibid., p. 194.

9. "Holiness Religion: Cultural Shock and Social Reorganization," *American Sociological Review*, 5 (1940), 740–47.

10. Ibid., p. 741.

11. *American Urban Communities*, (Harper & Row: New York, 1951), pp. 477–78.

12. *Millhands and Preachers*, (Yale University Press, New Haven, 1942).

13. Ibid., p. 136.

14. Ibid., p. 137.

15. Benton Johnston, "Do Holiness Sects Socialize in Dominant Values," *Social Forces*, 39 (1961–1962), 310.

16. "The Implications of Pentecostal Religion for Intellectualism, Politics,

and Race Relations," *The American Journal of Sociology*, 70 (1965), 404.

17. Russell R. Dynes, "Church-Sect Typology and Socio-Economic Status," *American Sociological Review*, 20 (1955), 559.

18. "Anomie and the 'Quest for Community': The Formation of Sects Among the Puerto Ricans of New York," *The American Catholic Sociological Review*, 21 (1960), 29.

19. *Culture and Personality Aspects of the Pentecostal Holiness Religion*, Mouton, The Hague, 1965.

20. "The Pentecostal Immigrants: A Study of an Ethnic Central City Church," *Journal for the Scientific Study of Religion*, 4 (1965), 183–97.

21. *The Ghost Dance: Origins of Religion*, Doubleday, Garden City, 1970, p. 287.

22. "En guise d'introduction, ou comment se sauver de l'anomie et de l'aliénation: Jesus People et Catholiques Pentecostaux," *Social Compass*, 21 (1974), 238.

23. "A Note on Relative Deprivation Theory as Applied to Millenarian and Other Cult Movements," reprinted in *Reader in Comparative Religion*, ed. William A. Lessa and Evon Z. Vogt, 2nd ed., Harper & Row, New York, 1965, p. 538. Relative deprivation theories had been applied in the two volumes, *The American Soldier*, of the four volume work, *Studies in Social Psychology in World War II*, Princeton University Press, Princeton, 1949. cf. also *Continuities in Social Research*, ed. Robert K. Merton and Paul F. Lazarsfeld, Free Press, Glencoe, Illinois, 1950, pp. 42–53, where the use of relative deprivation by the authors of *The American Soldier* is analyzed.

24. Glock, "The Role of Deprivation in the Origin and Evolution of Religious Groups," *Religion and Social Conflict*, p. 27.

25. "Affective Deprivation as a Factor in Crisis Movement Formation: A Current Example" (paper presented at the meeting of the Society for the Scientific Study of Religion, San Francisco, 1973). McGuire further develops this line of thought in chapter eleven of "People, Prayer and Promise: An Anthropological Analysis of a Catholic Charismatic Covenant Community" (Ph.D. diss., Ohio State University, Department of Anthropology, 1976).

26. Virginia H. Hine, "The Deprivation and Disorganization Theories of Social Movements," *Religious Movements in Contemporary America*, ed. Irving I. Zaretsky and Mark P. Leone, Princeton University Press, Princeton, 1974, p. 652.

27. Russell R. Dynes, "Rurality, Migration, and Sectarianism," *Rural Sociology*, 21 (1956), 28. Dynes's methodology can be criticized. Glock and Stark fault Dynes's research both in sample design and return rate. The sampling frame was the city telephone directory. That, however, gives a sampling biased against both the geographically mobile and the lower class who do not have telephones. Charles Y. Glock and Rodney Stark, *Religion and Society in Tension*, Rand McNally, Chicago, 1965, p. 189, n. 14. For the leads to the research of Dynes, Goldschmidt, Beers and Heflin, Giffin and Powles, I am indebted to Hart M. Nelsen and Hugh P. Whitt, "Religion and the Migrant in the City: A Test of Holt's Cultural Shock Thesis," *Social Forces*, 50 (1972), 379–84.

28. "Class Denominationalism in Rural California Churches," *The American Journal of Sociology*, 49 (1944), 354.

29. H. W. Beers and C. Heflin, "The Urban Status of Rural Migrants, *Social Forces*, 23 (1944), 36.

30. R. Giffin, "Appalachian Newcomers in Cincinnati," *The Southern Appala-*

chian Region: A Survey, ed. Thomas R. Ford, University of Kentucky Press, Lexington, 1962, p. 83.

31. W. E. Powles, "The Southern Appalachian Migrant: Country Boy Turned Blue-Collarite," *Blue-Collar World: Studies of the American Worker*, ed. Arthur B. Shostak and William Gomberg, Prentice-Hall, Englewood Cliffs, 1964, pp. 273–74.

32. Nelsen and Whitt, "Religion and the Migrant in the City: A Test of Holt's Cultural Shock Thesis," p. 381. Also worthy of note is William F. Whyte, *Street Corner Society*, University of Chicago, Chicago, 1943. Whyte's research demonstrates that sometimes social disorganization is more perceived than real. He intended to study the slum because he assumed it was socially disorganized. After prolonged study he found that it was highly organized but the patterns were not those of the middle class.

33. "Educational and Economic Composition of Religious Groups: An Analysis of Poll Data," *The American Journal of Sociology*, 48 (1942–1943), 574–79. The data were gathered by the American Institute of Public Opinion and the Office of Public Opinion Research.

34. Ibid., p. 579.

35. *Middletown*, Harcourt, Brace, New York, 1929, 344–70.

36. "Prestige Classes in a New York Rural Community," *Cornell University Agricultural Experiment Station, Memoire 260* (March, 1944), 4–5, 9–10, 15–21, and 36–38 (reprinted in *Class, Status and Power*, ed. Reinhard Bendix and Seymour Lipset, Free Press of Glencoe, 1953, pp. 190–203).

37. *Elmtown's Youth*, John Wiley, New York, 1949, pp. 83–120; Hollingshead, "Selected Characteristics of Classes in a Middle Western Community," *American Sociological Review*, 12(1947), 385–395. Hollingshead's research is based on a sample of adolescents rather than on the entire population of the area studied.

38. "Church Membership and Church Attendance in Madison, Wisconsin," *American Sociological Review*, 14 (1940), 384–389.

39. *Democracy in Janesville*, Harper & Row, New York, 1949, 153–54.

40. *The Religious Factor*, Doubleday, Garden City, 1961, 102–03.

41. "Some Social Status Criteria and Church Membership and Church Attendance," *The Journal of Social Psychology*, 49 (1959), 53–64.

42. Lenski, *The Religious Factor*, p. 44n.

43. "The Major Dimensions of Church Membership," *Review of Religious Research*, 2 (1960), 154–161.

44. Ibid., p. 159.

45. *Social Class in American Protestantism*, Rand McNally, Chicago, 1965.

46. Ibid., pp. 177–204. cf. also Demerath, "Social Class, Religious Affiliation, and Styles of Religious Involvement," *Class, Status, and Power*, 1966, pp. 388–94.

47. Charles Y. Glock, Benjamin Ringer, Earl R. Babbie, *To Comfort and to Challenge*, University of California Press, Berkeley, 1967, p. 98.

48. "Social Correlates of Religious Interest," *American Sociological Review*, 18 (1953), pp. 538, 540.

49. Ibid., p. 538.

50. Ibid., p. 544.

51. Walter Hollenweger, *The Pentecostals*, trans. R. A. Wilson, Augsburg Publishing House, Minneapolis, 1972, pp. 75–110; Hollenweger, "Pentecostalism and the Third World," *Dialog*, 9 (1970), 122–29; Christian Lalive

d'Epinay, *Haven of the Masses*, Friendship Press, New York, 1969; David B. Barrett, *Schism and Renewal in Africa*, Oxford University Press, Nairobi, 1968.

52. Hine, "The Deprivation and Disorganization Theories of Social Movements," p. 648.
53. Luther P. Gerlach and Virginia H. Hine, *People, Power, Change: Movements of Social Transformation*, Bobbs-Merrill, Indianapolis, 1970, p. 97.
54. Hine, "The Deprivation and Disorganization Theories of Social Movements," p. 651.
55. Gerlach and Hine, *People, Power, Change*, p. 97.
56. Ibid., p. 81.
57. *Church Growth in Mexico*, Eerdmans, Grand Rapids, 1963, pp. 98–99. Cf. pp. 102–03, 122, 132.
58. "Embodied Access," *Doomsday Cult*, Prentice Hall, Englewood Cliffs, New Jersey, 1966, pp. 90–110.
59. "Whereas Christians in Japan are reluctant to call upon their neighbors for evangelistic purposes, a survey of Soka Gakkai converts conducted by students at Tokyo University found that initial contact with the faith was made through the following channels: 35 percent by neighbours, 16.4 percent by relatives, 16.2 percent by colleagues at place of work, 12.8 percent by customers, 4.8 by a senior friend, and 14.8 percent by a miscellany of 'other' means. By far the most successful evangelistic thrust was made through neighbourhood contacts." *Stranger in the Land: A Study of the Church in Japan*, Lutterworth Press, London, 1967, p. 146.
60. Bultena, "Church Membership and Church Attendance in Madison, Wisconsin," p. 387.
61. Stanley C. Plog, "UCLA Conducts Research on Glossolalia," *Trinity*, 3 (1964), 38–39.
62. E. Mansell Pattison, "Speaking in Tongues and About Tongues," *Christian Standard*, 99 (February 15, 1964), 4.
63. Hine, "The Deprivation and Disorganization Theories of Social Movements," p. 655.
64. Ibid., pp. 656, 657.
65. The mean occupational level of the sample is well above that of the average of the area which is principally metropolitan Minneapolis-St. Paul. It is surely above that of a statistically random sample of participants in the larger classical Pentecostal movement.
66. Hine, "The Deprivation and Disorganization Theories of Social Movements," p. 660.
67. Gerlach and Hine, *People, Power, Change*, p. xxi.
68. "Spirit-Filled Catholics: Some Biographical Comparisons," *Social Compass*, 21 (1974), 311–24.
69. Ibid., p. 311.
70. Ibid., p. 312.
71. Ibid., p. 318.
72. Ibid., pp. 318–20.
73. "Sources of Recruitment to Catholic Pentecostalism," *Journal for the Scientific Study of Religion*, 13 (1974), 49–64. The data were gathered by a questionnaire distributed to three Michigan groups, with two hundred thirty-one questionnaires returned. Additional data were obtained by participating over an eight-month period in weekly meetings in Ann

Arbor and in the monthly Michigan Days of Renewal. The same questionnaire was sent to a probability sample of Catholic students attending the University of Michigan in Ann Arbor. This population was a prime target for evangelization and recruitment.

74. Ibid., p. 52.
75. Ibid., p. 56.
76. Ibid., p. 57.
77. Aberle, "A Note on Relative Deprivation Theory as Applied to Millenarian and Other Cult Movements," p. 539.
78. Glock, "The Role of Deprivation in the Origin and Evolution of Religious Groups," p. 26.
79. Gerlach and Hine, *People, Power, Change*, p. 97.

CHAPTER 3

1. This question is posed with greater urgency when the groups are markedly enthusiastic. It is only certain classical Pentecostal groups of a rather specific socio-economic and/or ethnic background which allow entirely unrestrained and uninhibited behavior. In most classical Pentecostal groups, in the Protestant neo-Pentecostal and Catholic charismatic groups there are restraints either in the form of a leader or nonformal understanding of what is acceptable. For classical Pentecostal and neo-Pentecostal groups cf. Luther P. Gerlach and Virginia H. Hine, *People, Power, Change: Movements of Social Transformation*, Bobbs-Merrill, Indianapolis, 1970, 14–15. For Catholic groups cf. Jim Cavnar, *Participating in Prayer Meetings*, Word of Life Publishers, Ann Arbor, 1974.
2. "The Speaking in Tongues and the Church," Episcopal diocese of Los Angeles, p. 5.
3. Ibid., p. 6.
4. "Report of the Special Commission on Glossolalia" to the Right Reverend Gerald Francis Burrill, Bishop of Chicago, December 12, 1960, p. 4.
5. "A Report on Glossolalia," p. 2. This is reprinted in "Towards a Mutual Understanding of Neo-Pentecostalism," ed. Walter Wietzke and Jack Hustad, Augsburg Publishing House, Minneapolis, 1973, 7–11.
6. Ibid.
7. Ibid.
8. "Report of the Field Study Committee on Speaking in Tongues," Commission on Evangelism of the American Lutheran Church, p. 9.
9. Ibid.
10. Ibid., p. 12.
11. Ibid., p. 13.
12. "A Statement with Regard to Speaking in Tongues," *Reports and Actions of the Second General Convention of the American Lutheran Church*, 1964, Exhibit J, pp. 162–64. This is reprinted in "Towards a Mutual Understanding of Neo-Pentecostalism," pp. 12–13.
13. Ibid.
14. Ibid.
15. "Pastoral Letter," Bishop James A. Pike, Bishop of California, May 2, 1963, p. 3.

16. Ibid., p. 4.
17. Ibid.
18. Ibid., p. 3.
19. Recounted in a letter to the author from J. B. Anderson, dated May 24, 1971. Also present during the conversation was Pastor Joseph Ottoson, a Lutheran minister.
20. *Trinity*, 1 (Christmastide 1961–1962), 8–11. Cf. also Stone, "California Episcopalians Receive Pentecostal Baptism," *Pentecostal Testimony*, 46 (June, 1962), 8–9. The "revival" in the Episcopal Church is described in Walter Hollenweger, *The Pentecostals: The Charismatic Movement in the Churches*, Augsburg Publishing House, Minneapolis, 1972, pp. 4–6. More extensive documentation can be found in Hollenweger, "Handbuch der Pfingstbewgung" (Ph.D. diss., University of Zürich, 1965, 02a.02.206).
21. Ibid., 08.417.001
22. "Preliminary Report, Study Commission on Glossolalia," Division of Pastoral Services, Diocese of California, May 2, 1963, p. 12.
23. Ibid.
24. Ibid.
25. "Glossolalia and Possession: An Appeal to the Episcopal Study Commission," *Journal for the Scientific Study of Religion*, 4 (Fall, 1964), 88. Sadler criticizes the study for its dominance of Freudian categories and the easy movement from theological assertion to psychological judgment. These factors become "an obstruction to genuine understanding." Ibid., p. 89.
26. *Voodoo in Haiti*, Oxford University Press, New York, 1959, p. 135.
27. S. F. Nadel, "A Study of Shamanism in the Nuba Mountains," *Royal Anthropological Institute of Great Britain and Ireland, Journal*, 76, part 1 (1946), 37. Cf. also Mircea Eliade, *Myths, Dreams and Mysteries*, Harper & Row, New York, 1960, p. 78; Eliade, *Shamanism: Archaic Techniques of Ecstasy*, Princeton University Press, Princeton, 1964, pp. 23–32. I. M. Lewis reviews the conflicting views and takes a position similar to that of Nadel and Eliade. Cf. Lewis, *Ecstatic Religion: An Anthropological Study of Spirit Possession and Shamanism*, Pelikan Books, Baltimore, 1971, pp. 178–205.
28. "Preliminary Report," p. 12.
29. Ibid., pp. 14–15.
30. Ibid., p. 17.
31. "Sixth International Conference," *New Covenant*, 2 (July, 1972), 2.
32. "Report of the Committee on Doctrine of the National Conference of Catholic Bishops," submitted to the bishops in their meeting in Washington, D.C., November 14, 1969. This report is printed in Edward O'Connor, *The Pentecostal Movement in the Catholic Church*, Ave Maria Press, Notre Dame, Indiana, 1971. The present reference is found on page 291.
33. Ibid., p. 292.
34. Ibid., pp. 292–293.
35. "Minutes of the 181st General Assembly (1969) of the United Presbyterian Church in the USA," p. 310.
36. Ibid.
37. Ibid., p. 311.
38. Ibid.
39. "Report of the Special Committee on the Work of the Holy Spirit," The United Presbyterian Church in the United States of America, Office of

the General Assembly, Philadelphia, 1970, p. 15. The report is not on glossolalia or speaking in tongues, as were the three Episcopal and the American Lutheran reports, but on the "Work of the Holy Spirit."

40. Ibid., p. 15.
41. Ibid.
42. Ibid.
43. Ibid., p. 11.
44. Ibid.
45. Ibid., p. 12
46. Ibid., p. 55.
47. *The Assembly's Digest*, The Presbyterian Church in the United States, 1965, p. 9.
48. Ibid.
49. Ibid.
50. Ibid., p. 10.
51. Ibid.
52. Ibid.
53. Ibid., p. 11.
54. Ibid.
55. Ibid., pp. 11–12.
56. Ibid., p. 12.
57. Ibid.
58. The report appeared in printed form but has no indication of publisher or place.
59. "The Person and Work of the Holy Spirit," p. 14.
60. Ibid., p. 15.
61. Ibid.
62. Ibid.
63. "Declaration of the Bishops of Puerto Rico on the Pentecostal Movement," translated from *El Imparcial*, June 15, 1972.
64. Ibid.
65. Ibid.
66. Ibid.
67. Ibid.
68. Ibid.
69. Ibid.
70. "The Charismatic Movement and Lutheran Theology," a Report of the Commission on Theology and Church Relations of the Lutheran Church-Missouri Synod, January, 1972.
71. Ibid., p. 23.
72. "The Charismatic Movement and Lutheran Theology," pp. 14, 28.
73. "Das Abendmahl im Neuen Testament und in der frühen Kirche," Kühne Verlag, Wetzhausen, 1969; "Charisma und Amt," Calwer Verlag, Stuttgart, 1967²; "Gemeinde ist Anders: Verwirklichung neutestamentlicher Gemeindeordnung innerhalb der Volkskirche," Calwer Verlag, Stuttgart, 1966; *Gifts and Graces: A Commentary on 1 Corinthians 12–14*, trans. Herbert Klassen, Eerdmans, Grand Rapids, 1967; *Glossolalia: Wert und Problematik des Sprachenredens*, Kühne Verlag, Hanover, 1967²; "Gottesdienst Heute," Calwer Verlag, Stuttgart, 1968; *Im Kraftfeld des Heiligen Geistes*, R. F. Edel, Marburg an der Lahn, 1968; Kilian McDonnell and Arnold Bittlinger, "The Baptism in the Holy Spirit as an Ecumenical

Problem," Charismatic Renewal Services, Notre Dame, 1972.

74. Twelve Missouri Synod pastors involved in the renewal within the Lutheran Church-Missouri Synod have taken the occasion of "The Charismatic Movement and Lutheran Theology" to explain to the Synod how they understand the charismatic renewal in "Lutherans, the Spirit, the Gifts, and the Word," published privately in a tentative form in 1973. The twelve pastors do not conceive of this publication as a reply to the Synod's pamphlet but rather as an attempt to enter into dialogue with the Synod. This publication, which the author has seen only in its tentative form, contains some witness material, theological and exegetical explanations, and some practical pastoral suggestions. The psychological dimension of the renewal is not discussed. Copies of this material are available from Rev. Delbert Rossin, 1727 Kaneville Road, Geneva, Illinois.

75. Kilian McDonnell, "The Relationship of the Charismatic Renewal to the Established Denominations," *Dialog*, 13 (1974), 223–29.

76. *Touched By the Spirit*, Augsburg, Minneapolis, 1975. Tormod Engelsviken, a Norwegian scholar, has spent time at the Institute for Ecumenical and Cultural Research, Collegeville, Minnesota, and at Wartburg Seminary, Dubuque, developing a theology of the charismatic renewal which is authentically Lutheran.

77. "Lutheran Theologians Discuss Doctrine of the Holy Spirit," *Lutheran Charismatic Renewal Newsletter*, 1 (January 1975), 3.

78. Ibid.

79. "Policy Statement Regarding the Neo-Pentecostal Movement," p. 1.

80. Ibid.

81. Ibid., p. 2.

82. Ibid.

83. Ibid., p. 3.

84. Ibid.

85. Three questions were asked. "Is it your opinion that the baptism with the Holy Spirit which once took place on Pentecost occurs within the Christian Church also today?" "Do you believe that you have received this baptism? "Do you think that you have received one or more of the special charismatic gifts which God gave the Apostles in the early church?" The student was asked to check one of five possible answers to each of these three questions: No, Uncertain, No Opinions, Reasonably Certain, Yes. The student was asked to comment on each question and to sign the questionnaire.

86. *L'Osservatore Romano*, October 11, 1973.

87. Ibid.

88. Published as a paper by the Lutheran Church in America, 231 Madison Avenue, New York City.

89. Ibid., p. 19.

90. Ibid., p. 17.

91. Ibid.

92. Ibid., p. 8.

93. Ibid., p. 9.

94. "The Charismatic Movement within the Church of Scotland," Report of the Panel on Doctrine, May 1974, p. 17.

95. Ibid.

96. Ibid., p. 2.
97. Ibid., p. 3.
98. Ibid., p. 7.
99. Ibid., p. 8.
100. Ibid., p. 18.
101. Ibid., p. 15.
102. Ibid., p. 13.
103. Ibid., p. 9.
104. Ibid., p. 15.
105. Ibid., p. 9.
106. Ibid.
107. Ibid., p. 15.
108. Ibid., p. 16.
109. Ibid.
110. "Message des Evêques de l'Inter-Ouest du Quebec sur le Renouveau Charismatique Catholique," vol. 6, no. 140, *Orientations Pastorales*, November 1974.
111. Publications Office, United States Catholic Conference, 1312 Massachusetts Avenue N.W., Washington, D.C.
112. Ibid., p. 1.
113. Ibid., p. 3.
114. Ibid.
115. Ibid.
116. Ibid., p. 4.
117. Ibid., p. 5.
118. Ibid., p. 6.
119. "Message of the Canadian Bishops Addressed to all Canadian Catholics," Publications Service, Canadian Catholic Conference, 90 Parent Avenue, Ottawa.
120. "Theological and Pastoral Orientations on the Catholic Charismatic Renewal," *Word of Life*, Ann Arbor, Michigan, 1974. This document, prepared under the direction of Cardinal Suenens of Belgium, was issued by an international team of theologians and lay leaders who met in Malines, Belgium, in May 1974. A second international team of theological consultants gave suggestions which were incorporated into the final text. The consultants include Yves Congar, Avery Dulles, Michael Hurley, Walter Kasper, René Laurentin, Joseph Ratzinger. The Malines Document has no official standing but has been widely accepted as an authoritative statement.
121. "Message of the Canadian Bishops Addressed to All Canadian Catholics," p. 3.
122. Ibid., p. 4.
123. Ibid., p. 5.
124. Ibid.
125. Ibid., p. 6.
126. Ibid., p. 10.
127. Ibid.
128. *L'Osservatore Romano*, May 20, 1975. English text of the address in *New Covenant*, 5 (July 1975), 23–25.
129. Ibid., p. 23.
130. Ibid., p. 24.

131. Ibid., p. 25.
132. Ibid.
133. "Au Fil du Temps," *Pastoralia: Communications de l'Archevêché de Malines—Bruxelles*, Juin-Juillet, 1975, p. 87.
134. Quoted in Bert Ghezzi, "A Joyful Pilgrimage: Report on the 1975 International Conference," *New Covenant*, 5 (July 1975), 18.
135. "A collective letter from the Episcopacy of Panama concerning the movement of renewal in the Spirit, directed to priests, religious and lay people who work in apostolic movements," August 15, 1975.
136. Ibid.
137. Ibid.
138. Ibid.
139. Ibid.
140. Ibid.
141. "1975's Top News: Ethical Dilemmas," *Christian Century*, 92 (1975), 1195.
142. Reprinted in *The National Courier*, November 18, 1975.
143. Ruthann Garlock and John Galey, "Will Ouster Create More Conflict," ibid.

CHAPTER 4

1. " 'Possession' in a Revivalistic Negro Church," *Journal for the Scientific Study of Religion*, 1 (1961), 204–13.
2. "Personality, Pentecostalism, and Glossolalia: A Research Note on Some Unsuccessful Research," *Canadian Review of Sociology and Anthropology*, 5 (1968), 38.
3. " 'Possession' in a Revivalistic Negro Church," p. 209: "A Culture or sub-culture composed of either hysterics or schizophrenics would be difficult to imagine."
4. Ibid., p. 92.
5. *Hypnosis and Related States*, International Universities Press, New York, 1959. ". . . psychiatric patients are on the whole poorer subjects [for hypnosis] than those judged by ordinary standards to be 'normal' " (p. 78).
6. *Hypnotic Induction of Anxiety*, Charles C. Thomas, Springfield, Illinois, 1964, pp. 207, 327, 331.
7. Ernest R. Hilgard, Josephine R. Hilgard, *Hypnotic Susceptibility*, Harcourt, Brace and World, New York, 1965.
8. Ibid., p. 295. Cf. also pp. 331, 342, 349, 374.
9. C. L. Hull, *Hypnosis and Suggestibility: An Experimental Approach*, D. Appleton-Century, New York, 1933.
10. "Altered States of Consciousness," *Trance and Possession States*, ed. Raymond Prince, Proceedings of Second Annual Conference, R. M. Bucke Memorial Society, March 1966, Montreal, 1968, p. 89.
11. Alland, " 'Possession' in a Revivalistic Negro Church," p. 213.
12. Ibid., p. 211.
13. Ibid., p. 209. David M. Beckmann, "Trance: From Africa to Pentecostalism," *Concordia Theological Monthly*, 45 (January, 1974), 11–26, argues that "trance, of which speaking in tongues is a stylized form, is a gift which

Afro-Americans brought with them into Christianity" (p. 11). Beckmann has six theses: "1. Outside the Christian tradition the religious cult in which trance is sought as evidence of spirit possession is characteristic only of African culture. Trance in African cults is strikingly similar to trance in American Christianity. 2. Within the Christian tradition there were only a few minor instances of trance attributed to the Holy Spirit before the Second Great Awakening. Trance was usually attributed to demons. 3. The widespread occurrence of trance during the Second Great Awakening was associated with the first major successes in evangelism among Afro-American slaves. 4. Some of the earliest documents of Afro-American religion report the continued incidence of trance. 5. Pentecostalism began in a revival among Afro-Americans. 6. Pentecostal missions have generally been best received in those parts of the world most influenced by Africa" (pp. 11–12).

Beckmann's position merits further attention but as presented in this article it lacks conviction. For instance, his definition of trance as "an altered state of consciousness accompanied by agitation or activity" would not correspond to a large number of Pentecostals and charismatics who are in trance but are neither agitated nor engaged in "activity." He seems to confuse cultural factors which are facilitating with those which are determining. Also cultural similarities do not mean cultural dependence. To assert that the origins of the classical Pentecostal movement in the United States was black is to oversimplify. The beginnings were interracial. Finally, the exceptions to his own theses which he himself cites greatly weaken his own position. However, Beckmann has pointed to an aspect of the Pentecostal movement which still has to be reckoned with, namely the importance of black Africa for the church of the future in general and Pentecostalism in general. cf. Alland, " 'Possession' in a Revivalistic Negro Church," p. 209. Alland's research is more interesting than convincing. There are no longitudinal studies of persons before and after their Pentecostal involvement, no time-sequence interviews after such involvement, and no control groups. Like many other studies reviewed here, Alland's research suggests topics for further research but does not give scientifically verifiable answers.

14. James N. Lapsley and John H. Simpson, "Speaking with Tongues," *The Princeton Seminary Bulletin*, 58 (February, 1965), 6.
15. Margaret J. Field, *Search for Security*, Northwestern University Press, Evanston, Illinois, 1960, p. 19.
16. "Trance," an unpublished paper presented at the annual meeting of the Central States Anthropological Society, Chicago, April 27–29, 1967, p. 4.
17. *Speaking in Tongues: A Cross-Cultural Study of Glossolalia*, The University of Chicago Press, Chicago, 1972, p. 8.
18. Ibid., p. 124.
19. Goodman, "Phonetic Analysis of Glossolalia in Four Cultural Settings," *Journal for the Scientific Study of Religion*, 8 (1969), 238.
20. *Tongues of Men and Angels: The Religious Language of Pentecostalism*, Macmillan, New York, 1972, p. 33.
21. "Glossolalia as Regressive Speech," *Language and Speech*, 16 (January–March, 1973), 85–86.
22. "Toward a Typology of Formal Communicative Behaviors: Glossolalia,"

Anthropological Linguistics, vol. 9, no. 8 (1967), 7; cf. also Stanley C. Plog, "UCLA Conducts Research on Glossolalia," *Trinity,* 3 (Whitsuntide, 1964), 38–39.

23. H. B. English and A. C. English, *A Comprehensive Dictionary of Psychological and Psychoanalytic Terms,* Longmans Green, New York, 1958.

24. "The Trance," *Comprehensive Psychiatry,* 8 (1967), 11–12. Using the more comprehensive category of "Altered States of Consciousness," Ludwig defines them in the following somewhat confusing fashion: "Mental states . . . which can be recognized subjectively by the individual himself (or by an objective observer of the individual) as representing a sufficient deviation, in terms of subjective experiences or psychological functioning, from certain general norms as determined by the subjective experience and psychological functioning of that individual during alert, waking consciousness" ("Altered States of Consciousness," *Trance and Possession States,* pp. 69–70).

25. T. X. Barber and D. S. Calverley, " 'Hypnotic Behavior' as a Function of Task Motivation," *Journal of Psychology,* 54 (1962), 363–89.

26. "Trance," p. 5.

27. "Hypnosis and the Concept of the Generalized Reality-Orientation," *American Journal of Psychotherapy,* 13 (1959), 591. "I was reading a rather difficult scientific book which required complete absorption of thought to follow the argument. I had lost myself in it, and was unaware of the passage of time and of my surroundings. Then, without warning, something was intruding upon me; a vague, nebulous feeling of change. It all took place in a split-second, and when it was over I discovered that my wife had entered the room and had addressed a remark to me. I was then able to call forth the remark itself which had somehow etched itself into my memory, even though at the time it was spoken I was not aware of it" (p. 591).

28. Erika Bourguignon and Louanna Pettay, "Spirit Possession, Trance and Cross-Cultural Research," *Proceedings of the Annual Meeting of the American Ethnological Society,* (1964), 40.

29. Ibid., p. 39.

30. Bourguignon, "The Self, the Behavior Environment and the Theory of Spirit Possession," *Context and Meaning in Cultural Anthropology,* ed. Melford E. Spiro, Free Press, New York, 1965, p. 45. Field, *Search for Security,* pp. 55–56, holds that there seems to be no more reason to suppose that dissociation is necessarily hysterical than to suppose that laughter is hysterical.

31. *Glossolalia: Wert und Problematik des Sprachenredens,* 2nd ed., Kühne Verlag, Hanover, 1967, p. 10.

32. "Speaking in Tongues and About Tongues," *Christian Standard,* 99 (February 15, 1964), 4.

33. *Speaking in Tongues: A Cross-Cultural Study of Glossolalia,* pp. 72, 87–125.

34. Ibid., p. 123.

35. *The Psychology of Speaking in Tongues,* Harper & Row, New York, 1972, p. 53.

36. "Behavioral Science Research on the Nature of Glossolalia," *Journal of the American Scientific Affiliation,* 20 (September, 1968), 80.

37. "The Sociolinguistics of Glossolalia" (master's thesis, Hartford Seminary Foundation, 1966, p. 91).

172   CHARISMATIC RENEWAL AND THE CHURCHES

38. "Glossolalia as Learned Behavior," *Canadian Journal of Theology*, 15 (January, 1969), 60.
39. Ibid., p. 62.
40. Kildahl, *The Psychology of Speaking in Tongues*, pp. 37–39.
41. Samarin, "Glossolalia as Learned Behavior," p. 62.
42. Ibid., p. 64.
43. Luther P. Gerlach and Virginia H. Hine, *People, Power, Change: Movements of Social Transformation*, Bobbs-Merrill, Indianapolis, 1970, p. 113.
44. L. M. Vivier, "Glossolalia" (Ph.D. diss., University of Witwatersrand, 1960, p. 436). This dissertation is available on microfilm at such libraries as University of Chicago, Union Theological Seminary, St. John's University, Collegeville, Minnesota.
45. "Interim Report on the Study of the Pentecostal Movement Conducted by the Anthropology Department of the University of Minnesota," research report, University of Minnesota, 1967.
46. Wolfram, "The Sociolinguistus of Glossolalia," p. 20.
47. *De la Glossolalie chez les Premiers Chrétiens et des Phénomènes Similaires*, Georges Bridel, Lausanne, 1910.
48. Ibid., p. 111.
49. Ibid., pp. 112–13.
50. Ibid., pp. 14, 142.
51. Ibid., p. 232. Lombard's formulation is: "Au point de vue de la psychologie du language, le parler en langues offre un caractère d'infantilisme et d'émotivité. . . ."
52. *Das Zungenreden, geschichtlich und psychologisch Untersucht*, J.C.B. Mohr (Paul Siebeck), Tübingen, 1911, pp. 101ff.
53. Ibid., p. 114.
54. Ibid.
55. "Transformation Symbolism in the Mass," *Psychology and Religion: West and East*, 2nd ed. (*The Collected Works of C. G. Jung*, vol. 11), Princeton University Press, Princeton, 1969, p. 284.
56. Oskar Pfister, *Die Psychologische Enträselung der Religiösen Glossolalie und der Automatischen Kryptographie (Sonderabdruck aus dem Jahrbuch für Psychoanalytische und Psychopathologische Forschungen*, III Band), Franz Deuticke, Leipzig und Wien, 1912, p. 94.
57. Ibid.
58. *Speaking with Tongues, Historically and Psychologically Considered*, Yale University Press, New Haven, 1927, pp. 165–66.
59. Ibid., p. 160.
60. Ibid., pp. 162, 168.
61. Ibid.
62. Virginia H. Hine, "Pentecostal Glossolalia: Toward a Functional Interpretation," *Journal for the Scientific Study of Religion*, 8 (Fall, 1969), 213.
63. Anton Boisen, "Economic Distress and Religious Experience: A Study of the Holy Rollers," *Psychiatry*, 2 (1930), 194.
64. *Religion in Crisis and Custom: A Sociological and Psychological Study*, Harper & Row, New York, 1945, p. 71.
65. Ibid., p. 90.
66. Ibid., pp. 93–94.
67. Ibid., p. 94.
68. "Economic Distress and Religious Experience: A Study of the Holy Rollers," p. 190.

69. L. M. Vivier, "Glossolalia." Vivier tested a group of glossolalics and had two control groups. The first control group believed in glossolalia but as a matter of fact did not practice it, while the second control group came from the orthodox reformed church or traditionalists who did not believe in glossolalia. All three groups filled out two questionnaires: one more biographical and the other related more specifically to the religious background. Tests administered were the Willoughby Test, the Thematic Apperception Test, tests for suggestibility (including the Body or Postural Sway Test; arm or hand levitation, Cevreal Pendulum), and the Rosenzweig Picture Frustration Test.

70. Fifteen of the twenty-four glossolalics were originally members of the non-Pentecostal church which furnished subjects for the control group of Christians who did not speak in tongues. Further, eleven of the members of the control group of pretongue speakers were originally members of the non-Pentecostal church. James T. Richardson suggests that Vivier has actually studied persons who are in various stages of moving from a community in which glossolalia was not allowed to another community where it was the norm. Cf. "Psychological Interpretations of Glossolalia: A Reexamination of Research," *Journal for the Scientific Study of Religion*, 12 (1973), 199–207.

71. Vivier, "Glossolalia," p. 432.

72. *Sects and Society*, University of California Press, Berkeley, 1961, p. 113.

73. Vivier, "The Glossolalic and his Personality," *Beiträge zur Ekstase*, ed. T. H. Spoerri, S. Karger, Basel, 1968, p. 169.

74. Ibid. "It was felt that this test [Willoughby] would give an overall picture of the general level of neuroticism of the different groups, as well as for intragroup comparison between the frequent and the non-frequent speakers in tongues. . . . This is a test for persistent unadaptive anxiety reactions, i.e., for neuroticism, and the neuroticisms revealed by the questionnaire relate mainly to common types of social situations" (Vivier, "Glossolalia," p. 210). James Richardson misreads Vivier. He interprets Vivier to say that the "Test Group [glossolalics] was more anxious, had more difficulty in nervous control, was more unstable" ("Psychological Interpretations of Glossolalia: A Reexamination of Research," p. 204). Richardson is interpreting Vivier in terms of the unprinted doctoral dissertation. Reporting on the Willoughby test, Vivier says that "the Test Group [glossolalics] is significantly more sensitive than Control B [traditionalists who do not believe in glossolalia]" ("Glossolalia," p. 337). Richardson concluded that because the glossolalics were more sensitive they were therefore more neurotic. This is an unwarranted deduction. Vivier continues: "As regards the factor of unadaptive anxiety there is no significant difference" (p. 337). "The three groups are similar in the general tendency to repression" (p. 344). However, "Test Group and Control Group A are more likely to use the mechanism of repression in frustrating situations" (p. 343). Vivier is much more clear when he reviews the same research in his essay, "The Glossolalic and his Personality," in *Beiträge zur Ekstase*, a publication of which Richardson is not aware, where Vivier says that "glossolalia is clearly not associated with neuroticism" (p. 169).

Richardson rightly quotes the dissertation as saying that glossolalics are more superstitious. It should be noted that Vivier uses a psychiatric category, not a theological one. Part of the working definition of his superstition category is "a belief in supernatural forces both evil and good" (p. 331).

75. "The Glossolalic and his Personality," p. 169; "Glossolalia," p. 364.
76. "The Glossolalic and his Personality," p. 170.
77. Ibid. Malony et al. note that "it is suggestive, but not conclusive, to know that glossolalics are *less* suggestible than controls (Vivier, 1960) if one does not control for social class, prior exposure and/or group expectancy." See H. Newton Malony, Nelson Zwaanstra, and James W. Ramsey, "Personal and Situational Determinants of Glossolalia: A Literature Review and Report of Ongoing Research," paper presented at the International Congress of Religious Studies, Los Angeles, 1972.
78. "The Glossolalic and his Personality," p. 170.
79. "Glossolalia," p. 432.
80. "The Glossolalic and his Personality," pp. 173–74.
81. "Glossolalia," pp. 432–33.
82. Carl Jung, *Civilization in Transition*, trans. R. F. C. Hull, Pantheon Books, New York, 1964, p. 265.
83. "The Glossolalic and his Personality," p. 174.
84. John B. Oman, "On 'Speaking in Tongues': A Psychological Analysis, *Pastoral Psychology*, vol. 14, no. 139 (1963), 49.
85. Ibid., p. 51.
86. Ibid., p. 49.
87. Kiev, "Psychotherapeutic Aspects of Pentecostal Sects Among West Indian Immigrants to England," *British Journal of Sociology*, 15 (1964), 135.
88. "Beliefs and Delusions of West Indian Immigrants to London," *British Journal of Psychiatry*, 109 (1963), 362. Cf. also Kiev, "The Study of Folk Psychiatry," *Magic, Faith and Healing: Studies in Primitive Psychiatry*, ed. Ari Kiev, Free Press, New York, 1964, pp. 3–35.
89. Kiev, "Beliefs and Delusions of West Indian Immigrants to London," p. 363.
90. T. H. Spoerri. *Sprachphänomene und Psychose*, S. Karger, Basel, 1964, p. 133.
91. "Ekstatische Zustände bei Schizophrenen," *Beiträge zur Ekstase*, ed. T. H. Spoerri, S. Karger, Basel, 1968, pp. 115–36.
92. *Tongue Speaking: An Experiment in Spiritual Experience*, Doubleday, Garden City, New York, 1964, pp. 194–95.
93. Ibid.
94. Ibid., p. 208.
95. Ibid., p. 199.
96. Ibid., pp. 207–08.
97. Ibid., pp. 203, 206–09.
98. Ibid., pp. 209–10.
99. *Culture and Personality Aspects of the Pentecostal Holiness Religion*, Mouton and Co., The Hague, 1965.
100. Ibid., p. 97.
101. Ibid., p. 103.
102. Ibid., pp. 36, 47.
103. Ibid., p. 105.
104. Cohn, "Personality, Pentecostalism, and Glossolalia: A Research Note on Some Unsuccessful Research," p. 38; Hine, "Pentecostal Glossolalia: Toward a Functional Interpretation," p. 215.
105. *Battle for the Mind: A Physiology of Conversion and Brainwashing*, Harper & Row, New York, 1959, pp. 51–75.

106. Ibid., 119–41; 143–217. A critique of *Battle for the Mind* is given by D. Martyn Lloyd-Jones, "Conversions: Psychological and Spiritual," Inter-Varsity Press, London, 1959.

107. *Persuasion and Healing: A Comparative Study of Psychotherapy,* Johns Hopkins Press, Baltimore, 1961.

108. Ibid., p. 76.

109. Ibid., pp. 81–82.

110. "Psychopathology and Religious Commitment," *Review of Religious Research,* 12 (1971), 167.

111. "UCLA Conducts Research on Glossolalia," pp. 38–39.

112. Ibid., p. 39.

113. Lapsley and Simpson, "Speaking in Tongues: Token of Group Acceptance and Divine Approval," *Pastoral Psychology,* 15 (May, 1964), 54–55.

114. Lapsley and Simpson, "Speaking in Tongues: Infantile Babble or Song of the Self?" *Pastoral Psychology,* 15 (September, 1964), 18.

115. Ibid., p. 19.

116. Ibid., p. 20.

117. Leonhard Steiner, *Mit Flogenden Zeichen,* Verlag Mission für das volle Evangelium, Basel, 1954, pp. 195–202.

118. Lapsley and Simpson, "Speaking in Tongues: Infantile Babble or Song of the Self?" pp. 20–21.

119. Ibid., p. 24.

120. Ibid.

121. "Speaking in Tongues and About Tongues," p. 100.

122. Ibid.

123. Ibid., p. 101.

124. Ibid., p. 100.

125. Ibid.

126. "Behavioral Science Research on the Nature of Glossolalia," p. 81.

127. Ibid., pp. 80–81.

128. Ibid., p. 76.

129. Ibid.

130. "Ideological Support for the Marginal Middle Class: Faith Healing and Glossolalia," *Religious Movements in Contemporary America,* ed. Irving I. Zaretsky and Mark P. Leone, Princeton University Press, Princeton, 1974, pp. 418–55.

131. Ibid., p. 422.

132. Ibid., p. 445.

133. Ibid., pp. 446–47.

134. Ibid., p. 446.

135. Ibid.

136. Nathan L. Gerrard and Louise B. Gerrard, "Scrabble Creek Folk," (unpublished multilithed manuscript, 1966). A much abbreviated report of this research can be found in Nathan L. Gerrard, "The Serpent-handling Religions of West Virginia," *TransAction,* 6 (May, 1968), 22–28. Cf. also Nathan L. Gerrard, "The Holiness Movement in Southern Appalachia," *The Charismatic Movement,* ed. Michael P. Hamilton, Eerdmans, Grand Rapids, 1975, pp. 159–71.

137. Nathan and Louise Gerrard, "Scrabble Creek Folk," p. 55.

138. Ibid., p. 69.

139. Ibid., p. 67.

140. Ibid., p. 56.

141. Ibid., p. 70.
142. Ibid., pp. 80–81.
143. Ibid., p. 67. For present purposes Weston La Barre's *They Shall Take Up Serpents*, University of Minnesota Press, Minneapolis, 1962, is not specific enough to be helpful. La Barre attempts a psychiatric analysis of a subculture, that of the snake handlers. This is done in strongly Freudian categories and is nonspecific. No statistical studies were made and only one snake handler, a Reverend Barefoot, is analyzed in detail.
144. Gerrard, "The Holiness Movement in Southern Appalachia," p. 171.
145. Nathan and Louise Gerrard, "Scrabble Creek Folk," p. 56.
146. "Psychological Interpretations of Glossolalia: A Reexamination of Research," p. 205.

CHAPTER 5

1. "A Socio-Psychological Study of Glossolalia," *Glossolalia*, Frank Stagg, E. Glenn Hinson, Wayne E. Oates, Abingdon Press, Nashville, 1967, pp. 76–99.
2. Ibid., p. 77.
3. Oates, *The Holy Spirit and Contemporary Man*, Baker Book House, Grand Rapids, Michigan, 1968, p. 56.
4. Ibid., p. 55.
5. "A Socio-Psychological Study of Glossolalia," p. 89.
6. Ibid., pp. 90–91.
7. Ibid., p. 93.
8. Ibid., p. 95.
9. "Behavioral Science Research on the Nature of Glossolalia," *Journal of the American Scientific Affiliation*, 20 (1968), 83–84.
10. "Trance and Dissociation: A Cross-Cultural Study in Psychophysiology" (master's thesis, University of Minnesota, 1966, pp. 80–82).
11. "The Pentecostal Movement: Three Perspectives," *Scholastic*, 109 (April 21, 1967), 15–17, 32.
12. Ibid., p. 16.
13. Ibid., p. 17.
14. Ibid., p. 16.
15. Ibid., p. 17.
16. *Tongues of Men and Angels: The Religious Language of Pentecostalism*, Macmillan, New York, 1972, p. 235.
17. Ibid., p. 2. As a definition this is defective because there are a number of persons who speak in tongues who do not consider tongues to be a true language. This would not be difficult to document.
18. Ibid., pp. 127, 178.
19. Ibid., p. 211.
20. Ibid., p. 127.
21. Ibid., p. 227.
22. Ibid., p. 113.
23. Ibid., p. 25.
24. Ibid., p. 231.
25. Ibid., p. 227.

26. Ibid.
27. Ibid., p. 228.
28. Ibid.
29. Samarin, "Variation and Variables in Religious Glossolalia," *Language in Society*, 1 (1972), 121–30.
30. Samarin, *Tongues of Men and Angels*, p. 72.
31. Ibid., p. 52.
32. Ibid., p. 51.
33. Ibid., pp. 22–23.
34. Ibid.
35. Ibid., p. 204.
36. Ibid.
37. Ibid., p. 198.
38. Ibid., p. 234.
39. Ibid., p. 210.
40. Ibid., p. 234.
41. Ibid., p. 117.
42. Ibid., p. 233.
43. Ibid., pp. xiii–xiv.
44. "Some Secular Implications of the Pentecostal Denomination" (master's thesis, University of Minnesota, 1969).
45. Two psychological tests were used, The Conceptual Systems Test and Dean's Alienation Scale.
46. "Some Personality Correlates of Religious Attitudes as Determined by Projective Techniques," *Psychological Monographs*, 66 (1952), 3–26.
47. Sorem, "Some Secular Implications of the Pentecostal Denomination," pp. 56–60.
48. Ibid., p. 58.
49. Ibid., p. 61.
50. "Pentecostal Glossolalia: Toward a Functional Interpretation," *Journal for the Scientific Study of Religion*, 8 (1969), 211–26.
51. *People, Power, Change: Movements of Social Transformation*, Bobbs-Merrill, Indianapolis, 1970.
52. "Pentecostal Glossolalia: Toward a Functional Interpretation," p. 217.
53. Ibid.
54. Ibid., p. 218.
55. Ibid., p. 225.
56. Gerlach and Hine, *People, Power, Change*, p. xxi.
57. Ibid., p. 70.
58. Ibid., p. 110.
59. Ibid., p. 131.
60. Ibid., p. 181.
61. Ibid., p. 160.
62. Ibid., p. 164.
63. This must be understood in the context of the sampling. Most of the sampling is made up of classical Pentecostals and Protestant neo-Pentecostals. Many of the latter, though not all, had come under the influence of classical Pentecostal theology and culture. A very small part of the sampling were Catholic charismatics.
64. *The Catholic Cult of the Paraclete*, Sheed and Ward, New York, 1975, p. 64.
65. Gerlach and Hine, *People, Power, Change*, p. 16.

178 CHARISMATIC RENEWAL AND THE CHURCHES

66. Ibid., p. 127.
67. Ibid., p. 128.
68. Ibid.
69. Ibid., p. 110.
70. Ibid., p. 114.
71. Ibid., p. 126.
72. Ibid., p. 5.
73. Ibid., p. 81.
74. Ibid., p. 79.
75. Ibid., pp. 89, 93–94.
76. Ibid., p. 97.
77. Ibid., p. 81. "Hiddens" are those who have adopted the Pentecostal-charismatic approach to the gospel and the Christian life but do not want this publicly known.
78. Ibid., pp. 81–82.
79. Ibid., pp. 94–95.
80. Ibid., p. 39.
81. Ibid., pp. 6–7, 10–11, 35. Susan L. Bergquist (1973), in her study of Catholic charismatics, remarked on the same kind of authoritarianism, not as asserted by the leaders but as attributed to them by their followers. "Certain individuals would at one time point out to me the dangers of 'spiritual elitism' only to follow this warning with reference to a particular person (leader) with great respect, admiration and perhaps even adoration. The respect and admiration seems fitting, but in a few cases I felt as though certain individuals are being 'sacralized' to the point where they are elevated above human fallibility" ("The Revival of Glossolalic Practices in the Catholic Church: Its Sociological Implications," *Perkins Journal*, 26 (1973), 37). Bergquist's conclusions do not carry much conviction. Her study is based on attendance at a Catholic "charismatic Mass" in Los Angeles and on hearing Catholics praying over children in Dallas. She was herself prayed over. In addition to this, she undertook depth interviews with thirteen Catholic charismatics from Orange County in California and the Dallas area in Texas. However interesting, this sampling cannot be the conveyer of any scientific knowledge.
82. Gerlach and Hine, *People, Power, Change*, pp. 38–39.
83. Ibid., p. 39. Cf. Dorothy Emmet, *Function, Purposes and Powers*, Macmillan, London, 1958.
84. Gerlach and Hine, *People, Power, Change*, p. 35.
85. *Haven of The Masses*, Lutterworth Press, London, 1969.
86. Ibid., p. 87.
87. Ibid.
88. *People, Power, Change*, pp. xx–xxi.
89. "A Phonemic Analysis of Nine Samples of Glossolalic Speech," *Psychonomic Science*, 22 (1971), 81. A phoneme is the smallest unit of speech that distinguishes one utterance from another in all the variations that it displays in the speech of a single person or dialect as a result of modifying influences (as neighboring sounds and stress).
90. Daniel C. O'Connell and Ernest T. Bryant, "Some Psychological Reflections on Glossolalia," *Review for Religious*, 31 (1972), 975.
91. Ibid.
92. Ibid.

93. *Tongues of Men and Angels,* p. 102.
94. "Some Psychological Reflections on Glossolalia," p. 976.
95. Ibid.
96. Ibid.
97. "Social and Personality Correlates of Pentecostalism: A Review of the Literature and a Comparison of Pentecostal Christian Students with non-Pentecostal Christian Students" (diss., University of Waikato, New Zealand, 1972).
98. The following tests were administered: Student Attitude Inventory, Religious Orientation Scale, the Congalton-Havinghurst Scale, Religious Autobiographical Questionnaire, and the 16 Personality Factor Test. Fifteen of the subjects were Anglican; twelve, Presbyterian; six, Roman Catholic; five, Baptist; four, Brethren; five, classical Pentecostal; two, Methodist; and three belonged to no church.
99. "Social and Personality Correlates of Pentecostalism," p. 52.
100. "Relationship Between Glossolalia and Mental Health," available from the National Institute of Mental Health, Bethesda, Maryland.
101. Kildahl, *The Psychology of Speaking in Tongues,* Harper & Row, New York, 1972, pp. 50, 44.
102. Ibid., p. 46.
103. Ibid., p. 48.
104. Ibid., p. 49.
105. Ibid., p. 51.
106. Ibid., p. 55.
107. Ibid., pp. 54–55.
108. "Lecture on Glossolalia" (paper delivered at the University of Berkeley, 1966).
109. "Trance States and Ego Psychology," *Trance and Possession States,* ed. Raymond Prince, Proceedings of Second Annual Conference, R. M. Bucke Memorial Society, March 1966, Montreal, 1968, p. 60.
110. *The Psychology of Speaking in Tongues,* p. 59.
111. Ibid., pp. 66–75.
112. Ibid., p. 86.
113. Ibid., p. 74.
114. Ibid., p. 85, Cf. also Kildahl, "Psychological Observations," *The Charismatic Movement,* ed. Michael P. Hamilton, Eerdmans, Grand Rapids, 1975, p. 140.
115. *The Psychology of Speaking in Tongues,* p. 59.
116. "The Glossolalic and his Personality," *Beiträge zur Ekstase,* ed. T. H. Spoerri, S. Karger, Basel, 1968, pp. 170–171.
117. *The Psychology of Speaking in Tongues,* pp. 36, 53, 59.
118. Samarin, "Glossolalia as Regressive Speech," *Language and Speech,* 16 (1973), 77–89; Alexander Alland, "Possession in a Revivalistic Negro Church," *Journal for the Scientific Study of Religion,* 1 (1961), 204–13.
119. "Behavioral Science Research on the Nature of Glossolalia," p. 84.
120. ". . . occasional regressions in the service of the ego can be tolerated by the adult ego if its functions are unimpaired. We also know that the healthy ego, for certain purposes, has to be able to abandon itself to the id (as in sleep and in sexual intercourse). There are also other less well known situations, in which the ego itself induces a temporary discarding of some of its most highly differentiated functions. To do so, not only

without impairment of normal function but even to its benefit, is an achievement that has to be learned. The child, up to a certain age, is not capable of using this mechanism, or feels threatened by its attempted use" (*Essays on Ego Psychology*, International Universities Press, New York, 1965, p. 177).

121. *The Psychology of Speaking in Tongues*, p. 39. In a letter to the editor, William E. Welmers, Professor of African Languages at the University of California, denies that tongues is a real language. His emotional response to the question places his scientific judgment somewhat in doubt: ". . . when Christians publicize, propagate, and endeavor to perpetuate an apparent manifestation of psychological instability and an obvious blasphemy as a special 'gift of the Holy Spirit' I cannot refuse to apply my knowledge and training to the problem" (*Christianity Today*, 8 [November 8, 1963], 128).

122. *Tongues of Men and Angels*, p. 113. One linguist is reported to have said that he would need sixteen pages of transcription to verify the presence of a true language. Cf. Laurence Christenson, "Speaking in Tongues," Bethany Fellowship, Minneapolis, 1968, p. 24. There have been attempts to collect the accounts when speaking in tongues was recognized as a foreign language. Cf. Ralph W. Harris, *Spoken by the Spirit*, Gospel Publishing House, Springfield, Missouri, 1973. Harris quotes from personal witnesses and from printed accounts in classical Pentecostal publications. From a purely scientific point of view these accounts are of little value. There are no controls and the situations in which languages were recognized are often ones which would be suspect to a scientist. Whatever the problems of scientific verification, however, a theologian would not want to deny all possibility of a real language being spoken.

123. "Final Progress Report: Glossolalia and Mental Health," a research project supported by the Behavioral Sciences Research Branch of the National Institute of Mental Health, 1971, p. 7.

124. *The Psychology of Speaking in Tongues*, p. 86.

125. Samarin, "Forms and Functions of Nonsense Language," *Linguistics*, 50 (1969), 74. Samarin remarks that "subjects who have listened to samples of pseudo-language rank them closer to real language than to nonlanguage" (p. 71).

126. "Toward a Typology of Formal Communicative Behaviors: Glossolalia," *Anthropological Linguistics*, 9 (1967), 2–3, 5.

127. "Speaking in Tongues and About Tongues," *Christian Standard*, 99 (1964), 4.

128. "Wie alle Charismen ist auch das Charisma des Sprachenredens ein natürliches Phänomen," *Glossolalia: Wert und Problematik des Sprachenredens*, Kühne Verlag, Hanover, 1967, p. 11.

129. *The Psychology of Speaking in Tongues*, pp. 6–7, 62, 67–68.

130. There is no report on how the groups were equated or matched. Were they matched on various characteristics according to the group means? Were the standard deviations similar? Were the subjects each matched with another subject? Were they matched by medians?

131. One could mention Nathan Gerrard, L. M. Vivier, William Samarin, Luther P. Gerlach and Virginia H. Hine, and the independent publication of Hine. It would not be valid for Kildahl to object that his research was confined to Protestant neo-Pentecostals, while these above men-

tioned studies have a broader scope. Kildahl has a section on Cutten who is not dealing with Protestant neo-Pentecostals.

132. *The Psychology of Speaking in Tongues*, p. 50.

133. Susan L. Bergquist, "The Revival of Glossolalic Practices in the Catholic Church: Its Sociological Implications," p. 37. James C. Logan, "Controversial Aspects of the Movement," *The Charismatic Movement*, ed. Michael P. Hamilton, Eerdmans, Grand Rapids, 1975, p. 39.

134. Arnold Ludwig, "The Trance," *Comparative Psychiatry*, 8 (1967), 9.

135. "Multidimensional Analysis of 'Hypnotic Behavior,'" *Journal of Abnormal Psychology*, 74, (1969), 214. In an independent study Barber comes to these conclusions: "A substantial proportion of the variance in behaviors that have been traditionally associated with the word *hypnotism* is due to a set of subject variables (subjects' attitudes, expectancies, and motivations toward the test-situation and toward the experimental tasks) and a set of instruction-suggestion variables (wording and tone of instructions, direct suggestions, and inquiry questions)" ("An Empirically-Based Formulation of Hypnotism," *The American Journal of Clinical Hypnosis*, 12 (1969), 123). In a later article Barber took an even more radical stand on hypnosis. Barber thinks that hypnosis and the hypnotic state "have no clearly defined referents; they can be used, after the fact, to explain every conceivable finding. . . . Since no test has been able to demonstrate the existence of a hypnotic state, there is no reason to assume that there *is* such a state" ("Who Believes in Hypnosis?" *Psychology Today*, 4 [July, 1970], 84).

136. "Altered States of Consciousness," *Trance and Possession States*, Raymond Prince, ed., 70.

137. Barber and Calverley, "Multidimensional Analysis of 'Hypnotic' Behavior," *Journal of Abnormal Psychology*, vol. 74, 217.

138. "Altered States of Consciousness," *Trance and Possession States*, ed. Raymond Prince, Proceedings of Second Annual Conference, R. M. Bucke Memorial Society, March, 1966, Montreal, 1968, pp. 82–83.

139. *The Psychology of Speaking in Tongues*, pp. 50–59. Significant here is the research of Rodney Stark. He notes that many social scientists are inclined to regard conservative religious beliefs as abnormal ("Psychopathology and Religious Commitment," *Review of Religious Research*, 12 [1971] 172). There is a widespread assumption that authoritarianism is a major source of religious commitment. This assumption is then given a psychopathological interpretation (p. 173). Ever since the publication of *The Authoritarian Personality* (T.W. Adorno et al., Harper & Row, New York, 1950), authoritarianism has become one of the most heavily worked concepts in social science. It refers to rigidities in the personality structure and to the inability to tolerate ambiguity or ambivalence. This book was falsely interpreted as maintaining that there is an empirical basis for a strong positive relationship between religious orthodoxy and authoritarianism. Frymier (1959), Siegman (1962), Photiadis and Johnson (1963), and Stark (1971) have reported no relationship between authoritarianism and various forms of religious commitment. Stark's conclusion is that "the widespread assumption that authoritarianism is positively related to conventional religious orthodoxy is falsified among both Protestants and Catholics" ("Psychopathology and Religious Commitment," p. 174). Stark's perspective is not the same as Kildahl's but his

research should make one hesitate in accepting the kind of relationship Kildahl asserts exists between the authoritarian leader and the seeker after tongues. More research is needed.

140. James C. Logan, "Controversial Aspects of the Movement," p. 39; Josephine Massyngberde Ford, "The Charismatic Gifts in Worship," ibid., p. 123.

141. Smet, "Survey of Scientific Literature on Tongue-Speaking" (paper read at the international Pentecostal-Catholic dialogue, Venice, May 20–26, 1975); Bennett, "The Gifts of the Spirit," *The Charismatic Movement,* ed. Michael P. Harrington, Eerdmans, Grand Rapids, 1975, pp. 25–26.

142. Hine, "Pentecostal Glossolalia: Toward a Functional Interpretation," p. 220; Morton Kelsey, *Tongue Speaking: An Experiment in Spiritual Experience,* Doubleday, Garden City, New York, 1964, pp. 13–14, 163; Samarin, *Tongues of Men and Angels,* pp. 22–23, 51–52; personal letter to the author by Dr. William Backus, Senior Clinical Psychologist, Hennepin County Hospital, Minneapolis, Minnesota.

143. "Our data pose a problem with regard to the hypnosis theory, as we have found that tongue speaking occurs frequently in solitary situations. After the initial experience of glossolalia, most Pentecostals speak with tongues as frequently, if not more frequently, alone in private prayer as in group situations where hypnosis could be practised. Auto-suggestion and self-hypnosis are commonly used to explain this fact. Twenty-three percent of our questionnaire respondents, however, experienced the Baptism of the Holy Spirit and spoke with tongues for the first time when they were alone. This would suggest a sophisticated and calculated use of post-hypnotic suggestion during previous group meetings, and this we did not observe" ("Pentecostal Glossolalia: Toward A Functional Interpretation," p. 218). Cf. also Vivier, "The Glossolalic and his Personality," pp. 173–174.

144. Samarin, *Tongues of Men and Angels,* 52–58.

145. *The Psychology of Speaking in Tongues,* p. 78.

146. Kildahl, "Psychological Observations," p. 129.

147. "Interim Report on the Study of the Pentecostal Movement Conducted by the Anthropology Department of the University of Minnesota," 1967, p. 5.

148. Smet, "Survey of Scientific Literature on Tongue-Speaking," p. 48.

149. "Glossolalia" (Ph.D. diss., University of Witwatersrand, Johannesburg, 1960), p. 435; "The Glossolalic and his Personality," p. 170.

150. "Glossolalia as Learned Behavior," *Canadian Journal of Theology,* 15 (1969), 64.

151. Hine and Olila, "Interim Report on the Study of the Pentecostal Movement," pp. 3–11.

152. Gerlach and Hine, *People, Power, Change,* pp. 79–97. Cf. also Hine and Olila, "Interim Report on the Study of the Pentecostal Movement." In ranking the factors in the order of importance which influenced the two hundred thirty-nine persons to seek the baptism in the Holy Spirit and tongues, the following order was noted: "an individual who talked to me about it privately (not necessarily a leader)," attending a small group meeting, attending services of a Pentecostal church, attending a large revival meeting, mass media, reading literature or tracts, parents' example or teachings, seeing the change in someone's life, no influence at all,

other. Samarin prints some of the data from this unpublished report (*Tongues of Men and Angels*, pp. 48–49).

153. "Recruitment and Organization in a Racially Mixed Pentecostal Church" (paper read at the annual meeting of the Central States Anthropological Society, University of Chicago, April 27–29, 1967).

154. "Social and Personality Correlates of Pentecostaliam," pp. 52–53. Though Donald McGavran is not concerned with the psychological dimensions of Pentecostalism he also mentions preexisting social relations as an important factor in the growth of classical Pentecostalism in Mexico. Cf. Donald McGavran, John Huegel, and Jack Taylor, *Church Growth in Mexico*, Eerdmans, Grand Rapids, Michigan, 1963, p. 122.

155. H. Newton Malony, Nelson Zwaanstra, and James W. Ramsey, "Personal and Situational Determinants of Glossolalia: A Literature Review and Report on Ongoing Research" (paper presented at the International Congress of Religious Studies, Los Angeles, 1972, p. 5).

156. Hine, "Pentecostal Glossolalia," p. 218.

157. "Glossolalia," p. 435.

158. "The Glossolalic and his Personality," p. 170.

159. Hine, "Pentecostal Glossolalia," p. 218.

160. "Who Believes in Hypnosis?" p. 27.

161. "Final Progress Report: Glossolalia and Mental Health," p. 4.

162. *The Psychology of Speaking in Tongues*, pp. xi., 47.

163. Book review in *Sisters Today*, 44 (August–September, 1972), 42–43. In a letter to Laurence Christenson which Christenson quotes in his review of Kildahl's book, Ṣamarin says that the book is "rich in assertions, especially derogatory ones, and weak in substantiations. Competent scholars in these fields (psychology, sociology, linguistics) will not be able to accept this book as a scholarly and scientific one. It is unfortunate that the general reader will not be so perceptive" ("Book News Letter of Augsburg Publishing House," No. 440 [September–October, 1972], 4. James T. Richardson criticizes Kildahl for the smallness of his sampling plus the absence of time-series data ("Interpretations of Glossolalia: A Reexamination of Research," *Journal for the Scientific Study of Religion*, 12 [1973], 205). On page 20 of his book, Kildahl speaks of the twenty glossolalics and the twenty nonglossolalics who were given psychological tests. While Kildahl matched his groups on some characteristics, some confusion has resulted from the discovery of persons who had engaged in some minimal glossolalia among those whom the research had considered nonglossolalics. The number of nonglossolalics was thus reduced to thirteen. Kildahl appeals to his wide experience outside the research design to make up for this deficiency (p. 41, n. 3). Richardson is in error in saying that Kildahl has no time-series data. On page 41 Kildahl refers to some time-series tests. However the data are so meagre and the reporting so minimal as to justify Richardson's reading.

164. H. Newton Malony, Nelson Zwaanstra, and James W. Ramsey, "Personal and Situational Determinants of Glossolalia,"

165. Ibid., p. 5.

166. Ibid., p. 6.

167. Ibid., p. 9.

168. "Psychological Interpretations of Glossolalia," p. 206.

169. Ibid.

170. "An Interpretive Comparison of Elements of the Pentecostal and Underground Church Movements in American Catholicism," *Sociological Analysis*, 35 (1974), 58.
171. McGuire, "Sharing Life in the Spirit: The Function of Testimony in Catholic Pentecostal Commitment and Conversion" (paper presented at the meeting of the Society for the Scientific Study of Religion, Milwaukee, 1975, p. 5). The author studied seven Catholic Pentecostal groups by participant observation in northern New Jersey between 1971 and 1975. This was supplemented by interviewing key members.
172. Ibid., p. 7.
173. Ibid., p. 9.
174. Ibid., p. 11.
175. Ibid., p. 15.
176. Ibid., p. 13.
177. Ibid., pp. 8–9.

CHAPTER 6

1. Writing of classical Pentecostalism, Steve Durasoff says: "The Pentecostal meeting may indeed have attracted the mentally unstable, for in the mystical aspects and the little understood manifestations of the charismatic gifts, they were able to find opportunities for the disordered self-expression that they sought" ("An Abstract of the All-Union Council of Evangelical Christians—Baptists in the Soviet Union: 1944–1966," [Ph.D. diss., New York University, 1967, p. 214]). ". . . Pentecostalists themselves believe that though in some cases speaking in tongues may be nothing but hysteria, yet in genuine cases it is a sign of the power of the Holy Spirit taking hold of individual lives" (Bryan Green, *Pentecost*, no. 69 [September–November, 1964], 15). Cf. also D. Paul Fleisch, *Die Pfingstbewegung in Deutschland*, Heinr. Feesche Verlag, Hanover, 1957, p. 41.
2. Frank Bartleman, *How Pentecost Came to Los Angeles* (published privately by Bartleman, Los Angeles, 1925, p. 90).
3. Ibid., p. 80.
4. Ibid., p. 81.
5. Ibid., p. 112.
6. Ibid., p. 110.
7. Ibid., p. 112.
8. Donald Gee, "Wheat, Tares and 'Tongues'," *Pentecost*, no. 67 (December 1963–February 1964), 17.
9. Pastor J. Paul, "Vortrag von Pastor Paul auf der III. Pfingstkonferenz in Mülheim," *Pfingstgrüsse*, 2 (December, 1909), 3.
10. Walter J. Hollenweger, "Christentum ohne Sheuklappen," *Kirchenbote*, Zürich, September 16, 1966, p. 2.
11. *The Wind Bloweth Where it Listeth*, Bethany Fellowship, Minneapolis, 1968, p. 58.
12. "Pentecostal Glossolalia: Toward a Functional Interpretation," *Journal for the Scientific Study of Religion*. 8 (1969), 217.
13. Ibid., p. 218.
14. Book review of Kildahl's *The Psychology of Speaking in Tongues* in *Sisters Today*, 44 (August–September, 1972), 44.

15. *Review of Religious Research*, 12 (1971), 167.
16. Ibid., p. 165.
17. Ibid., p. 167.
18. Michael I. Harrison, "Sources of Recruitment to Catholic Pentecostals," *Journal for the Scientific Study of Religion*, 13 (1974), 62; John Lofland, *Dooms-day Cult*, Prentice-Hall, Englewood Cliffs, 1966. After recruitment deep involvement in the renewal may lead to diminishing of ties to outsiders, as is true of other movements.
19. Meredith B. McGuire, "An Interpretive Comparison of Elements of the Pentecostal and Underground Church Movements in American Catholicism." *Sociological Analysis*, 35 (1974), 58.
20. Presented at the Sixth International Conference on the Catholic Charismatic Renewal in the Catholic Church, South Bend.
21. Samarin, *Tongues of Men and of Angels*, Macmillan, New York, 1972, pp. 42–43.
22. Ibid., pp. 18–19.
23. "Social and Personality Correlates of Pentecostalism: A Review of the Literature and Comparison of Pentecostal Christian Students with non-Pentecostal Students" (diss., University of Waikato, New Zealand, 1972, p. 52).
24. Virginia H. Hine, "Pentecostal Glossolalia: Toward a Functional Interpretation," p. 225.
25. John P. Kildahl, *The Psychology of Speaking in Tongues*, Harper & Row, New York, 1972, p. 51.
26. James T. Richardson, "Psychological Interpretations of Glossolalia: A Reexamination of Research," *Journal for the Scientific Study of Religion*, 12 (1973), 205.
27. Donald T. Campbell and Julian C. Stanley, *Experimental and Quasi-Experimental Designs for Research*, Rand McNally, Chicago, 1963, p. 7.
28. Sheed and Ward, New York, 1975.
29. Campbell and Stanley, *Experimental and Quasi-Experimental Designs*, p. 3.

BIBLIOGRAPHY

Aberle, David. "A Note on Relative Deprivation Theory as Applied to Millenarian and Other Cultic Movements." In *Reader in Comparative Religion*, 2nd ed. Edited by William A. Lessa and Evon Z. Vogt. Harper & Row, New York, 1965.

Adorno, T. W., et al. *The Authoritarian Personality*. Harper & Row, New York, 1950.

Alland, Alexander. " 'Possession' in a Revivalistic Negro Church." *Journal for the Scientific Study of Religion* 1 (1961): 204–213.

Barber, Theodore X. "Who Believes in Hypnosis?" *Psychology Today* 4 (July, 1970): 2–27, 84.

Barber, Theodore X, and Calverley, David S. " 'Hypnotic Behavior' and a Function of Task Motivation." *The Journal of Psychology* 54 (1962): 363–89.

———. "Multidimensional Analysis of 'Hypnotic Behavior.' " *Journal of Abnormal Psychology* 74 (1969): 209–20.

Bartleman, Frank. *How Pentecost Came to Los Angeles*. Published privately by Bartleman, Los Angeles, 1925.

Beckmann, David M. "Trance: From Africa to Pentecostalism." *Concordia Theological Monthly* 45 (January, 1974): 11–26.

Beers, H. W., and Heflin, C. "The Urban Status of Rural Migrants." *Social Forces* 23 (1944): 32–37.

Bergquist, Susan L. "The Revival of Glossolalic Practices in the Catholic Church: Its Sociological Implications." *Perkins Journal* 30 (1973): 256–65.

Bittlinger, Arnold. *Das Abendmahl im Neuen Testament und in der frühen Kirche*. Kühne Verlag, Wetzhausen, 1969.

———. *Gemeinde ist Anders: Verwirklichung neutestamentliche Gemeindeordnung innerhalb der Volkskirche*. Calwer Verlag, Stüttgart, 1966.

———. *Gifts and Graces: A Commentary on 1 Corinthians 12–14*. Eerdmans, Grand Rapids, 1967.

————. *Glossolalia: Wert und Problematik des Sprachenredens.* Kühne Verlag, Hanover, 1967.

————. *Gottesdienst Heute.* Calwer Verlag, Stüttgart, 1968.

Boisen, Anton T. "Economic Distress and Religious Experience." *Psychiatry* 2 (1939): 185–94.

————. *The Exploration of the Inner World.* Harper & Row, New York, 1936.

————. *Religion in Crisis and Custom: A Sociological and Psychological Study.* Harper & Row, New York, 1945.

Bourguignon, Erika. "The Self, the Behavioral Environment, and the Theory of Spirit Possession." *Context and Meaning in Cultural Anthropology.* Edited by Melford E. Spiro. Free Press, New York, 1965.

Bourguignon, Erika, and Pettay, Louanna. "Spirit Possession, Trance and Cross-Cultural Research." *Proceedings of the Annual Meeting of the American Ethnological Society* 1964: 38–49.

Brown, L. B. "The Structure of Religious Belief." *Journal for the Scientific Study of Religion* 5 (1966): 259–72.

————. "Some Attitudes Surrounding Glossolalia." *Colloquium* 2 (1967): 221–28.

Bryant, Ernest, and O'Connell, Daniel. "A Phonemic Analysis of Nine Samples of Glossolalic Speech." *Psychonomic Speech* 22 (1971): 81–83.

Bultena, Louis. "Church Membership and Church Attendance in Madison, Wisconsin." *American Sociological Review* 14 (1940): 384–89.

Burchinal, Lee G. "Some Social Status Criteria and Church Membership and Church Attendance." *Journal of Social Psychology* 49 (1959): 53–64.

Buss, Arnold, H. *Psychopathology.* John Wiley and Sons, New York, 1966.

Cantril, Hadley. "Educational and Economic Composition of Religious Groups: An Analysis of Poll Data." *American Journal of Sociology* 48 (1942–1943): 574–79.

"The Charismatic Movement and Lutheran Theology." A Report of the Commission on Theology and Church Relations of the Lutheran Church-Missouri Synod, January, 1972.

"The Charismatic Movement in the Lutheran Church in America." The Commission on Worship of the Lutheran Church in America, 1974.

Christenson, Larry, et al., "A Theological and Pastoral Perspective on the Charismatic Renewal in the Lutheran Church," unpublished paper, 1975.

Cohn, Werner. "Personality, Pentecostalism, and Glossolalia: A Research Note on Some Unsuccessful Research." *Canadian Review of Sociology and Anthropology* 5 (1968): 36–39.

Cutten, George Barton. *Speaking with Tongues: Historically and Psychologically Considered.* Yale University Press, New Haven, 1927.

Demerath III, N. J. *Social Class in American Protestantism.* Rand McNally, Chicago, 1965.

Dreger, Ralph. "Some Personality Correlates of Religious Attitudes as Determined by Projective Techniques." *Psychological Monographs* 66 (1952): 3–26.

Durasoff, Steve. "An Abstract of the All-Union Council of Evangelical Christians—Baptists in the Soviet Union: 1944–1966." Ph.D. dissertation, New York University, 1967.

Dynes, Russell R. "Church-Sect Typology and Socio-Economic Status." *American Sociological Review* 20 (1955): 555–60.

————. "Rurality, Migration, and Sectarianism." *Rural Sociology* 21 (1956): 25–28.

Edel, R. F. *Im Kraftfeld des Heiligen Geistes.* Marburg an der Lahn, 1968.

Eliade, Mircea. *Myths, Dreams and Mysteries.* Harper & Row, New York, 1960.
————. *Shamanism: Archaic Techniques of Ecstasy.* Princeton University Press, Princeton, 1964.

Elinson, Howard. "The Implications of Pentecostal Religion for Intellectualism, Politics and Race Relations." *American Journal of Sociology* 70 (1965): 403–15.

English, H. B., and A. C. *A Comprehensive Dictionary of Psychological and Psychoanalytic Terms.* Longmans Green, New York, 1958.

Field, Margaret J. *Search for Security.* Northwestern University Press, Evanston, Illinois, 1960.

Fleisch, D. Paul. *Die Pfingstbewegung in Deutschland.* Heinr. Feesche Verlag, Hanover, 1957.

Frank, Jerome D. *Persuasion and Healing: A Comparative Study of Psychotherapy.* Johns Hopkins Press, Baltimore, 1961.

Fukuyama, Yoshio. "The Major Dimensions of Church Membership." *Review of Religious Research* 2 (1960): 154–61.

Gee, Donald. "Wheat, Tares and 'Tongues'." *Pentecost* no. 67 (December 1963–February 1964): 17.

Gerlach, Luther P., and Hine, Virginia H. "Five Factors Crucial to the Growth and Spread of a Modern Religious Movement." *Journal for the Scientific Study of Religion* 7 (1968): 23–40.

————. *People, Power, Change: Movements of Social Transformation.* Bobbs-Merrill, Indianapolis, 1970.

Gerrard, Nathan L. "The Serpent-Handling Religions of West Virginia." *TransAction* 6 (May, 1968): 22–28.

————. "The Holiness Movement in Southern Appalachia." *The Charismatic Movement.* Edited by Michael P. Hamilton. Eerdmans, Grand Rapids, 1975.

Gerrard, Nathan L., and Louise B. "Scrabble Creek Folk." Multilithed manuscript. Charleston, West Virginia, 1966.

Giffin, R. "Appalachian Newcomers in Cincinnati." In *The Southern Appalachian Region: A Survey.* Edited by Thomas R. Fold. University of Kentucky Press, Lexington, 1962.

Gill, Merton, and Brenman, Margaret. *Hypnosis and Related States: Psychoanalytic Studies in Regression.* International Universities Press, New York, 1959.

Glock, Charles Y., Ringer, Benjamin, and Babbie, Earl R. *To Comfort and To Challenge.* University of California Press, Berkeley, 1967.

Glock, Charles Y., and Stark, Rodney. *Religion and Society in Tension.* Rand McNally, Chicago, 1965.

Goldschmidt, Walter R. "Class Denominationalism in Rural California Churches." *American Journal of Sociology* 49 (1944): 348–55.

Goodman, Felicitas. "Phonetic Analysis of Glossolalia in Four Cultural Settings." *Journal for the Scientific Study of Religion* 8 (1969): 227–39.

————. "Glossolalia: Speaking in Tongues in Four Cultural Settings." *Confinia Psychiatrica* 12 (1969): 113–29.

————. *Speaking in Tongues: A Cross-Cultural Study of Glossolalia.* The University of Chicago Press, Chicago, 1972.

Green, Bryan. *Pentecost* no. 69 (September-November, 1964): 15.

Hallenbeck, Wilbur, C. *American Urban Communities.* Harper & Row, New York, 1951.

Harper, Charles L. "Spirit-Filled Catholics: Some Biographical Comparisons." *Social Compass* 21 (1974): 311–324.

Harris, Ralph W. *Spoken by the Spirit.* Gospel Publishing House, Springfield, Missouri, 1973.

Harrison, Michael I. "Preparation for Life in the Spirit: The Process of Initial Commitment to a Religious Movement." *Urban Life and Culture* 2 (1974): 387–414.

———. "Sources of Recruitment to Catholic Pentecostalism." *Journal for the Scientific Study of Religion* 13 (1974): 49–64.

Hilgard, Ernest R., and Josephine R. *Hypnotic Susceptibility.* Harcourt, Brace and World, New York, 1965.

Hine, Virginia H. "The Deprivation and Disorganization Theories of Social Movements." *Religious Movements in Contemporary America.* Edited by Irving I. Zaretsky and Mark P. Leone. Princeton University Press, Princeton, 1974.

———. "Pentecostal Glossolalia: Toward a Functional Interpretation." *Journal for the Scientific Study of Religion* 8 (1969): 211–26.

Hine, Virginia H., and Olila, James H. "Interim Report on the Study of the Pentecostal Movement Conducted by the Anthropology Department of the University of Minnesota." Research report, University of Minnesota, Minneapolis, 1967.

Hockett, Charles P. "The Problem of Universals in Language." In *Universals in Language.* Edited by J. H. Greenberg. M.I.T. Press, Cambridge, 1963.

Hollenweger, Walter J. "Christentum ohne Sheuklappen." *Kirchenbote.* Zürich, September 16, 1966, p. 2.

———. "Handbuch der Pfingstbewegung." Ph.D. dissertation, University of Zürich, 1965.

———. *The Pentecostals: The Charismatic Movement in the Churches.* Augsburg Publishing House, Minneapolis, 1972.

Hollingshead, August B. *Elmtown's Youth.* John Wiley, New York, 1949.

———. "Selected Characteristics of Classes in a Middle Western Community." *American Sociological Review* 12 (1947): 385–95.

Holt, John B. "Holiness Religion: Cultural Shock and Social Reorganization." *American Sociological Review* 5 (1940): 740–47.

Hull, C. L. *Hypnosis and Suggestibility: An Experimental Approach.* D. Appleton-Century, New York, 1933.

Jaquith, James R. "Toward a Typology of Formal Communicative Behaviors: Glossolalia." *Anthropological Linguistics* 9, no. 8 (1967): 1–8.

Johnston, Benton. "Do Holiness Sects Socialize in Dominant Values?" *Social Forces* 39 (1961–1962): 309–16.

Jung, Carl. *Civilization in Transition.* Translated by R.F.C. Hull. Pantheon Books, New York, 1964.

———. *Psychology and Religion: West and East. The Collected Works of C. G. Jung.* Vol. 11. Princeton University Press, Princeton, 1969.

Kaufman, Harold. "Prestige Classes in a New York Rural Community." *Cornell University Agricultural Experiment Station, Memoire 260* March 1944: 4–5, 9–10, 15–21, 36–38.

Kelsey, Morton. *Tongue Speaking: An Experiment in Spiritual Experience.* Doubleday, Garden City, New York, 1964.

Kiev, Ari. "Beliefs and Delusions Among West Indian Immigrants to London." *British Journal of Psychiatry* 109 (1963): 356–63.

———. "The Study of Folk Psychiatry." In *Magic, Faith, and Healing: Studies in Primitive Psychiatry.* Edited by Ari Kiev. Free Press, New York, 1964.

Kildahl, John P. "Psychological Observations." In *The Charismatic Movement.* Edited by Michael P. Hamilton. Eerdmans, Grand Rapids, 1975.

———. *The Psychology of Speaking in Tongues.* Harper & Row, New York, 1972.

Kildahl, John P., and Qualben, Paul A. "Final Progress Report: Glossolalia and Mental Health." Research project supported by the Behavioral Sciences Research Branch of the National Institute of Mental Health, 1971.

———. "Relationship Between Glossolalia and Mental Health." National Institute of Mental Health, Bethesda, Maryland. 1971.

Le Barre, Weston. *They Shall Take Up Serpents: Psychology of the Southern Snake-Handling Cult.* University of Minnesota Press, Minneapolis, 1962.

Lapsley, James N., and Simpson, John H. "Speaking in Tongues." *The Princeton Seminary Bulletin* 58 (February, 1965): 3–18.

———. "Speaking in Tongues: Infantile Babble or Song of the Self?" *Pastoral Psychology* 15 (September, 1964): 16–24.

———. "Speaking in Tongues: Token of Group Acceptance and Divine Approval." *Pastoral Psychology* 15 (May, 1964): 48–55.

Lee, Robert. *Stranger in the Land: A Study of the Church in Japan.* Lutterworth Press, London, 1967.

Lenski, Gerhard. *The Religious Factor.* Doubleday, Garden City, 1961.

———. "Social Correlates of Religious Interest." *American Sociological Review* 18 (1953): 533–44.

Levitt, E., Persky, H., and Brady, J. P. *Hypnotic Induction of Anxiety.* Charles C. Thomas, Springfield, Illinois, 1964.

Lewis, I. M. *Ecstatic Religion: An Anthropological Study of Spirit Possession and Shamanism.* Pelikan Books, Baltimore, 1971.

Lloyd-Jones, D. Martyn. "Conversions: Psychological and Spiritual." Inter-Varsity Press, London, 1959.

Lofland, John. *Doomsday Cult.* Prentice Hall, Englewood Cliffs, New Jersey, 1966.

Lombard, Emile. *De la Glossolalie chez les Premiers Chrétiens et des Phénomènes Similaires.* Georges Bridel, Lausanne, 1910.

Ludwig, Arnold M. "Altered States of Consciousness." In *Trance and Possession States.* Edited by Raymond Prince. Proceedings of Second Annual Conference, R. M. Bucke Memorial Society, 1966, Montreal, 1968.

———. "The Trance." *Comprehensive Psychiatry* 8 (1967): 7–15.

"Lutherans, The Spirit, The Gifts, and The World." Published privately in a tentative form in 1973.

Malony, H. Newton, Zwaanstra, Nelson, and Ramsey, James W. "Personal and Situational Determinants of Glossolalia: A Literature Review and Report of Ongoing Research." Paper presented at the International Congress of Religious Studies, Los Angeles, 1972.

Martin, Ralph. *Unless the Lord Build the House.* Ave Maria, Notre Dame, 1971.

Martraux, Alfred. *Voodoo in Haiti.* Oxford University Press, New York, 1959.

McDonnell, Kilian, and Bittlinger, Arnold. "The Baptism in the Holy Spirit as an Ecumenical Problem." Charismatic Renewal Services, Notre Dame, 1972.

McGavran, Donald. *Church Growth in Mexico.* Eerdmans, Grand Rapids, 1963.

McGuire, Kenneth. "People, Prayer and Promise: An Anthropological Analysis of a Catholic Charismatic Covenant Community." Ph.D. dissertation, Department of Anthropology, Ohio State University, Columbus, 1976.

———. "Affective Deprivation as a Factor in Crisis Movement Formation: A Current Example." Paper presented at the meeting of the Society for the Scientific Study of Religion, San Francisco, 1973.

McGuire, Meredith B. "An Interpretive Comparison of Elements of the Pentecostal and Underground Church Movements in American Catholicism." *Sociological Analysis* 35 (1974): 57–63.

———. "Sharing Life in the Spirit: The Function of Testimony in Catholic Pentecostal Commitment and Conversion." Paper presented at the meeting of the Society for the Scientific Study of Religion, Milwaukee, 1975.

Meares, Ainslie. "Theories of Hypnosis." In *Hypnosis in Modern Medicine*. 3rd ed. Edited by Jerome M. Schneck. Charles C. Thomas Publisher, Springfield, Illinois, 1963.

Montague, George T. "Baptism in the Spirit and Speaking in Tongues: A Biblical Appraisal." *Theology Digest* 21 (1973): 342–60. "The Spirit and His Gifts." Paulist Press, New York, 1974.

Moore, John. "God Has No Grandsons." *Month* 8 (1975): 171–76.

Morentz, Paul. "Lecture on Glossolalia." Multilithed paper, University of California, Berkeley, 1966.

Mosiman, Eddison. *Das Zungenreden, geschichtlich und psychologisch Untersucht.* J.C.B. Mohr (Paul Siebeck), Tübingen, 1911.

Nadel, S. F. "A Study of Shamanism in the Nuba Mountains." *Royal Anthropological Institute of Great Britain and Ireland Journal* 76, part 1 (1946): 25–37.

Nelsen, Hart M., and Whitt, Hugh P. "Religion and the Migrant in the City: A Test of Holt's Culture Shock Thesis." *Social Forces* 50 (1972): 379–84.

Nouwen, Henri. "The Pentecostal Movement: Three Perspectives." *Scholastic* 109 (April 21, 1967): 15–17, 32.

Oates, Wayne E. "A Socio-Psychological Study of Glossolalia." In *Glossolalia*. Frank Stagg et al. Abingdon Press, Nashville, 1967.

O'Connell, Daniel C., and Bryant, Ernest T. "Some Psychological Reflections on Glossolalia." *Review for Religious* 31 (1972): 174–77.

Oman, John B. "On 'Speaking in Tongues': A Psychological Analysis. *Pastoral Psychology* 14, No. 139 (1963): 48–51.

Palmer, Gary. "Trance." Paper presented at the annual meeting of the Central States, Anthropological Society, Chicago, April 27–29, 1967.

———. "Trance and Dissociation: A Cross-Cultural Study in Psychophysiology." Master's thesis, University of Minnesota, Minneapolis, 1966.

Parsons, Anne. "The Pentecostal Immigrants: A Study of an Ethnic Central City Church." *Journal for the Scientific Study of Religion* 4 (1965): 183–97.

Pattison, E. Mansell. "Ideological Support for the Marginal Middle Class: Faith Healing and Glossolalia." In *Religious Movements in Contemporary America*. Edited by Irving I. Zaretsky and Mark P. Leone. Princeton University Press, 1974.

Pattison, E. Mansell. "Behavioral Science Research on the Nature of Glossolalia." *Journal of the American Scientific Affiliation* 20 (1968): 73–86.

———. "Speaking in Tongues and About Tongues." *Christian Standard* 99 (February 15, 1964): 3–5.

Pattison, E. Mansell, and Casey, Robert L. "Glossolalia: A Contemporary Mystical Experience." In *Clinical Psychiatry and Religion*. Edited by E. Mansell Pattison. *International Psychiatry Clinics*. Vol. 5. Little, Brown and Co., Boston, 1968.

Paul, Pastor J. "Vortrag von Pastor Paul auf der III. Pfingstkonferenz in Müheim." *Pfingstgrüsse* 2 (December, 1909): 3.

"The Person and Work of the Holy Spirit, with Special Reference to 'the Baptism in the Holy Spirit.'" Report to the Presbyterian Church in the U.S., submitted to the General Assembly, 1971.

Pfister, Oskar. *Die Psychologische Enträselung der Religiösen Glossolalie und der Automatischen Kryptographie. Sonderabdruck aus dem Jahrbuch für Psychoanalytische und Psychopathologische Forschungen.* III Band. Franz Deuticke, Leipzig und Wein, 1912.

Pike, Bishop James A. "Pastoral Letter." May 2, 1963.

Pin, Emile Jean. "En guise d'introduction, ou comment se sauver de l'anomie et de l'aliénation: Jesus People et Catholiques Pentecostaux." *Social Compass* 21 (1974): 227–39.

Plog, Stanley C. "UCLA Conducts Research on Glossolalia." *Trinity* 3 (Whitsuntide, 1964): 38–39.

Poblete, Renato, and O'Dea, Thomas F. "Anomie and the 'Quest for Community': The Formation of Sects Among the Puerto Ricans of New York." *American Catholic Sociological Review* 21 (1960): 18–36.

Pope, Liston. *Millhands and Preachers.* Yale University Press, New Haven, 1942.

Powles, W. E. "The Southern Appalachian Migrant: Country Boy Turned Blue-Collarite." In *Blue-Collar World: Studies of the American Worker.* Edited by Arthur B. Shostak and William Gomberg. Prentice-Hall, Englewood Cliffs, 1964.

"Preliminary Report, Study Commission on Glossolalia." Division of Pastoral Services, Diocese of California, May 2, 1963.

"Report of the Field Study Committee on Speaking in Tongues." Commission on Evangelism of the American Lutheran Church, 1972.

"Report of the Special Commission on Glossolalia." To the Right Reverend Gerald Francis Burrill, Bishop of Chicago, December 12, 1960.

"Report of the Special Committee on the Work of the Holy Spirit." The United Presbyterian Church in the United States of America, Office of the General Assembly, Philadelphia, 1970.

Richardson, James T. "Psychological Interpretations of Glossolalia: A Reexamination of Research." *Journal for the Scientific Study of Religion* 12 (1973): 199–207.

Roth, Richard A. "Recruitment and Organization in a Racially Mixed Pentecostal Church." Paper read at the annual meeting of the Central States Anthropological Society, University of Chicago, April 27–29, 1967.

Sadler, A. W. "Glossolalia and Possession: An Appeal to the Episcopal Study Commission." *Journal for the Scientific Study of Religion* 4 (Fall, 1964): 84–90.

Samarin, William J. "Evolution in Glossolalic Private Language." *Anthropological Linguistics* 13 (1971): 55–57.

_____. "Forms and Functions of Nonsense Language." *Linguistics* 50 (1969): 70–74.

_____. "Glossolalia as Learned Behavior." *Canadian Journal of Theology* 15 (1969): 60–64.

_____. "Glossolalia as Regressive Speech." *Language and Speech* 16 (1973): 85–86.

_____. "Language in Resocialization." *Practical Anthropology* 17 (1970): 269–79.

_____. "The Linguisticality of Glossolalia." *The Hartford Quarterly* 8 (1968): 49–75.

———. *Tongues of Men and Angels: The Religious Language of Pentecostalism*. Macmillan, New York, 1972.

———. "Variation and Variables in Religious Glossolalia." *Language in Society* 1 (1972): 121–30.

———. Book review of Goodman's *Speaking in Tongues*. *Language* 50 (1974): 207–12.

———. Book review of Kildahl's *The Psychology of Speaking in Tongues*. *Journal of Psycholinguistic Research* 2 (1973): 171–74.

———. Book review of Kildahl's *The Psychology of Speaking in Tongues*. *Sisters Today* 44 (August–September, 1972): 42–43.

Sargant, William. *Battle for the Mind: A Physiology of Conversion and Brainwashing*. Harper & Row, New York, 1959.

Shor, Ronald E. "Hypnosis and the Concept of the Generalized Reality-Orientation." *American Journal of Psychotherapy* 13 (1959): 582–602.

Sorem, Anthony M. "Some Secular Implications of the Pentecostal Denomination." Master's thesis, University of Minnesota, 1969.

"The Speaking in Tongues and the Church." Commission Report to the Episcopal Bishop of Los Angeles, Francis Eric Bloy, April, 1960.

———. *Sprachphänomene und Psychose*. Edited by T. H. Spoerri. S. Karger, Basel, 1964.

Stark, Rodney. "Psychopathology and Religious Commitment." *Review of Religious Research* 2 (1971): 165–76.

"A Statement with Regard to Speaking in Tongues," *Reports and Actions of the Second General Convention of the American Lutheran Church*, 1964, Exhibit J, 162–164; reprinted in "Towards a Mutual Understanding of Neo-Pentecostalism," 12, 13.

Steiner, Leonhard. *Mit Folgenden Zeichen*. Verlag Mission für das volle Evangelium, Basel, 1954.

Stevenson, Ian. Book review of Morton T. Kelsey's *Tongue Speaking*. *Journal of the American Society for Psychical Research* 60 (1966): 300–03.

Stone, Jean. "California Episcopalians Receive Pentecostal Baptism." *Pentecostal Testimony* 46 (June, 1962): 8–9.

———. "What is Happening Today in the Episcopal Church?" *Trinity* 1 (Christmastide 1961–1962): 8–11.

Sutcliffe, J. P. " 'Credulous' and 'Skeptical' Views of Hypnotic Phenomena: Experiments on Esthesia, Hallucination, and Delusion." *Journal of Abnormal and Social Psychology* 62 (1961): 189–200.

Ullmann, Leonard P. and Krasner, Leonard. *A Psychological Approach to Abnormal Behavior*. Prentice-Hall, Englewood Cliffs, 1969.

van der Walde, Peter. "Trance States and Ego Psychology." In *Trance and Possession States*. Edited by Raymond Prince. Proceedings of Second Annual Conference, R. M. Bucke Memorial Society, March 1966, Montreal, 1968.

Vivier, L. M. "Glossolalia." Ph.D. dissertation, University of Witwatersrand, Johannesburg, 1960.

———. "The Glossolalic and His Personality." *Beiträge zur Ekstase*. Edited by T. H. Spoerri. S. Karger, Basel, 1968.

Waldegrave, Charles. "Social and Personality Correlates of Pentecostalism: A Review of the Literature and a Comparison of Pentecostal Christian Students with Non-Pentecostal Christian Students." Dissertation, University of Waikato, New Zealand, 1972.

Warburton, Rennie T. "Holiness Religion: An Anomaly of Sectarian Typologies." *Journal for the Scientific Study of Religion* 8 (1969): 130–39.

Warner, W. Lloyd. *Democracy in Jonesville.* Harper & Row, New York, 1949.

Weitbrecht, H. J., "Ekstatische Zustände bei Schizophrenen." *Beiträge zur Ekstase.* Edited by T. H. Spoerri. S. Karger, Basel, 1968.

Welmers, William E. "Letter to the Editor." *Christianity Today* 8 (November 8, 1963): 128.

Wietzke, Walter, and Hustad, Jack, eds. "A Report on Glossolalia." Reprinted in "Towards a Mutual Understanding of Neo-Pentecostalism," Augsburg Publishing House, Minneapolis, 1973.

Wilson, Bryan. *Sects and Society.* University of California Press, Berkeley, 1961.

Wolfram, Walter. "The Sociolinguistics of Glossolalia." Master's thesis, Hartford Seminary Foundation, 1966.

Wood, William W. *Culture and Personality Aspects of the Pentecostal Holiness Religion.* Mouton, The Hague, 1965.

Worsley, Peter. *The Trumpet Shall Sound.* MacGibbon and Kee, London, 1957.

Yinger, J. M. *Religion, Society and the Individual.* Macmillan, New York, 1957.

INDEX

Aberle, David, 18, 24–25, 34, 35, 36, 37, 38
abnormal psychology, abnormality, 13–14, 43, 48, 68, 79–109, 117, 129, 142, 144, 149, 157 (see also maladjustment, imbalance)
abstract painting, 9, 49
acceptability, social, 14–16, 81, 86, 112, 142
alienation, cultural, 23; religious, 24, 37–38
Alland, Alexander, 79–80, 81, 103, 108, 109, 112, 121, 132
Allen, A. A., 23–24
Anderson, J. B., 46
anomie, 24, 27, 120
anthropology, cultural, 2, 48, 83; and Pentecostalism, 3, 20, 48, 102, 104, 116, 118, 121–28, 130, 137, 138, 144, 149
Authoritarian Personality, The, 179 n.139
authority figures, 61, 81, 99, 126–27, 130–31, 135–38, 143, 144, 150, 153–54

Babbie, Earl R., 30
Backus, William, 136

baptism, 1, 11, 16, 36, 45, 47, 50, 55, 58, 59, 60, 61, 63–64, 66–67, 71, 72, 81, 86–87, 92, 121, 129, 142, 146, 153
Barber, Theodore X., 135, 138
Beers, H. W., 27
behavioral sciences and Pentecostalism, 13, 14, 128–29, 130, 152
Bennett, Dennis, 136
Bergquist, Susan L., 176 n.81
Bernardin, Archbishop, 70, 77–78
Bible, the, 44, 47, 53, 56, 65, 75, 76, 77, 78, 88
Biblical allusions:
    MATTHEW, the end, *11;* 3:11, *55*
    MARK 1:8, *55;* 16:8, *104;* 16:17, 2
    LUKE 3:16, *55*
    JOHN, 3:5, *11;* 6:63, *11;* 8:28, *136;* 15:15, *136;* 20:23, *11*
    ACTS, 1:5, *55;* 1:8, *36;* 2, *43, 75, 156;* 2:3–4, *2;* 5:38–39, *51;* 8, *55;* 8:17, *11;* 10, *55;* 10:46, *2;* 17:28, *12;* 19, *55;* 19:6, *2, 11*
    ROMANS, 8:2, 14, 26, *12;* 12:5–8, *6*
    I CORINTHIANS, 12, *64;* 12–14, *2, 10;* 12:7, *6;* 12:16, *10;* 12:27–28, *6;* 12:-30, *7;* 12:31, *6;* 14:5, 29, 32, *7;* 14:-40, *68*
Bittlinger, Arnold, 61, 84, 133–34
Bloy, Francis Eric, 42–43

Boisen, Anton, 20, 21–22, 23, 34, 40, 89–90, 91, 96, 107–8
Bourguignon, Erika, 14, 83
Brady, J. P., 80
Brand, Eugene, 66
Brenman, Margaret, 80
Bryant, Ernest T., 116, 128–29, 143
Bultena, Louis, 28, 29, 37
Burchinal, Lee G., 29

Calverley, David S., 135
Campbell, Donald T., 150
Cantril, Hadley, 27–28
Carrillo, Alday Salvador, 15
catalepsy, 89
Catherine of Siena, 12
Catholic Biblical Quarterly, The, 10, 15
Catholic Cult of the Paraclete, The (Fichter), 150
charism(a), 2, 5–9, 56, 68, 69, 71, 78, 88, 126–27, 129, 131, 133–34, 141, 143, 155 (see also gifts of the Spirit)
charismatic pilgrimage, the, 15, 71–73
charismatics, see Pentecostalism
Christ, commitment to, 3, 6, 11, 12, 42–43, 65, 69, 71, 73; second coming of, 35
Christenson, Larry, 62, 63
Christian Century, 73–74
Church in the Modern World, The, 15
church-sect theory, the, 18–20, 24, 26, 36–37, 39
Cohn, Werner, 80
confirmation, 1, 58
Constitution on the Church, The, 15
control, 6–7, 45, 48–49, 68, 81, 82, 92, 94, 99, 101, 117, 125
conversion, 38, 58, 61, 63, 66–67, 73, 96–97, 118, 123, 141, 144
cult movements, 24–25
culture conflict, 22, 31, 103, 154
culture shock, 18, 20, 22, 27, 37
Cursillo movement, the, 59
Cutten, George Barton, 88–89, 107, 108, 112

Demerath, N. J. III, 30
demonic, the, 45, 84, 99–100
D'Epinay, Christian Lelive, 127
deprivation, 18, 25, 34, 35–37, 38, 143, 158 n.5; affective, 25–26; cultural, 15, 16; economic, 15, 16, 17, 18, 19, 20, 21, 22, 23–24, 25, 27–31, 32, 33–35, 37, 39, 40, 79, 80, 89, 100, 107, 108, 113, 122, 126, 130, 141, 153; ethical, 21, 21; power, 36; psychological, 13, 14, 79–80, 103, 107, 113, 125, 146, 152; relative, 24–26, 34, 35, 36, 37, 38; social, 16, 18, 20, 21, 23–24, 25, 30, 32, 33–37, 39, 100, 107, 108, 122, 125, 126, 130, 141, 153
disorganization, 18, 34, 143; social, 20, 21, 22, 24, 31–33, 34, 36, 37, 122, 125, 126; among American Indians, 32
dispensationalism, 60, 78
dissociation, psychological, 81, 82, 83, 100, 118
Dreger, Ralph, 120
Durkheim, Emile, 24
Dynes, Russell R., 24, 27

ecstasy, 57, 59, 68, 82, 87–88, 94, 101, 113, 118, 149
ecumenism, 98, 109, 111–12; false, 60, 69, 70, 71
Elinson, Howard, 23–24
elitism, 70, 176 n.81
Emmet, Dorothy, 126
emotionalism, in Pentecostalism, 14, 16, 24, 43, 51, 71, 86, 87, 89–90, 92, 95–98, 100–1, 105–6, 108, 114, 118, 142, 144, 145–46, 147, 153; in reaction to Pentecostalism, 51, 146–47, 178 n.121
epilepsy, 81, 83
Eucharist, the, 1, 11, 69
evil spirits, see demonic
exorcism, 46

fanaticism, 145
Fichter, Joseph, 124, 150
Francis of Assisi, 12
Frank, Jerome D., 97–98, 108
Freudianism, 88
Fukuyama Yoshio, 29–30
Full Gospel Men's Voice (magazine), 47
fundamentalism, 22, 41–42, 47, 56, 69, 70, 71, 78, 87, 100, 103, 125

Gamaliel, 51
Gelpi, Donald, 15
Gerlach, Luther, 32, 34, 36, 38, 61, 85–86, 101, 118, 121–28, 135, 137, 138, 139, 141, 143

Gerrard, Nathan and Louise, 14, 91, 104–7, 109, 139

Giffin, R., 27

gifts of the Spirit, 2, 3, 6–9, 41, 43, 46, 59, 63, 67–68, 69, 70, 74, 84, 99, 117, 129, 133–34, 154–56 (see also charism)

Gill, Merton, 80

Glock, Charles Y., 25, 30

glossolalia: as gift of the Holy Spirit, 2, 43, 46, 57, 60, 84, 99, 117, 129, 132, 133–34, 146, 154–55; divine aspect of, 67; not necessarily religious, 47, 101; as miracle, 67–68; control of, 48–49, 68, 81, 82, 94, 99, 101, 117, 125; frequency of, 32, 35, 91–92, 125, 132, 139; private, 49, 55, 86, 92, 101, 114, 121, 138, 141, 154; induced, 57, 124–25, 129, 131–32, 141, 144; spontaneous acquisition of, 85–86, 102, 117, 124, 133, 135–36, 154; as a learned behavior, 81, 83–86, 102, 115–17, 121, 124, 129, 132, 133, 154–55; as a "natural" ability, 84, 119, 129, 133–34, 143, 155; and true language, 9–11, 44–45, 85, 101, 115–19, 128, 132–33, 143, 155; as linguistic symbol, 116, 143; as "cradle speech", 113; as reinstating of experience, 93; "not normative for salvation", 44; not always highly emotional, 101; and the demonic, 99–100; and mental imbalance, 48, 61; "not associated with neuroticism", 91–92; as therapy, 91, 94, 95, 96, 108, 118–19; not confined to one personality type, 122–23, 131, 142, 148, 154; broad based social support of, 98, 147, 152

Goldschmidt, Walter R., 27

Goodman, Felicitas, 81, 84–85

Hallenbeck, Wilbur C., 23

Hansen, Olaf, 62–63

Harper, Charles L., 34, 36–37

Harrison, Michael I., 34, 37, 38, 141

Hartmann, H., 132

Hatt, 36

Heflin, C., 27

Hilgard, Ernest and Josephine, 80

Hillmer, Mark, 62

Hine, Virginia H., 14, 31–32, 34, 35, 36, 38, 61, 85–86, 101, 118, 121–28, 135, 136, 137, 138, 139, 140, 141, 143, 146–47, 149, 150

Hocken, Peter, 15

Holiness Movement, the, 2

Hollingshead, August B., 28, 29, 36

Holt, John B., 18, 22–23, 24, 27, 31, 34, 37

holy rollers, the, 22, 90

Hull, C. L., 80

hypnosis, 49, 80, 81, 82–83, 87–88, 113, 121, 129, 130–31, 135–38; group, 54

hysteria, 48, 60, 80, 81, 82, 83, 87, 88, 89, 94, 95, 100, 102, 104, 107, 125

imbalance, mental, 48

Incarnation, the, 156

initiation, Christian, 1, 58

irrationality, 43, 49, 95, 101 (see also nonrationality)

Irving, Edward, 67

Jaquith, James R., 82, 133

Jensen, Richard, 62

Jesus Freaks, the, 24

Johnson, Benton, 23

Jung, Carl, 88, 93, 94–95, 108

Jungkuntz, Theodore, 62

Kaufman, Harold, 28

Kelsey, Morton, 91, 93, 94–95, 96, 100, 108, 136

Kiev, Ari, 91, 93–94, 108, 112

Kildahl, John P., 38, 61, 66, 81, 85, 99, 117, 129, 130–39, 143, 144, 149–150

La Barre, Weston, 24

Lapsley, James N., 81, 99–100, 108–9, 113

leaders, see authority figures

Lebeau, Paul, 15

Lee, Robert, 33

Lenski, Gerhard, 28–29, 30

Lester, Andrew D., 113

Levitt, E., 80

Lofland, John, 33

Logos (periodical), 47

Lombard, Emile, 87, 93, 101, 113, 118

Ludwig, Arnold, 80, 82, 115, 135–36

Luther, Martin, 63

Lynd, Robert and Helen, 28

Lyonnet, Stanislaus, 15

maladjustment, psychological, 20, 21, 32, 36, 44, 112, 122, 143
Malines Document, the, 4, 70
Malony, H. Newton, 137, 139–40, 144
Martin, Ralph, 146
Mary, 69, 73
McDonnell, Kilian, 62
McGavran, Donald, 33, 139
McGuire, Kenneth, 25–26
McGuire, Meredith, 34, 38, 141–42, 144, 148
McKinney, Bishop Joseph, 51
Menzies, William W., 52, 112
Métraux, Alfred, 48
ministry, 6–7, 11, 23–24
miracles, the miraculous, 6, 7–9, 12, 23–24, 67–68, 71, 116, 119, 143–44, 155
Montague, George T., 10, 15
Morentz, Paul, 131
Mosiman, Eddison, 87–88, 94, 108
Mühlen, Heribert, 15

Nadel, S. F., 48
Nelsen, Hart M., 27
Newman, John Henry Cardinal, 13
New Testament, see Bible
Niebuhr, H. Richard, 18
nonrationality, 49 (see also irrationality)
normality, psychological, 13–14, 21, 43, 53–54, 68, 81, 82, 83, 100, 106, 116, 120, 123, 145, 152, 153
Nouwen, Henri, 114–15, 142

Oates, Wayne E., 34, 112–14, 142
objectivity of researchers, 106–7, 109, 134
O'Connell, Daniel C., 116, 128–29, 143
O'Dea, Thomas, 24
Olila, James, 86, 137, 138
Oman, John B., 93, 108–9

Palmer, Gary, 81, 113–14
paranoia, 48
Parsons, Anne, 24
Pattison, E. Mansell, 34–35, 84–85, 100–4, 109, 113, 116, 121, 132, 133, 140
Paul, 6, 10, 113, 133–34
Paul VI, Pope, 15–16, 60, 64–65, 71–

72, 73, 75, 78
Pavlov, I. P., 96
Pentecostalism, Catholic, 3, 4, 10, 11–13, 15–16, 18, 24, 25, 36–38, 42, 49–52, 53, 59–61, 64–65, 69–73, 74, 76, 77–78, 98, 101, 111, 114, 124, 130, 133–35, 140, 141–42, 146, 147–48, 151; in Canada, 70–71, 78; in Puerto Rico, 59–60, 77
Pentecostalism, classical, 2, 3, 10, 11, 13, 14–16, 19–20, 21–22, 32–33, 35, 37, 42, 47, 52, 58, 59, 67, 72, 81, 83, 86–87, 89–92, 93–94, 95–96, 97, 100–1, 103–8, 109, 111–12, 115, 120, 125, 126, 127, 130, 131, 133–35, 142, 145–46, 147
Pentecostalism, neo- or Protestant, 3, 10, 11, 13, 15, 16, 18, 34, 35, 42–49, 50, 51, 52–59, 60–64, 65–68, 73–78, 86–87, 89, 98, 99, 100–1, 103, 108–9, 111–12, 115, 118, 120, 124, 130–39, 146
Pentecostalism, in the Protestant Churches:
BAPTIST, SOUTHERN, 73–75, 78
EPISCOPAL, 3, 15, 42–43, 46–49, 50, 73–74, 75, 76, 98–99, 115, 125, 136
LUTHERAN, 3, 15, 42–46, 50, 60–66, 73–74, 75–76, 77, 78, 125; American Lutheran Church, 43–46, 75–76, 130; Lutheran Church in America, 65–66; Missouri Synod, 60–64, 77, 78
PRESBYTERIAN, 3, 15, 42, 50, 52–59, 66–68, 73–74, 76, 125; Church of Scotland, 66–68, 76; Presbyterian Church in the United States, 52, 55–59, 76; United Presbyterian Church, 52–54, 57, 76, 101
People, Power, Change (Gerlach and Hine), 121
Persky, H., 80
Pethrus, Lewis, 146
Pettay, Louanna, 14, 83
Pfister, Oskar, 88, 93, 113
Piaget, Jean, 112–13
Pike, Bishop James, 46–47, 75
Pin, Emile Jean, 24
Plessis, David du, 52
Plog, Stanley C., 34, 98–99, 109
Poblete, Renato, 24
Pope, Liston, 23

possession, 48, 80, 83
poverty, the poor, 17, 20, 27–31, 34
prayer, 2, 3, 9, 10, 16, 51–52, 55, 60, 65, 69, 71, 72, 73, 83, 86, 92, 102–3, 114, 117, 125, 128–29, 133, 141, 143
Preus, Robert, 63
prophecy, prophets, the prophetic, 2, 6–7, 12, 17, 46, 63, 68, 70, 84, 87
psychology, and Pentecostalism, 2, 3, 5–6, 8–9, 10, 11, 13–14, 16, 18, 19, 41–43, 44, 46–49, 52–54, 58–59, 61, 66, 68, 71–72, 75, 79–109, 112–15, 117, 118, 121–22, 123, 128, 129–40, 142–44, 146–47, 148–56
Psychology of Speaking in Tongues, The (Kildahl), 130–39

Qualben, Paul A., 61, 130, 131, 133, 136, 137, 138
Quanbeck, Warren, 62

Ramsey, James W., 139–40, 144
regression, psychological, 14, 22, 88, 94, 107, 129, 132
religion; and insecurity, 14, 17; and psychology, 53–54, 58–59, 147, 152; and sociology, 58, 179 n.139
research design, 150
research, future, 150–56
Richardson, James T., 107, 140–41, 144, 150, 151–52
Ringer, Benjamin, 30
Roth, Richard A., 137

sacraments, the, 12, 55, 58, 63, 73
Sadler, A. W., 48
Samarin, William, 10, 14, 34, 81–82, 85, 101, 115–19, 129, 132, 133, 135, 136, 137, 138–39, 143, 144, 147, 149, 151
sanctification, 41–42, 58, 61
Sargant, William, 96–97, 108
schizophrenia, 48, 80, 93–94, 95, 107, 108, 119
shamans, shamanism, 14, 48
Shor, Ronald E., 83
Simpson, John H., 81, 99–100, 108–9, 113
Smet, Walter, 136, 137
snake handling, 97, 103–7, 109
social acceptability, see acceptability
Social Sources of Denominationalism, The

(Niebuhr), 18
Society for Pentecostal Studies, The, 112
sociology, and Pentecostalism, 3, 8, 17–40, 90, 102, 118, 130, 137, 141–42, 144, 149
Soka Gakkai, 33
Sorem, Anthony M., 119–21
Spirit, gifts of the, see gifts
Spittler, Russell, 112
Spoerri, T. H., 94
Stanley, Julian C., 150
Stark, Rodney, 97, 147, 179 n.139
status, 21, 23, 25, 29, 30, 34, 36, 38, 111
Steinberg, Hardy, 52
Stone, Jean, 47, 99
Suenens, Leo Cardinal, 15–16, 72, 148
suggestion, suggestibility, 49, 54, 80, 81, 82, 86, 87–88, 91, 108, 121, 135, 136–37, 138, 153
Sullivan, Francis, 15
Sullivan, Harry Stack, 112–13
supernatural, the, supernaturalizing, 8, 9, 13, 67, 68, 84, 93, 116, 119, 124, 133–34, 143–44, 154–56
Synan, Vinson, 72, 112

Teresa of Avila, 12
theology, and Pentecostalism, 3–6, 8, 9, 10–13, 15–16, 42–43, 45–46, 47, 50, 53, 57–59, 61–64, 65–66, 67, 70–71, 73, 74–78, 84, 104, 111–12, 132–34, 136, 143–44, 147, 152, 155–56
Thompson, William P., 52, 76
tongues: not the charismatic issue, 11, 50–51, 57, 124; in total life of the Church, 12–13, 51–52, 57
trance, 45, 79–83, 87, 97, 99, 115, 125, 135, 146, 149, 153
Trinity (periodical), 47, 99
Troeltsch, Ernst, 17–18, 19, 26

unconscious, the, 87–88, 94–95, 108

Vatican Council II, 15, 65, 69
Vekan, Jan van der, 15
Vivier, L. M., 86, 90–93, 94, 96, 108, 112, 132, 136, 137, 138, 139, 150, 152
Voice (magazine), 47

Walde, Peter H. van der, 131
Waldegrave, Charles, 129–30, 137,

Waldegrave *(cont.)*
144, 149
Warner, W. Lloyd, 28, 36
Watterson, Douglas, 75
Weber, Max, 17, 18, 19, 26, 126
Weitbrecht, H. J., 94
Whitt, Hugh P., 27
Williams, J. Rodman, 52, 112
Wilson, Bryan, 90
Wolfram, Walter, 10, 85, 86, 133

Wood, William W., 24, 95–96, 97, 100, 108, 112
World War II, 14, 28, 86, 111, 147

Xavier, Francis, 12
xenoglossolalia, 116

Zaleski, Bishop Alexander M., 49
Zwaanstra, Nelson, 139–40, 144